AMERICAN
INDIAN
MYTHS
& MYSTERIES

AMERICAN
INDIAN
MYTHS
& MYSTERIES

Vincent H. Gaddis

🕉

cap. &

Chilton Book Company/Radnor, Pennsylvania

Library of Congress Cataloging in Publication Data
Gaddis, Vincent H
    American Indian myths & mysteries.

    Includes bibliographical references and index.
    1. Indians of North America—Miscellanea.
2. Indians—Miscellanea.   3. Folk-lore, Indian.
I. Title.
E77.G14   1977   970'.004'97   76-51215
ISBN 0-8019-6409-1

1 2 3 4 5 6 7 8 9 0   5 4 3 2 1 0 9 8 7

Contents

Introduction:
Our Indian Heritage

A SMALL ARMY entered the village of Hotevilla, a Hopi Pueblo in northeastern Arizona. They were not cavalrymen riding horses and brandishing swords as in times long past. They were not infantrymen marching with rifles. No, the invaders consisted of workmen led by the superintendent of the Hopi Indian Agency. They were riding on tractors, road graders, earth-moving equipment and trucks loaded with logs. It was the early morning of May 20, 1968.

The alarmed villagers left their homes and stood beside the road, wondering, resenting this intrusion into their quiet hamlet and tranquil lives. Chief Dan Katchongva and a group of the pueblo's elder religious leaders gathered in the center of the road, and the caravan came to a halt. "Why do you come with all the big machines?" asked the chief.

The superintendent smiled. "This is a great day for your village," he explained. "You're going to have electricity and telephones. These logs will be power line poles. Sewers and water pipes will be placed in the ground for the benefit of your people."

"No!" said the chief, shaking his head. "We don't need these things. This is our sacred village and these things will defile it. We have our good spring water and our oil lamps. We are satisfied."

"But this is progress," protested the superintendent. "These improvements will be for your health and convenience. They will be good for the Hopi."

"No," said one of the leaders. "It will mean not progress, but destruction for the Hopi. Our youth will become restless and they will leave to enter the white man's world. It will mean taxes that we can't pay. We will lose our homes and no more Hopi. We have health. We can take care of ourselves. In the ancient ways lies our strength, our survival."

The superintendent impatiently waved his hands, then reached into a pocket and removed a paper. "You cannot stop our work," he announced. "This is a petition for public utilities here with ninety names on it."

"We Hotevilla Hopis didn't sign your paper," insisted a leader. "We haven't asked for anything from the government."

As the argument continued, some of the Hopi traditionalists began checking the names on the petition. More than half the names were unknown to the village men. Others were recognized as families who had moved away a generation ago, some to live in the cities of the white men. A few were Hopi followers of the white men's ways who lived in or near the village, and some of their names had been written more than once.

Early in the afternoon a now-angry superintendent decided to end the stalemate. The tractors and trucks began moving forward. With cries of rage, the Hopi fought the invasion with their bodies. Men flung themselves on the road in the path of the heavy vehicles and were dragged away by workmen. Screaming women tried to climb aboard the trucks and were shoved off violently.

All through the warm afternoon the struggle continued. There were scuffles and fist fights. Women jumped into holes to prevent the log poles from being erected. One log struck a woman and knocked her unconscious. Finally the workmen and their equipment left the village.

That evening prayers for deliverance were offered in the kivas. Chief Katchongva sent messages to influential white friends of the Hopi requesting their help. These friends sent telegrams to federal and state officials and newspaper editors. The chief and his interpreter were taped for an appearance on the Steve Allen television show. The Bureau of Indian Affairs ordered the superintendent to suspend operations. The Bureau added that it had acted on a petition for public utilities, and the tribe should now resolve the issue among its own members.

The leaders agreed that the best way to resolve the issue was to have the Hotevilla Hopis and their tribal neighbors vote on the question. In the final count there were 98 votes for the utilities, but 130 against.

The following day the superintendent was back with his work-men and equipment. The leaders met him in the road and showed him the vote tally. He ignored it. The vote was meaningless, he in-sisted, since it was limited to a small number, and a majority of the tribe could be named from anywhere.

Now the battle of a week before was repeated. Men trying to stop the labor and machines were seized and shoved to the sides of the road. Women were yanked out of the post holes they had jumped into. Despite the violance, no one was seriously hurt. By sundown an ugly row of poles lined the road from the pueblo to the schoolhouse.

"I know you people are figuring on staying up all night to take down the poles and burn them," the superintendent told the vil-lagers. "We've strung live wires on these poles. If you try to take them down, you'll get burned or electrocuted. I warn you that if anyone gets hurt or killed, I will not be responsible." The villagers didn't know if the wires were live or not, but the elders wouldn't permit them to take any chances.

"If these things remain," said Chief Katchongva bitterly, "our pueblo will become just another village like all the others, a honky-tonk as the white men say, with tourists and shops and taverns selling strong drink. The Great Spirit will leave us, and there will be no more peace, no more Hopi honoring their fathers. There will be no more ceremonies, no more butterfly dances in the plaza, no more kachinas performing their spirit world rituals. This is almost the last pueblo where the ancient ways are remembered."

In the months that followed, the white friends of the Hotevilla Hopis joined in the struggle, with pleas to authorities to end the in-vasion of pueblo privacy. Meanwhile, the parents refused to send their children to the school operated by the Bureau of Indian Af-fairs. Early in 1969 the agency superintendent was replaced by a more sympathetic official. The utility poles were removed, and the ditches for sewer and water lines were filled in. The battle had been won—at least temporarily.

The struggle between the modern and traditional worlds of the North American Indians is being lost by those who seek to retain the old ways. As the old die, the philosophies and the cultural val-ues that once bridged the generations are being forgotten. So many of the young have entered the white man's world and adopted his ways and goals.

On the other hand, a minority of the young in some tribes are

beginning to take an interest in the traditions. While much of the Indian heritage has been lost, there is a great deal that can be saved. There are old men and women who remember the lore of their ancestors, who have been keepers of the traditional flame. With educational opportunities will come not only visions of a brighter tomorrow, but appreciation of a great and colorful yesterday.

The Indian's philosophy is no anachronism in today's world. He has always been a partner with nature, not a destroyer of it. Sensitive to the rhythms of mother earth, he can teach us. We are only now beginning to appreciate the relevance of this philosophy to our existence. We may yet learn some lessons about restoring the balance between man and his environment.

In the ritual worship of ancient days, in the legends about trees, lakes, mountains and canyons, the Indian reveals his understanding of the spiritual force of nature. This force creates the beauty of earth and sky, the basic unity and coherence of all life. In exploitation lies extinction. The land and the people who dwell upon it must live in harmony.

The misunderstood native American is both the victim of prejudice and the object of veneration. There are western towns where the Indians barely outrank dogs in the minds of some whites. On the other hand, there has been so much of a romantic aura surrounding the heroic red man that he has become the subject of a whole mythology in American and European literature. These extreme stereotypes must be replaced by knowledge and understanding. We must learn to know the Indian as he is—a human with the frailties and strengths, the vices and virtues common to all mankind.

The redskin stereotype is that he is taciturn, that he speaks in clipped monosyllables and rarely smiles. Around white men, especially strangers, he often speaks only when necessary, but among his own people he can be a fun-loving individual. He is so loquacious that he will travel many miles to a council meeting or pow-wow that can last for days.

Another myth is that his reflexes are slower and he is not as sensitive to pain as are whites. Actually the Indian considers it a point of honor to keep his pain to himself. He is trained from infancy to hide his emotions. And how the term "Indian giver" originated remains a mystery. There are as many generous Indians as among other peoples, and among Sioux, for example, generosity ranks

first among the four cardinal virtues. The other three are physical courage, bravery in battle and moral integrity.

The belief that Indian women are virtual slaves to their husbands is nonsense. In earlier times the home and all the activity involved in it had been her exclusive domain. The husband's duties were to provide the food, to hunt and fish, and to protect his hunting grounds. He possessed his clothes, his horse and his weapons. His wife owned the buffalo skins, the teepee poles, the cooking utensils and other furnishings. The man was little more than a visitor in her home.

Today the Indian woman still insists she is the mistress of her home. She will perform laborious tasks while her husband sits nearby, but if any man, white or red, tries to help her, he will receive a vehement rebuff. Such an attempt will be considered an encroachment on her special sphere of influence.[1]

The greatest error of all was made by Christopher Columbus. When he made his landfall at San Salvador, he thought he had reached the East Indies, so he called the inhabitants of the New World Indians. To distinguish the American from the East Indian the words Amerind and Amerindian have been coined. These names are being increasingly used by scientists and writers, and will be used in this book.

As the United States observes its Bicentennial, it is interesting to note that the Iroquois Confederacy, a self-governing league of six tribes, may have influenced the colonial Continental Congress.

They were the People of the Long House—the eastern woodland tribes who spoke Iroquoian languages. Originally they had fought one another as well as others, but in the middle of the sixteenth century there appeared two great humane leaders, brilliant men who hated the stupidities and sorrows of war, prophets who had visions of a united defense against aggressive outsiders and the tranquil fruits of peace. As with all reformers, they had to overcome indifference and suspicion.

Deganawidah was born among the Hurons on the north shore of Lake Ontario. Growing into manhood, he heard reports of the numerous conflicts on the lake's south side that threatened to destroy the Iroquoian people. He was troubled. As he walked the forest trails and fished on the quiet lakes and streams, he developed his "Message of Peace and Power." He crossed Lake Ontario to the country of the Onondagas, to a place near modern Syracuse to begin his mission. Unfortunately, he had a speech impediment. He needed a spokesman and a disciple who would share his ambition, and he found him in Hiawatha.

Hiawatha was a Mohawk who happened to be living among the Onondagas. Henry W. Longfellow immortalized his name, while Deganawidah is almost forgotten. But the poet used only the name, and all of the other material in his narrative is of Algonquin origin. With the fervor of Deganawidah's vision expressed in Hiawatha's spellbinding oratory, they traveled from village to village, sometimes separately to save time but usually together, overcoming the stubborn resistance of suspicious chiefs, bringing their doctrine of peace and power to the campfire councils. They spoke and the people listened.

Thus was established the Great Peace of the eastern woodlands, the Iroquois Confederacy. It included the Mohawks, Oneidas, Onondagas, Cayugas and Senecas. These were the Five Nations, who became known as the Six Nations after they were joined by the Tuscaroras who had been driven north from the Carolinas. On the shore of Lake Onondaga Deganawidah planted the Tree of Peace with branches pointing in all directions. On its summit he placed the symbol of military preparedness—the Eagle that Sees Afar. There followed the numerous councils during which the genius of Deganawidah, assisted by his brilliant speechmaker Hiawatha, worked out the details of an alliance so comprehensive, detailed, and advanced that it is forever a pinnacle in the history of statesmanship.

"I think no institutional achievement of mankind exceeds it in either wisdom or intelligence, accepting the limits of its time and place," writes John Collier, the noted Indian authority, in his book *Indians of the Americas.* "An idea and an intention, among the Iroquois, wrought out a social institution, a system of greatness in human relationships, a system for evoking maximum genius and for socializing it, and a role of women in society, which may well stand today as the most brilliant creation in the record of man. Then from a world unknown, a ravenous race swept in a dark age for the native life which was hurled into the pit by cannon, by rum, by money, by unconscionable intrigue." [2]

The Confederacy exerted an extraordinary influence on American history, a startling fact when we consider that its population at its height was only about 16,000 men, women and children. As Paul A. W. Wallace, historian and editor of *Pennsylvania History*, states in *American Heritage*, there might be no United States or Canadian partner in the British Commonwealth today if the Confederacy had not sheltered our forefathers during the long struggle with France in America.[3] And they held two mighty European empires in check until well into the eighteenth century.

In addition to maintaining peace among the nations and a united defense against their enemies, the Confederacy provided services to refugees from displaced tribes. All Indians could come under the protection of the league and many of them did. Those who were destitute, who had been driven from their homelands by warfare or the advance of the whites, were fed and cared for as they passed from village to village to final locations designated by the council. Special care was given the sick and the aged.

Laws for the punishment of crimes were established. Attention, however, was paid to the victims of crimes. Part of the punishment of convicted criminals was to pay the victims (or the victim's family in the case of homicides) certain amounts of valuable wampum.

Iroquois women were liberated. Ancestral descent was reckoned in the female line, and there was equality of the sexes in all social relationships and even leadership. Moreover, women of the Iroquoian tribal group could vote centuries before their white sisters. The mothers in lines of descent which possessed hereditary chieftainship rights nominated the forty-nine civil chiefs of the Confederacy. Popular vote (male and female) followed in each tribe, subject to confirmation by the League's Grand Council of Chiefs.

While the governing council was composed of hereditary chiefs, the Confederacy's strength lay in its democracy. Authority flowed upward from the individual and family through the clan and tribe to the council, then the power for effective action flowed downward through the same channels. Its brilliant political structure contained many of those elements that were to become vital factors in American government, such as initiative, referendum and recall.

The Confederacy may have been one of the motivating forces behind the American Revolution. At a time when there was constant dissension and bickering among the colonies, it was an Iroquois chief who called the attention of the colonial leaders to the power-giving unity of the Six Nations.

Benjamin Franklin, speaking at the Albany Convention in 1754, made the first formal proposal for a political union:

It would be a strange thing if Six Nations of ignorant savages should be capable of forming a scheme for such an union, and be able to execute it in such a manner as that it has subsisted ages and appears indissoluble; and yet that a like union should be impracticable for ten or a dozen English colonies, to whom it is more necessary and must be more advantageous, and who cannot be supposed to want an equal understanding of their interests.

No agreement was reached by the representatives of the colonies present, but this convention laid the groundwork for the later Constitutional Convention which united the colonies.[4]

For more than two centuries the Confederacy withstood the assaults of its enemies; then it was overcome by the sheer might of the white invasion. Each sunrise brought more and more Europeans, and each sunset was symbolic of the league's decline. It was not only the loss of their land. In the struggles between French, Dutch and English, each nationality enlisted the support of Amerinds. Indian fought Indian in self-annihilation.

Yet the vitality of the Confederacy was great enough to prevent the Iroquois from being pushed west. They are still in the eastern states, most of them in New York. Others, remaining faithful to the British, moved to Canada during the American Revolution.

Remnants of the league exist today, most noticeably in Canada. It was on the Six Nations Reserve in Canada that Seth Newhouse in 1885 wrote for the first time the legend of Deganawidah and Hiawatha that had been preserved for centuries by oral tradition.

"The Six Nations will never die," an Iroquois friend told Paul A. W. Wallace. And Wallace points out that the Confederacy's strength still exists, not in numbers or voting power, but in a united moral faith inspired by the founding legend and nourished not only by past victories but also by defeats.

John Lawson, an English surveyor and traveler in America, wrote in 1714 of the Indians of the Iroquois group: "They will walk over deep brooks and creeks, on the smallest poles, and that without any fear or concern. Nay, an Indian will walk on the ridge of a barn or house and look down the gable-end and spit upon the ground, as unconcerned as if he was walking on terra firma." [5]

One hundred seventy-two years later, in 1886, contractors came to the Mohawk Reservation on the St. Lawrence River near Montreal. They planned to erect a bridge across the river, and they offered the Amerinds jobs on the project in return for rights to the necessary land. It was a deal—the Mohawks wanted the work and the bridge builders needed their labor to keep wage costs down. In those days seamen accustomed to climbing the masts of sailing vessels were among the few who had the nerve to work at high altitudes, and they demanded and received high salaries. So the experienced sailors would construct the high iron, while the Mohawks would serve as ground laborers.

As the project progressed, the iron workers were astonished to discover Amerinds peering curiously over their shoulders as they worked on the narrow girders high above the river. They learned what John Lawson had observed almost two centuries earlier—the Iroquois, and particularly the Mohawks, were absolutely fearless at high altitudes. By the time the bridge was built, many of the Indians had learned riveting and other steel construction skills. It was only natural that when there were other high iron jobs to be done, the Mohawks should come along and do them.

During the skyscraper-building boom during the 1920s, a number of Mohawks moved to New York. They have worked on every major high-rise and bridge project since, riveting steel and swinging the heavy girders into place at dizzying heights. There are about 700 men and their families in the city, most of them living in Brooklyn. Some of the workmen speak Iroquois on the job, and most have tribal as well as conventional names. Sons learn the trade from their fathers. They comprise, of course, only a small percentage of the total number of iron workers on a given job. Upon retirement some of the older men return to the reservation, but among the younger there is some intermarriage with whites, and knowledge of their tribal language and reservation associations is fading away.

But the Mohawk on the girder high above New York's concrete and steel canyons, proud of his tribal heritage and its colorful traditions, bridges two worlds. He breathes in a modern world of skyscrapers, atomic power and conquest of the moon, but within him flows the blood of his forefathers who once knew a free, uninhibited life, close to the nature they worshiped. Once their golden skins shone in the sunlight as they trod forest trails, hunted in the winding valleys and paddled their canoes over the pure clear waters of lakes and streams. But that was in another time long gone that has faded away like a dream.[6]

Part One

THE
HISTORICAL
MYSTERIES

"The present contains nothing more than the past," wrote Henri Bergson, the French philosopher, in his book Creative Evolution, *"and what is found in the effect was already in the cause."* Today some of the younger North American Indians are seeking a racial identity. As with the Blacks who, emerging from second-class citizenry, found dignity and pride in their history and ancestry, so the Amerindians are taking an interest in their past and traditions. Parallel with this awakening are the recent discoveries that offer evidence that the antiquity of man in the Americas is far greater than previously believed. Not only have the native Americans been here a long time, but some reached astonishingly high plateaus of culture.

I

Whence Came the Amerind?

THE MOJAVE DESERT between Los Angeles and Las Vegas stretches over sandy, desolate wastelands to sterile gray and purple hills. During the summers the 100-degree-plus heat laces the dry air with shimmering waves. Nights bring a penetrating cold, and when the rare rains come flash floods sweep down age-old river beds. But winter days can be sunny and pleasant, with moderate temperatures inviting the visitor to explore the trails and canyons so shrouded in timeless silence.

It was on such a day in December 1948 that Ritner Sayles made his great discovery. An amateur archeologist and dairy farmer, he had been performing a survey along the Mojave River bed for the San Bernardino County Museum. He decided to climb up a grade above the dry channel to get a wider view of the area. In so doing he found himself on a spot hallowed by eons of time.

Today the Mojave is a desert, but it was not always so. Sayles was standing on the shoreline of what had been a large lake in the Pleistocene epoch, a lake of blue waters surrounded by swampy land and tall grass inhabited by game. Surveyors, observing the archaic waterlines of the long vanished body of water, had named it Lake Manix. As he walked along the crest of the rise, Sayles noticed with surprise some stones. They had obviously been chipped by primitive man long ago.

So began the Calico Mountain archeological project near Barstow, three miles from the Calico Ghost Town on Interstate Highway 15. The late Dr. L. S. B. Leakey, renowned discoverer of the oldest known human remains at Olduvai Gorge in East Africa, believed that man came to America much earlier than the period assigned by most of his fellow archeologists. He persuaded the National Geographic Society to support the exploratory excavation.

The surface rocks and flakes were of relatively recent times, but Dr. Leakey suspected that the site had been an ancient workshop for making stone tools for many millennia. He indicated where the first master pit should be dug. Fragments of mastodon tusks appeared at thirteen feet. At fourteen feet the dedicated workers found the first artifacts buried in the alluvial soil, implements of chalcedony, jasper, and chert that offered sharp, long-lasting cutting edges.

Twenty-three feet down the fifteen-foot square shaft reached a hearth of thirteen boulders arranged in the form of a capital C. In the center of the semicircle the prehistoric hunters had built fires to warm themselves as they chipped their tools while sitting in the open space of the hearth ring. Tests with the rocks that had reflected the heat disclosed they had been heated to 400 degrees centrigrade on the sides facing the fire.

Estimated ages ranged from 20,000 years for the surface artifacts to 50,000 for the buried relics. But as the two master pits attained depths of well over thirty feet and artifacts continued to be found, surprise was succeeded by bewilderment. Dr. Thomas Clements, retired chairman of the geology department of the University of Southern California and project geologist, believes 100,000 years is the maximum age of the site. More than 100 scientists from all parts of the world attended the Calico International Conference at the San Bernardino County Museum in Bloomington, California, in October of 1970, where they listened to lectures and examined the evidence. The astonishing depth at which artifacts have been found, plus the nature of the soil, has led some geologists to believe that 200,000 to 500,000 years is a more probable estimate.[1]

A date of approximately 50,000 years for man in Southern California was confirmed in 1974. In 1929 the late Malcolm J. Rogers, a former director of the Museum of Man, Balboa Park, San Diego, discovered a skull, jawbone, ribs, and other bones at two sites in Del Mar and La Jolla near San Diego. Preserved by the long discarded clam and mollusk shells that had surrounded them, the remains had been exposed by erosion.

Early in 1974 an age of 48,000 to 50,000 years was announced by Dr. Jeffrey Bada, of the Scripps Institute of Oceanography, La

Jolla, after using a new technique of bone dating that he had developed. Primitive camp debris has since been recovered from the sites. The skull is on public view at the museum.

To the surprise of the scientists, the skull does not resemble those of ancient Amerinds of the northwest, Eskimos or the Mongoloid peoples of Asia, but more closely resembles those of an early race of man in Japan, according to Dr. Spencer L. Rogers, scientific director at the museum. Dr. George Carter, of Texas A. and M. University, who had requested the reexamination of the bones, has insisted that "the real antiquity of man in America was on the order of magnitude of 100,000 years." [2]

Soon after this discovery, Dr. Sheldon P. Applegate, associate curator at the Los Angeles County Museum of National History, announced the finding of evidence that man was in Mexico 50,000 years ago. A large number of obsidian and flint implements were found in fossil beds of that age at the southern tip of Baja California. [3]

Even older artifacts may have been discovered on America's east coast. Dr. Bruce E. Raemsch, professor of anthropology at Hartwick College, Oneonta, New York, reported in 1970 finding primitive tools along a ten-mile stretch surrounding a creek in eastern central New York. Various studies of the molded clay, quartzite and silicified limestone tools, together with the weathering profile and aged patina have set their age at a minimum of 70,000 years. [4]

More and more evidence currently being discovered supports the great antiquity of man in America, and a battle may be shaping up between the geologists and the anthropologists. In a report to the Geological Society of America, three scientists said they had uncovered evidence indicating man had been in Mexico as long as 250,000 years ago. Dr. Roald Frynell of Washington State University, Dr. Harold E. Malde and Virginia Steen-McIntyre, both of the U.S. Geological Survey, explained they had dated by several independent methods a number of stone tools found in an ancient Mexican river bed.

"We're confronted with a dilemma in which we have apparently sound geological data that lead to a head-on confrontation with apparently sound archeological data," Dr. Frynell told the geologists assembled in Dallas, Texas, November 12, 1973. [5]

Even at 100,000 years the awesome immensity of time stuns the mind. Pick up an artifact. Between the hand that chipped it in a dawn era and your own hand lies twenty times the length of man's known history. Since that stone became an implement, once-abundant species of animals have long been extinct, land masses have appeared and vanished, and the long winters of ice ages have come and gone.

Remarkable new "clocks" are making methods of determining the age of artifacts more accurate. The most common method has been radiocarbon dating, which can only be applied to organic matter. It is based on the fact that nitrogen in the atmosphere, bombarded by neutrons produced by cosmic rays, has some of its atoms transmuted into radioactive carbon-14. These atoms combine with oxygen to form carbon dioxide in the atmosphere. By photosynthesis these atoms are absorbed by plants, by animals that eat plants, and by animals that eat plant-eating animals, all having the same proportion of carbon-14 atoms as the atmosphere. This intake of radiocarbon ends with death, and it then proceeds to break down at a known rate until it disappears. The age of the matter can be determined by the amount still present, give or take a few centuries or decades. The method will not date much beyond 40,000 years of age, as by this time there is little left to be measured.

Discovery of this dating technique in 1949 was hailed with enthusiasm, and early tests confirmed accepted chronologies. Recently, however, radiocarbon analysis of the tree rings of California's bristlecone pines, some of which have been growing for almost 5,000 years and are the oldest living things on earth, revealed that the earth had experienced much heavier cosmic ray bombardments in ages past. Thus, organic remains formerly dated at 4,000 B.C., for example, were actually at least 600 years older. With this discovery the accepted chronologies of early man and his works have collapsed.

The new method used by Dr. Jeffrey Bada to date the 50,000-year-old San Diego Museum of Man skull (now known as the Del Mar man) is a process called aspartic-acid racemization. It is applied to bones and measures the ratio of D-amino acid to L-amino acid—the older the bone the larger proportion of D-amino acid. This method will date bones as far back as several hundred thousand years.

Other new dating techniques are the thermoluminescent process, which can date the age of ground-up pottery shards, and a method of determining the age of artifacts older than several thousand years. This latter procedure measures the extent to which radioactive potassium has decayed into argon gas in the volcanic strata in which they lie.[6]

Whence came the Amerindian?

The antiquity of all races is shrouded with mystery. Numerous migrations under Pleistocene skies followed the rise and fall of land masses, the glacial cycles, the hunts for game, and they have created a jigsaw puzzle that will never be fully solved. How infinitesimal is the knowledge we can discover in the stupendous immensity of ages gone!

We know so little about man's past that most orthodox anthropologists advocate easy and simple theories. Predicated upon the conventional belief that man's evolutionary birthplace is Asia (Dr. Leakey and his followers would say Africa), and that civilization had its beginnings in Egypt and the Tigris-Euphrates Valley about 6,000 years ago, it is the natural tendency to make of human history a recent development. The evidence for advanced cultures existing before what we call historic times is ignored. Archeology has been defined as the science concerned with unearthing the rubbish of the past and reburying it under a new rubbish of theory.

So we are told that while the evidence for man's existence goes back more than a million years in the Old World, paradoxically the first American came from Siberia to Alaska over the Bering Straits at a late period. Only a few years ago it was alleged that this first migration occurred about 10,000 years ago, and in the relatively short time since, Mongoloid man made his way through dense tropical jungles, deserts, and mountains the many thousands of miles to the southern tip of South America. Now as the result of more recent discoveries most anthropologists place the migration time as around 30,000 B.P. (Before Present).

No one knows when the first migration occurred or when the last ice age took place. While at present discoveries are lengthening the period of man's presence here, they are also shortening the time since the last glaciation. Not too many years ago it was given in the textbooks as about 30,000 years ago, but today it is believed to have been as recent as 12,000 to 15,000 years B.P.

Migration by the Bering Sea Strait (or "land bridge" during glaciation periods when sea levels were lowered) has been a theoretical sacred cow to many anthropologists, but it does not explain the origin of all Amerinds in America. It is true that natives of the Athabascan tribal group, which includes the Navajos, have Mongoloid characteristics and, along with the Eskimos, may have followed this route. They possess the "Mongoloid fold" on the inner canthus of the eye and the "Mongoloid spot," a bluish small pigment on the back just over the sacrum which usually disappears in adulthood. But even this evidence can be questioned.

Dr. Frank C. Hibben is professor and curator in the Department of Anthropology, University of New Mexico, and he goes along with the Bering Strait theory. However, as he points out in his book *Digging Up America*, there are Mongoloid or near-Mongoloid people all the way from Siberia to the far South Pacific, and in northern Europe as well as central Europe where such invasions as that of the Huns introduced Mongoloid stock. "Considering all these Mongoloid movements and mixtures, it is difficult, if not impossible, to try to pinpoint the origin of the American Indians by means of their physical type alone," he writes.[7]

There was no single great migration from northern Asia, but quite likely a series of small groups during the passage of millennia. Paul Radin in *The Story of the American Indian* suggests three invasions all from Asia, an Australian, a Melanesian, and a Mongolian, the latter being the last and probably the largest.[8]

As for the Bering Straits migrants eventually reaching the far destination of Tierra del Fuego, what was their incentive? There was no population pressure. About the time Columbus arrived on the scene, it is estimated that there were 15 million natives in the Americas, with about one million or less in what is now the United States and southern Canada. During the last glaciation there was an ice-free area just to the east of the Rocky Mountains and other areas to the south. At worst, ice age man would have had to go no farther than modern Mexico.

Nevertheless, the oldest and most advanced civilizations were in South America. A vast antiquity here is evident in the ruins under lava flows and at Lake Titicaca. Here the mysteries of countless ages await the study of skilled minds, and Latin American scientists who have led in the research are appalled at their own ignorance. And the trail of the totems is northward.

Perhaps the belief of an Asian birthplace for man arises from known history, but there is a vast unknown history. Man's oldest remains to date were found in Africa. If man does have a terrestrial birthplace, it could be somewhere on the slopes of the Andes, on the Argentine pampas or in the Amazon basin. There were migrations from the east, west and north. These new arrivals may have found man already here. The red man, then, would truly be the native American.

Untold centuries ago some immense catastrophe befell mankind, causing widespread loss of life and world-wide sorrow. The exact nature of this cataclysm is darkened by the ages, and memories of it have faded into myths. It could have been the Biblical flood. It could have been the last of a series of cosmic disasters that plagued earth as suggested by Immanuel Velikovsky, an upheaval of astronomical origin that changed our planet's surface and revolutionized human history. It could have been the sinking of a large land mass resulting in the legends of Atlantis, Mu, and Lemuria. Traditions of a great flood that apparently destroyed civilizations are associated with this dim memory.

Universal services of great solemnity to commemorate the disaster have been held since ancient times. Spanish missionary priests were astonished to discover that native Peruvian Indians as well as the Christians observe the feast of the dead on the same day—the second of November. It is no coincidence, since throughout the world in both hemispheres, other peoples hold their feasts to their ancestors around the beginning of November. This is true in Asia, Africa and America, and even in Australia the aborigines hold their three-day feast of the dead in the eleventh month.

It would seem that the widespread culture that suffered catastrophe had a calendar regulated by the star cluster Pleiades. These memorial observances are held at the zenith of the cluster in the constellation Taurus at midnight, or when it is directly overhead. The Pleiades can be observed as a mistylike group of stars, six of which are visible to the naked eye. There is a universal legend that originally there were seven stars and that one has been lost. The symbolism of the seven stars is to be found on ancient temples. The peculiar spectrum of Pleione has led astronomers to the belief that it formerly shone with a temporary brilliancy, and that this star is the lost Pleiad.

R. G. Halliburton, a Canadian scholar, has discovered traces of the Pleiad calendar throughout the world. In one of the most ancient of calendars, that of the Brahmins of Tirvalore, the name of November was *Kartica*, meaning "the month of the Pleiades." Still in use in Polynesia is a calendar year regulated by the rising of the cluster, or by the stars being visible all night long. In Australia,

Africa and North and South America the natives regard the Pleiades as beneficent stars and dance in their honor.

Halliburton asks why such apparently unimportant stars should have acquired such significance originally that they regulated a calendar. It was not merely because those stars announced spring and were "stars of rain," or because they were "for signs, and for seasons, and days, and years," but also because they were connected with the abode of the Deity and the spirits of the dead. Alcyone, the name of the brightest of the cluster, means a center or turning-point, and it seems the ancients believed that the Pleiades were the center of the universe, and Alcyone the central sun. Traces of these beliefs are still to be found among primitive peoples.[9]

Moving across the heavens like six jewels set in the velvet of night, the Pleiades, 350 light years in the awesome depths of space, have held the reverence of mankind for millennia. Job is considered the oldest book in the Bible and its origin is a mystery, but the author asks, already knowing the answer, "Canst thou bind the sweet influence of the Pleiades?"

Of all Amerindian flood legends, perhaps the most fascinating is one possessed by the Mayas. The *Chilam Balam*, of Mayan origin, which may be the oldest book on earth and certainly of the Americas, offers us a glimpse into the mists beyond known history. When fanatical Spanish priests burned it, a Quiche priest rewrote it from memory. Its allegorical style and archaic phrases are those of a vanished epoch, and it is a miracle that this lone survivor from a lost world has come down to us in this twentieth century.

A modern translator is A. M. Bolio, a full-blooded Mayan, linguist and scholar. He believes the original document was written by an eyewitness who escaped the great cataclysm, the sinking of a motherland. Perhaps the disaster is the same one that Egyptian priests in the Temple of Vulcan told Solon about, which retold by Plato became the legend of Atlantis. At any rate, from the great vistas of hoary antiquity comes this account of death and destruction.

A fiery rain fell, as ashes covered the heavens and trees trembled, crashing to the ground. And [the earth] shook, and the trees and rocks were thrown against one another. . . . [The people] ran to the shore-line screaming, where the tumultuous waves poured over them and buried them in the sands. Then cracked open great chasms, which yawned, swallowing falling temples and frantic hordes of running ones. Finally, in one vast, curving, green watery blow, curled back and came all the ocean . . . the sky began to fall down with steam and fire, and then all of the dry land sank into the engulfing waters.

Those who had escaped came to their places, knowing the annihilation was finished, and they were settled in their places. And a rainbow appeared as a sign that the destruction was over, and a new age was to begin.

New civilizations struck down their roots, the great yellow tree [Mayan color for the south] and the white tree [Mayan color for the north], and in memory of The Never-Forgotten Destruction, a bird sat upon the yellow tree and the white. And the footsteps of The Southerners echoed throughout the new land . . .[10]

Obviously, a civilization preceded this catastrophe, perhaps more than one, nor was this cataclysm the only one to plague man during his existence. It is generally believed that civilization progressed at a more or less steady rate from savagery to our present pinnacle, that civilized man has only lately appeared on the terrestrial scene. Perhaps this concept results from neo-Darwinism— evolution from simplicity to complexity—a belief unproven but unquestioned.

But the more we learn about the puzzling past and discover the artifacts of cultures long gone, the more we realize that there are crests and troughs of civilization, ups and downs with brilliant periods succeeded by dark ages. Moreover, there is a coexistence of cultures. At a time 15,000 to 20,000 years ago when Magdalenian cave men in Europe wore hides and hunted with crude spears, the rock drawings of Lussac-le-Chateau (Department of Vienne, France) reveal a cultured people who wore hats, trousers, petticoats, boots, and jackets with lapels and collars much like those we wear today. This discovery by Leon Pericard and Stephane Lwoff, two French archeologists, in strata containing cave man relics in 1937, was authenticated by the noted scholar Abbe Breuil. It is so disturbing to orthodoxy that the stones are kept under lock and key at the Musée de l'Homme in Paris.[11]

Concealing evidence that conflicts with accepted theory is common scientific skullduggery. For years the Smithsonian Institution has been accused of hiding in storage vaults things it doesn't like. In 1968 two Neanderthallike skulls with low foreheads and large brows were found in Minnesota. As for dating, University of Minnesota scientists said they were reluctant to destroy any of the material, although carbon-14 testing only requires the burning of one gram of bone. They were sent to the Smithsonian. Later Dr. Lawrence Angel, curator of physical anthropology at the institution, said he had no record of the skulls there, although he was sure they were not lost. We have a right to wonder whether some professional scientists mightn't find a really early date for the bones distressing.[12]

Coexistence of cultures exists today, with jet aircraft flying over peoples at a Stone-Age level in Brazil, the Philippines, Africa and Australia. Even in the United States we have the diversity of jet age sophistication and the Amish of Pennsylvania living an early nineteenth-century life.

Perhaps it is the myopic vision of North American anthropologists, with their obsession with the Bering Strait and northern latitudes, that causes the average North American citizen to picture all the Amerinds as painted, feathered barbarians riding to do battle at the Little Big Horn. But it is to the south—in Central and South America—that Amerind culture reached its zenith.

Here, where "the footsteps of the Southerners echoed throughout the new land" after some ancient catastrophe, was created the Chimu Empire with its capital city of Chan Chan covering eleven square miles. It was a complex of streets, buildings and palaces laid out in units or citadels, each one a separate city in itself. Within its vast domain stretching from modern Ecuador far south along the Peruvian coast and the Andes were fortresses, pyramids, irrigation systems and many cities that were smaller counterparts of Chan Chan.

Here too was the Incan Empire with its more than 7,000 miles of roads, suspension bridges over precipitous gorges, bridges of stone over major rivers and fortresses or guardhouses every ten miles or so. So stupendous and magnificent were some of their buildings that men who came later thought that they must have been built by some magical power. Each stone fitted like a cork in a bottle. The great fortress of Sacsahuaman, with its sixty-foot walls, was built of huge stone blocks, some weighing 200 tons, that fitted together so snugly that a knife blade could not be forced between them.[13]

The Great Wall of China is well known. Not so well known is the Great Wall of Peru. Beginning near the seacoast town of Chimbote, it stretches forty miles through the Andes, across valleys and up precipitous mountainsides, until it disappears among remote peaks and ridges. Made of stones cemented with adobe, the barricade is thirty feet high at some points. Its function is unknown, but it may have been erected by the Chimus in an effort to protect their highly cultured civilization.

Nor was the greatness of the Andean Amerinds limited to structures. They were far advanced in medicine and agriculture. *The American Heritage Book of Indians* tells us that the "textiles made by the Paracas and Nazca people of the Peruvian south coast represent, in the opinion of connoisseurs, the greatest textile art ever produced anywhere. They were woven from cotton and the wool of llamas, alpacas and vicunas into every sort of cloth from gauze and lace to brocade and tapestry, in every sort of color. Archeologists have classified as many as 190 hues in seven color ranges." [14]

And in Central America and southern Mexico were the mathematically skilled Mayas. Over many centuries from their pyramid observatories they had charted the movements of the sun, moon, stars and especially the planets. They devised an elaborate calendar more accurate than the Gregorian. The calculations by which they dated their monuments and buildings were so exact that they could not possibly be confused with any other during the next 374,440 years, a fantastic feat. They charted the revolution of the moon, the length of the Venus year, and the cycles of solar eclipses. What brilliant minds characterized these ancient scholars, whose very names have been forgotten!

It is in the south that the Amerindian can find his greatest sources for pride in his race and the accomplishments of his forefathers. And it is from the south that the totem trails came northward.

Whence came the Amerind?

"Who this race were, and whence they came," wrote William H. Prescott in his *Conquest of Peru*, "may afford a tempting theme for inquiry to the speculative antiquarian. But it is a land of darkness that lies far beyond the domain of history." [15]

Among North American Indians there is a widespread tradition of an eastern origin with arrival by sea. The woodland tribes of the United States believed that their ancestors once dwelt "toward the rising run." According to a Hopi legend, their progenitors came from the tropical south, but earlier there had been a great catastrophe. Some had saved their lives by living "under the sea," and others had survived by crossing the sea on huge reed rafts. The Delawares said they came from "the first land beyond the great ocean."

"At first," say the Iowa Amerinds, "all men lived on an island where the star of day is born." Sioux tradition also refers to an island toward the east or sunrise "where all the tribes were formerly one." They came to their new home in huge canoes after floating on the sea for weeks. The pre-Inca Chimus of South America believed their forefathers arrived by sea in a fleet of long canoes.[16]

I know of no legends among the tribes and peoples of the United States, Mexico, Central and South America that can be related to a western land bridge or Siberia. But why a land bridge? We are told that early man had to come to the Americas on foot because there were no vessels in those days. This is a belief in keeping with the accepted theory of evolutionary culture, but it ignores the crests and troughs of civilizations. Quite likely ice age hunters didn't have boats, but an increasing number of scholars are becoming convinced that not all Amerinds are descended from Siberian ice age hunters. We will probably never know when man first took to the sea.

In populating the South Pacific islands, the Polynesians in their double outrigger canoes sailed thousands of miles. They carried coconuts, they fished and caught rain water. With celestial navigation and charts constructed by tying sticks together in a series, these daring and skillful sailors defied the vast stretches of open sea.

It is not necessary for seaworthy craft to be large vessels. Men have crossed the oceans in boats little larger than bathtubs. Thor Heyerdahl and his balsawood raft, the *Kon-Tiki*, spanned the Pacific for 4,300 nautical miles from Peru to the Polynesian islands and duplicated the feat with a papyrus boat on the Atlantic to show that the Egyptians could have reached Mexico.

In 1966 William Verity, a Florida shipbuilder with pride in his Irish ancestors, sailed alone from Veracruz to Ireland in a twelve-foot sailboat to prove that Irish monks, led by St. Brandan, made it to Yucatan about 600 A.D. And in 1973 a dozen men with three cats, led by Vital Alsar, a Spanish navigator, floated three balsa rafts from Ecuador to Australia. The 8,500-mile voyage took 173 days.

As narrated in the *Chilam Balam*, the ancestors of the Mayans were the survivors of a great cataclysm who fled to the new land.

The Mayans, along with the Toltecs and other peoples of Central America, traced their origin to an island in the eastern sea named Aztlan or Atlan (and to what "lost continent" can be ascribed this name?). This tradition was confirmed by the early transcribers of Mayan records and in the Guatemalan Quiche-Mayan chronicle, the *Popul Vuh*.

Atlantis, fabled lost land of mystery and romance! Since the time of Solon, great lawgiver of classic Athens, and Plato, great Greek philosopher, it has been the subject of thousands of books, the tragic drama of an archaic holocaust, a tradition that will not die. There is an orthodox history of men and events, and there is a hidden history embodied in myth and legend. Troy was a myth until Heinrich Schliemann, who could not forget "the surge and thunder of the Odyssey," brought once more into the light of the sun the ancient walls and towers of Ilium. And so it may be with Atlantis.

Dimitri Rebikoff, oceanographer and marine explorer, noticed a rectangular object while flying over the Grand Bahama Bank in 1967. It appeared to be a man-made wall almost a quarter mile in length at a depth of around three fathoms of water. When he returned several weeks later he found that shifting sands had covered the site. Then, in the summer of the following year, Robert Brush, a Florida cargo pilot, reported sighting what looked like a sunken building not far from where Rebikoff had made his observation. It was a square structure in shallow water off the northern tip of Andros Island.

Since that time Rebikoff, the archeologist Pino Turrolla, and Dr. J. Manson Valentine, honorary curator of the Science Museum of Miami, have discovered sunken columns, pavements and walls apparently of buildings, along with suspicious bottom patterns around the chain of islands extending south from Bimini for sixty miles. One structure made of huge blocks of limestone measures sixty by 100 feet with walls three feet thick. Located near Bimini, it duplicates the floor plan of the Mayan Temple of the Turtles. Submerged for many centuries, the top edges of the stone blocks have been rounded off by weathering. At another location two parallel walls extending up from the sandy bottom are similar to the land causeways the Mayans built on the Yucatan Peninsula.[17]

Is this the location of Atlan—or Atlantis—home of an ancient civilization? Is this where the ancestors of the Central American Indians lived before the great catastrophe? And did the survivors of this cataclysm spread to the Old and New Worlds, remembering the destruction in myths and legends of an antediluvian age that exist in virtually all the civilized cultures of Asia, Europe and America?

"I believe there was an Atlantis," Dr. Valentine told a *Miami Herald* reporter (12 September 1968), "and not because of mythical references to it but because of fact. These consist of various pieces of evidence that I've personally found in explorations in Yucatan, South America, Mexico, and the West Indies." Referring to the Bahamian discoveries, he said: "Whether we have here an Atlantean or post-cataclysmic artifact of upwards of ten thousand years is too early to conjecture upon. But what seems certain is that the ruin is pre-Columbian, as established by its position relative to the present water level."

There is an occult tradition. It is that Atlantis flourished for thousands of years, survived two partial destructions that broke it up into islands, and was completely destroyed about 11,000 years ago. Poseidia, one of the last three major islands, will in time rise from the sea. This revelation and forecast, in part or in whole, has been given by a number of psychic sensitives such as Dresden Pythia, Joseph Leslie, Cheiro (Count Louis Hamon), and more recently by America's "Sleeping Prophet," the late Edgar Cayce.

Whatever was the cause of myth-shrouded Atlantis's demise, it was about eleven millennia ago that the ice age came to an end. From the melting ice and snow came torrents of water surging through the valleys to the sea. The sea level was raised an estimated 300 feet. If any ancient cities existed on low-lying islands or on continental coasts, they would have been inundated.

Edgar Cayce, in his strange trances, contacted what he called the Universal Unconscious, a timeless and spaceless realm of images, an earth memory, a reservoir of knowledge of the past, present, and future. At the Association of Research and Enlightenment at Virginia Beach, Virginia, there are 14,000 recorded transcripts of his psychic readings on file. More than 700 of these readings contain references to Atlantis.

In 1933 a reading referred to "the sunken portion of Atlantis, or Poseidia, where a portion of the temple may yet be discovered under the slime of ages of sea water—near what is known as Bimini, off the coast of Florida." And in 1940 he predicted that "Poseidia will be among the first portions of Atlantis to rise again.

Expect it in '68 and '69—not so far away." And upon Poseidia, he said later, there would be a temple containing records.

This emergence from the watery deep may seem overdue, but the timing of prophecies is rarely exact. It may happen. As custodians of transoceanic cables know, the bottom of the Atlantic is very unstable. An earthquake in 1960 violently raised a portion of the bottom 3,000 feet. Since then other parts have given birth to volcanic islands. Recent geological studies have revealed that the Mid-Atlantic Ridge is being slowly forced up by heat from the earth's interior.[18]

Dr. Valentine suggests that the Atlanteans may have been predominantly light-skinned, and the survivors may have been assimilated by the darker-hued Indians. This, he says, might explain why Pizarro found blond and red-headed Incas, and the lighter their color the higher up the social hierarchy they were. The Amerinds were already ancient inhabitants 11,000 years ago, and they may have added the *Chilam Balam* story of an escape from a catastrophe to their own historical lore. Thus, the two peoples may have become the Southerners whose footsteps echoed throughout the land.

Perhaps the Atlanteans had a superior culture at the time, and white was symbolic with advancement. The gods of old Mexico were bearded and white. Could Quetzalcoatl, the white god of the Aztecs, said to have taught them their arts and sciences, been an Atlantean?

Today we can only speculate. If Poseidia and its long-lost temple of records emerges from the abysmal grave, perhaps we will learn more.

2

Artifacts of a World Forgotten

BEYOND THE INTRICATE PUZZLE of the migrations of peoples, and before the dawn of the Egyptian and Mesopotamian cultures, there was an archaic civilization. Dim memories of its greatness were embodied in ancient traditions. Successive cataclysms have buried most of its artifacts beneath mud, lava, and sea water.

Writes W. J. Perry in his scholarly work *The Children of the Sun: A Study in the Early History of Civilization*, "The achievements of civilized man in preliterate times, prior to the building of the first cities in Neolithic antiquity, include a high development of the exact sciences and technologies." He adds that the cuneiform literature of Neolithic Mesopotamia reveals (1) access to raw materials in many far-off places, (2) development of land and sea travel, (3) domestic, urban and naval architecture, (4) skilled workmanship in ceramics and metallurgy, (5) the stratification of society into specialized guilds, (6) city planning, (7) an already ancient tradition of science and technology, (8) a system of international morality and law in addition to local regulations of law and order.[1]

Cyrus H. Gordon, in his book *Before Columbus: Links Between the Old World and Ancient America*, tells us that "Mesopotamia cherished a tradition that at the dawn of civilization, long before any period of history known to us, science stood at a level from which historic man has fallen. Oannes brought from the sea knowledge and technology above anything achieved (or, for that matter, achievable) by Sumer, Babylonia, Assyria or classical Greek antiquity." [2] Gordon

18

presents evidence that there was a civilization that antedated what we think of as classical civilizations, and that the science and technology of those civilizations were inherited from an earlier civilization of which we presently know almost nothing.

A report in *Time* magazine (26 February 1966) tells of the discovery of the ruins of a dwelling on the French Riviera during excavations for a new apartment building. Supported by upright beams, it was oval-shaped and about fifty by twenty feet in size. Its age was estimated at 200,000 years, at a time when, according to orthodox archeology, all men were at a primitive Stone-Age level and living in caves or in the open. Quite likely many men were at that level, just as they are today with our widely diversified parallel cultures. But how many crests and troughs of civilizations existed during the intervening 194,000 years up to the beginning of recorded history?

Orthodoxy seeks to maintain itself, and challenges to its conformity in beliefs and theories invite an onslaught. Gordon notes that there will be "irrational hostilities evoked by the topic of this book." [3] The vicious, bitter attacks by our leading archeologists and astronomers on Immanuel Velikovsky and his theories in the 1950s will long be remembered in the academic world. Personal vituperation was followed by efforts to suppress his books and threats to his publisher. But the science of the twenty-first century—and the twenty-second—will regard some current concepts much as we regard the astronomical Ptolemaic system of the fifteenth century.

Archeologists, however, are currently experiencing a revitalization and an acceleration in discovery. They have new tools: cesium magnometers and underground detectors, carbon-14 and other dating techniques, underwater exploration equipment. Most important of all is the airplane and aerial photography. Since World War II the number of discoveries made from the air is astonishing. Jungle-covered cities, sunken Mediterranean ports and monuments only recognizable from above have been found. In Iran a ground expedition spent a year and a half attempting to map a lost city in difficult terrain. In thirteen hours' flying time aerial photographs were taken that revealed about 400 sites, most of them in patterns visible only from the air.

Again, there are artifacts from older cultures that have survived the night of oblivion. There is the now famous map drawn in 1513 by the Turkish Admiral Piri Re'is, a fragment of a map of the world found in 1929 in the Palace of Topkapu in Istanbul. A full-size facsimile of the chart was reproduced in 1935 by the Turkish government and sent to the Library of Congress in Washington where photo-reproductions are available. It shows the Atlantic Ocean, the coasts of eastern America and West Africa, portions of western Europe and part of Antarctica. It was only a curiosity until Arlington H. Mallery, a retired engineer and map expert, and M. I. Walters, U.S. Navy Hydrographic engineer, interpreted its unique grid that had baffled earlier cartographers.

In a note written on the map, the admiral said he had used recent maps as well as charts "drawn in the days of Alexander." These latter maps were copies of far earlier ones, probably found in ancient Egypt, and they in turn were copies of still earlier charts, their origin lost in the mists of time. Quite likely there were similar maps, as well as other ancient knowledge, that were lost in Alexandria when the museum and library of 700,000 papyrus rolls were destroyed by fire in Julius Caesar's time, and again in 391 A.D. when the library in the Temple of Jupiter Serapis was burned by Christian fanatics.

The Piri Re'is map shows its part of the world with astonishing accuracy, especially when considering that it is the last of perhaps numerous copies. Upon checking U.S. Army surveys completed in 1953, Walters discovered that newly charted mountains were accurately placed on the map. In coastal locations where the admiral's map differed from modern maps, research disclosed that the older map shows where the coastlines were actually located about 7,000 years ago.

At a Georgetown University Forum in 1956 the Reverend Daniel Linehan, S. J., director of Weston Observatory and seismologist for the U.S. Navy's Antarctic explorations, said the seismic depth-soundings he supervised proved that the coastlines, mountains and other physical features of Antarctica were located exactly as shown on the map.

This was later confirmed by Lt. Col. Harold Z. Ohlmeyer as representative of U.S. Air Force map experts. He wrote: "The geographical detail shown in the lower part of the map agrees very remarkably with the results of the seismic profile made across the top of the icecap by the Swedish-British-Norwegian Antarctic Expedition of 1949. This indicates that the coastline had been mapped before it was covered by the icecap. The icecap in this region is now about a mile thick. We have no idea how the data on this map can be reconciled with the supposed state of geographical knowledge in 1513." [4]

The implications are that the map originally made was the result of a world-wide aerial survey. Even today, many of the locations charted are remote and almost inaccessible to land parties. This is evident in the mapping of inland mountain ranges which are positioned more accurately than an expedition on the surface would be capable of accomplishing.

Interpretation of the Piri Re'is map resulted in a widespread search for similar charts. They were found in museums, in old marine archives and in the families of seafaring folk where they had been handed down for many generations. In regard to Antarctica, care was taken that the representations were not the mythical southern continent of sixteenth-century mapmakers who believed it was needed to "balance" the land masses of the northern hemisphere. The most intensive study of these maps was made by Professor Charles H. Hapgood and his students at Keene State College, Keene, New Hampshire, as reported in Hapgood's book *Maps of the Ancient Sea Kings.* [5]

The most detailed Antarctic map was that of Oronteus Finaeus, a French mathematician and geographer, published in 1531, 300 years before the continent was discovered in 1820. It charts in general the coastlines, it locates within a few degrees the South Pole and the Ross Sea, and its positions of mountain ranges now under the ice correspond well with those discovered in recent years. River channels follow the present courses of the great glaciers, such as the Beardmore Glacier. An island is shown in a position corresponding to that of Ross Island on which Mount Erebus, Antarctica's only active volcano, is located. Of fifty geographical locations (mountains, capes, gulfs, bays and glaciers), a few are correctly positioned and others are off only a few degrees.

"In terms of the usual geological ideas, the map makes no sense," Hapgood writes. "It does make sense in terms of the theory of [my book] *Earth's Shifting Crust.* [6] By that theory Antarctica had a temperate climate during the last ice age in North America. It may have been during that time, therefore, that civilization existed, and even flourished there." [7]

He adds that the warm period ended about 6,000 years ago. If a civilization existed then, the climate change to cold would have brought it to an end and forced a migration of peoples from the freezing continent.

Another map, the original of which was charted by an unknown cartographer, a citizen of an unknown civilization at an unknown time, is the Niccolo Zeno map of Greenland. It was published in Venice in 1558, but had been in the Zeno family since 1402. Most of Greenland has been covered by a glacial sheet for millennia. This map, however, shows such land details as the mountainous parts of the northern area, depressed regions almost at sea level, and nearby islands along the coast now under ice.

The most interesting revelation is that Greenland is split into three islands by straits. This has been confirmed, along with other features, by soundings performed by Danish expeditions, French expeditions led by M. Paul-Emile Victor, and the U.S. Navy Hydrographic Office (now known as the U.S. Naval Oceanographic Office). It is obvious that the original map was drawn during some ancient period when the northern seas were relatively warm.

There are others. The Philippe Buache Map of 1737 shows a waterway across Antarctica dividing it into two huge islands. This division was not known until the International Geophysical Year of 1958 when modern ice-sounding devices located the split along a line of transantarctic mountains.

The Friseo Map, copied from an old Icelandic chart hundreds of years old in 1605, shows the American Atlantic coast north of Maine to Baffin Island. The Icelandic chart has been assumed to belong to a period around 1200 A.D. The North American coast could not have been mapped at that period by a known cartographer.

More startling is the Hadji Ahmed, a Turkish map of 1559. It shows in a fairly accurate replica the west coast of the Americas. Perhaps to the delight of the anthropologists who advocate the Mongoloid origin of Amerinds, it shows the famed land bridge between Alaska and Siberia. Does this mean that the original map was drawn near the end of the last ice age?

And there's the Ibn ben Zara map of the Mediterranean and Aegean Seas. It shows islands that once existed when the waters of earth's seas were lower during the end of the last glaciation.

Quite likely these maps were derived, at least in part, from a common source. And who were these skilled topographic surveyors and probably ancient airmen as well? Professor Hapgood speculates that the civilization responsible for the originals must have been as nearly advanced as our own. They must have had knowledge of the entire world. They must have had instruments for accurately determining longitude as well as latitude. They understood spherical trigonometry as applied to map projections. In short, these ancient cartographers must have been members of a highly organized society with a government possessing enormous resources. As for Antarctica, Hapgood thinks it unlikely that it was mapped for pure science. "It is commerce," he says, "that sets science in motion. It is, therefore, likely that Antarctica was exploited for commercial purposes when the climate made that possible." [8]

There are other artifacts, skills and advanced knowledge of prehistorical civilizations that may have survived the great destructions and appeared in later cultures. Rock crystal lenses with magnifying powers have been found in Crete and Asia Minor. The most remarkable was discovered in one of the royal tombs of Nineveh and is in the British Museum. And only the cast mirrors for the Mount Palomar Observatory are larger than the mass of glass weighing 8.8 tons found in 1966 in a cave near Haifa, Israel. The limestone blocks that formed the furnace have been identified, but what was the source of the tremendous heat that was required to melt the mass? [9]

The ancient Chinese made chain mail armor that was 85 percent aluminum. With their seismographs and a 3,000-year record of earthquakes, the Chinese discovered a four-stage cycle of increases in earthquake intensity. This record is currently being studied by western scientists since it appears capable of being used to predict major earthquake cycles. [10]

A wall painting in a temple at Dendera suggests that the ancient Egyptians used electricity. Two priests are pictured carrying a pair of objects similar to large electric light bulbs with heavy filaments. They are resting on pedestals which closely resemble modern insulators. Braided cables are attached to the bottoms of the lamplike objects and lead to what appears to be an altar. Another startling picture appears on an eighteenth dynasty papyrus scroll. It shows a globe which may represent the sun upheld on a pedestal that looks like a Van de Graaff electrostatic generator. [11]

There is evidence too of electroplating of metal. Four-thousand-year-old copper and bronze vessels and other art objects taken from Egyptian tombs have been found plated with antimony, a silverlike metal. If the Egyptians used electricity, was this knowledge the beginning of an embryo science or an inheritance from a higher technology that existed in a still more distant past?

Perhaps this explains how artists could paint tomb walls in great detail deep in solid rock beyond intricate passages. Obviously illumination was necessary, yet there are no tombs in which the slightest deposits from torches or oil lamps are found. It has been suggested that a series of mirrors could have directed sunlight into the many-angled passageways, but there is no mention in Egyptian writings of such a feat, nor have any such large mirrors ever been discovered.

A knowledge of electroplating could have passed from the Egyptians to the Sumerians and Babylonians and finally to the Parthians. The Parthians were undistinguished in anything except military tactics, yet among their artifacts have been found the famed "Baghdad Batteries." Quite a number of these primitive but practical batteries are now in museums, and it is believed they were used for electroplating by silversmiths.

Ivan T. Sanderson, in his book *Investigating The Unexplained*, tells of two ancient Amerindian artifacts. One is a gold pendant found during a "dig" in Cocle Province, Panama, and now in the Museum of the University of Pennsylvania, Philadelphia. It appears to represent a mechanical device with two cogwheels on an axle with a rocker arm between them. It very closely resembles what farmers and construction men call a backhoe. The other is a pre-Columbian gold model from the State Collection of Colombia. Unidentifiable with any known animal, fish or insect, it looks like a delta-winged aircraft. There are four similar objects in the Chicago Natural History Museum and one in the Smithsonian in Washington, D.C.

There is a surprising amount of evidence for highly advanced prehistoric cultures. "A true 'dark ages' apparently descended upon the Old World well before the rise of the Romans and not *after* their collapse," Sanderson writes. "Moreover, it seems to have descended upon the New World at about the same time, so that there were only memories left; but these memories were kept alive there for some two thousand more years because their local priesthoods were not extinguished until the arrival of the Spaniards. The priests of the truly 'ancient' (to us) world were manifestly a technological class (and probably worldwide), and they kept their knowledge to themselves—and so closely that, when threatened by aggressive temporal power, they had no defense but a sort of 'scorched earth' policy." [12]

Some writers present the theory that ancient astronauts visited the earth and taught early man some useful knowledge. Perhaps so.

No matter the source, the fact is that they possessed an advanced technology and erudition. And they were especially learned in mathematics and astronomy.

In 1900 a party of sponge-divers was driven by a storm to an anchorage near the Greek island of Antikythera. There, at a depth of 200 feet, they found the wreck of an ancient vessel. Greek archeologists were called to the site and the ship was explored. They found marble and bronze statues with well-proportioned, beautiful bodies and delicate, haunting faces representing the best in Hellenic artistry; pottery jars that had once contained fragrant Aegean wines; and an object, a mysterious object covered by a thick coating of calcified material.

The object was taken to the Greek National Museum in Athens where it was placed in storage as unidentified. From time to time some of the corrosion was removed and puzzled scientists examined it. Finally, in 1958, Dr. Derek Price of the Institute of Advanced Studies at Princeton noticed the object while visiting the museum. Removing more of the encrusted material, he discovered that it was a working model of the solar system, including the earth, sun, moon and planets—a precise, accurate astronomical computer with gears, wheels and dials that moved the celestial bodies through their orbits in correct relationship. Greek symbols and calibrations on the base explained the theory of the device and the various cycles of the sun and moon. Its age was estimated at about 100 B.C.

"Finding this device is like finding a jet plane in the tomb of King Tut," Dr. Price said. "This delicate, precisely made astronomical instrument is two thousand years old, made at a time when we thought they did not understand the solar system nor how to manufacture such an instrument, but there it is!" An article with photographs and detailed diagrams appeared in the *Scientific American*, June 1959.

How many other unidentified or mislabeled artifacts of ancient cultures are in the world's museums?

It is important to note that while an advanced astronomical knowledge could be gained by centuries of observation of movements in the mighty mainland of space beyond the earth, so precise was this ancient knowledge that one wonders if instrumentation was involved. Recently, new computations have been made of the ancient Mayan calendar system—calendars more exact than either the Gregorian or Julian calendars. The Mayans too plotted the movements of the sun, moon and planets, and as a result of their studies they devised a star calendar based on the rotation of the earth on its axis that was only .000069 of a day off each year!

There is evidence that the Greeks, the Mayans and others may have inherited some of this knowledge from an older world-wide culture. Look up at the splendor of the stellar universe, at the eternity of distant suns in the dark depths of space. You can see that it takes a lot of imagination to find connections between the accepted constellations and the stars they represent. You will see that by drawing imaginary lines between stars you could create literally thousands of figures that could be constellations. Why, then, are many constellations the same among scattered peoples in the ancient world?

Our modern constellation Scorpius had the identical name among the Mayans. Aquarius, the Water Bearer, was the god Tlaloc, Ruler of the Rains, in ancient Mexico. Orion, the Hunter, of Greece, Babylon and Egypt, in far away and long ago China was the Hunter of the Autumn Hunt. Also in old Cathay, the Babylonian sign Aries, the Ram, was the Sheep; Taurus, the Bull, was the Ox; and Sagittarius, the Archer, was the Horse. While the names are identical or similar, they do not always refer to the same constellation.

The Chinese-Tibetan calendar has the years of the Dragon, Snake, Rabbit, Dog and Monkey. In Central America the Aztec calendar gave these same names to days—the Alligator, Snake, Rabbit, Dog and Monkey.

All these similarities can hardly be coincidences. Regarding constellation names, the noted scientist Giorgio de Santillana, in his book *The Origins of Scientific Thought*, writes: "They were repeated without question substantially the same from Mexico to Africa and Polynesia—and have remained with us to this day." [13] There must have been a common source. It seems that early cultures derived the names from even older lists and adopted them to symbolize their own heavens. Ptolemy transmitted them from Hipparchus (130 B.C.) "as of unquestioned authority, unknown origin and unsearchable antiquity."

Long ago master designers and dedicated laborers built a zodiacal temple ten miles across near mystical Glastonbury, Somerset, England. Here may be the first "mighty labor of the Isle of Britain" of which the Welsh bards sang, and for thousands of years it lay covered with King Arthur's "mantle of invisibility." It was discovered when aerial photographs were taken and pieced together by the

British Government about the time of World War I. This great earthworks was brilliantly surveyed, construction of the huge earthwork figures taking advantage of the topography of hills, valleys, rivers and streams. How old is it? No one knows, but it is oriented to Taurus, so it must have been built during the period between 4419 B.C. and 2264 B.C. And who built this Round Table of the Stars with its thirty miles of circumference? Tradition says Hu the Mighty and his followers came "from the East in the Age of Ages" bringing the knowledge of the stars from Asia Minor. And here he laid out the sacred zodiac which is called, in the Welsh tongue, *Caer Sidi*. [14]

The greatest monument to ancient sophisticated knowledge is the Great Pyramid of Gizeh, attributed to Cheops (Khufu) although there is no definite proof that he built it. No one has yet come up with unassailable answers as to when it was erected, how it was built, and by whom. There is, however, no doubt that it was constructed as an astronomical observatory and a geodetic marker.

The meridian passing through the pyramid circles the planet, dividing the continents as well as the Pacific region into two equal parts; thus it can be considered a prime meridian like Greenwich. It is interesting to note that the prime meridian of the Piri Re'is map is Syene, Egypt.

The structure of the pyramid incorporates the value of *pi* as 3.1416, a more accurate value than that of the Greek mathematicians. The pyramid's base is a square whose perimeter is equal to the circumference of a circle whose radius is the pyramid's height. On display is the unit of measurement used by the builders, the "pyramidal inch." Unlike the French meter which is based on the meridian, it is a more accurate unit since it is based on the unchanging length of the polar axis. Fifty pyramidal inches makes a length of almost exactly one ten-millionth of the polar axis.

The pyramid is a calendar. The sum of its base sides gives the number of days in a year as 365, and, amazingly, adds the .2422 fraction of a day. It incorporates the geographical degrees of latitude and longitude. One minute of latitude at the equator equals 1,842.9 meters. The base of the monument has a perimeter intended to represent ⅛ minute of a degree, and twice the perimeter is 1,842.91 meters.

Approximately forty-five stories in height, the pyramid is composed of 2½ million stone blocks weighing from 2½ to twelve tons each. If its estimated weight of 600,000 tons is multiplied by one billion, we get the approximate weight of the earth. By adding together the diagonal lines of the pyramid's base we get a total of 25,826.6 which corresponds to the rotation of 25,827 years of the earth's polar axis.

Originally the pyramid was covered with white limestone facing stones that caused it to shine like a titanic beacon in reflected sunlight. At that time, it is believed by some writers, their slightly concave shape may have caused the monument to cast shadows of varying lengths to indicate the arrival of the spring equinox, the passing of the year and the hours of the day.

The builders incorporated their astronomical knowledge into their cyclopean monument. When its height is multiplied by ten million the total equals the approximate distance between the earth and the sun. One pyramidal inch multiplied by 100 million comes close to the distance covered by the earth in its orbit around the sun. The minor discrepancy may be due to variations that have occurred since the pyramid was built.

In the Great Pyramid's so-called King's Chamber there is a red granite coffer or sarcophagus. There is no evidence that it ever contained a body. Some scholars have suggested various meanings in its dimensions and volume, but accurate measurements cannot be made today since moronic, idiotic tourists have chipped pieces from it. Its sides, unlike all other sarcophagi, carry no pictured or hieroglyphic memorials or religious representations.

To fully outline the embalmed knowledge in this huge time capsule requires a book, and that book is Peter Tomkins's *Secrets of the Great Pyramid.* [15] The figures given are accurate to the last millimeter, as confirmed in a detailed and technical appendix in the book written by Dr. Livio Catullo Stecchini, considered the greatest living authority on ancient measurements. [16]

If no other artifacts existed, the Great Pyramid of Gizeh alone would be sufficient testimony to a former culture as advanced as or even in some ways surpassing our own in basic knowledge. With the passage of time, more of its secrets may come to light. Doubtless it was the first of Egypt's seventy pyramids and it is the largest—the only one to display mathematical and astronomical features. Quite likely it was erected by the same intellectuals who left a legacy of maps that eventually descended to Admiral Piri Re'is and others.

The builders made it a repository of scientific knowledge for an intervening period of history, to bridge the gap of a dark age that followed the destruction of one culture and the gradual development of a new one. Did they foresee their end and create this mammoth time capsule as their gift to posterity? Or was it the final accomplishment of a few survivors of the great catastrophe?

What startling stories in the history of man are hidden in the darkness of antiquity! The zenith of Egyptian civilization was reached about the end of the fourth millennium B.C., and it seemed to appear without any previous transitional stages as if it had been imported from elsewhere. Then, like the early cultures of South and Central America, it began to decline, to slowly retrogress. Its greatness was at its beginning.

And from what world-wide predecessor did the Egyptians and early Americans derive their cultural heritage? Surely the catastrophe that is only dimly remembered in the folklore of races must have been tremendous. Who were these people who have vanished so deeply into the maelstrom of time?

Whoever they were, they had attained greatness. As Peter Tomkins writes: "Whoever built the Great Pyramid, as the legends accurately report, knew how to make excellent charts of the stars with which to correctly calculate longitude, draw maps of the globe, and so travel at will across its continents and oceans."

With Marcus Aurelius, may we "Look at the yawning void of the future, and at that other limitless space, the past."

3

Mystery of the Megaliths

PERHAPS AT LEAST SOME of the Amerinds may have been here all the time, right from the beginning. Far from being late arrivals in the Americas, the antiquity of the red men in the so-called New World is so deep, dark and mysterious that the anthropologists who possess the most knowledge are appalled at their own ignorance.

One authority is Dr. John W. Sargent, of Oxford and Lima, leader of scientific expeditions to Peru for the British Museum. "After twenty-eight years spent in probing the past of Peru and Latin America in general, I feel that I know less today about it than I imagined I did when I began," he writes.[1] His studies have convinced him that man was living in South America some 200,000 years ago, and he agrees with the late Arthur Poznansky, the famed Bolivian savant, that the pre-Incan civilizations in the Andes probably date back some 18,000 years.

Such vast periods of time are anathema to the orthodox who cling to·traditional channels of belief. The discoveries that will replace current notions lie in the future when archeologists, instead of digging into Old World soil, get busy in Central and South America. Removing the dust from ancient America's past is needed, not only to correct present misconceptions but also for the just replacement of a great people's pride.

As in Egypt, the succeeding cultures of the Americas are a study in progressive decline. The most ancient civilizations were those most concerned with mathematical calculations and symbols dis-

30

playing a vast astronomical knowledge, long lost. This history is like a vast picture puzzle with only a few of the pieces finding their proper places.

At the dawn was the titan of them all—the Megalith. This was the one that timed the passing years and centuries with a calendar more accurate than our own. This was the one that terraced the hillsides now covered with jungle, engineered the finest dams, and built the best roads and bridges. Quite likely, too, it was the culture that left an astonishing heritage of food vegetation, and grew cotton in so many colors that it did not need to be dyed. These varieties of cotton, needless to say, have long been lost.

Titan is the proper word to describe the Megalithic culture, for they were the master builders in stone. Their bewildering engineering mastery was not confined to the Americas, but is found in many parts of the world. What relationships may have existed between the Herculean artisans in America, Europe, North Africa, the Near East and islands in the Pacific, we do not know. What they had in common was the ability to quarry, dress and erect Cyclopean blocks of stone and to build enormous earthworks.

Among the prehistoric monuments of England are Avebury, Stonehenge and the Glastonbury zodiac. On the plain of Carnac in Brittany are hundreds of standing stones arranged in straight lines. Megalithic structures are found throughout the Mediterranean region, in Crete, Greece, Sardinia, southern Spain, Malta and Egypt.

In Lebanon there is fallen grandeur at Baalbek with its ruins of the temples of Jupiter-Baal and Bacchus along with other structures and a great court. The immensity, the tremendous size of the architecture is awe-inspiring. After the visitor's initial surprise, Baalbek and its former splendor casts a spell of serenity. One dreams of its magnificent past, of the long gone worshipers of pagan gods who once thronged its courts, of the endless stream of humanity that flows through time into the great unknown. But here too is a mystery that we will meet many times in the Americas.

Three great stones are a part of the Temple of Jupiter platform or acropolis, each approximately sixty-four feet long, thirteen feet high and ten feet thick. They are in the middle course of the masonry twenty-three feet above the ground. *These stones weigh 1,200 tons apiece.* In the quarry about a half mile away is an even larger stone, quarried but never transported, weighing an estimated 2,000 tons. How were they moved and raised? In fact, why were they moved at all when they could have been cut into smaller blocks for easier transportation? Their massiveness was not necessary.[2]

Consider: according to the *Guinness Book of World Records*, the crane with the world's greatest and highest lifting capacity was installed in 1969 at Harland and Wolff's shipbuilding dock, Belfast, Northern Ireland. Built in West Germany, it spans 460 feet and can raise objects weighing 940 tons. Yet the Baalbek acropolis giants weigh 260 tons more than this crane's capacity.

Although their individual stones did not attain the tremendous weights of Baalbek, the Megalithic great-stone builders reached their peak, in size and number of structures as well as artistry, in Central and South America. And we should add mystery, for this race (or races) which preceded the Incas transported enormous granite, andesite and red porphyry blocks from quarries hundreds of miles away, across mountains and over rivers, and placed them on Andean mountaintops and plateaus. Many of these rocks weigh 150 to 200 tons. They are built into temples, fortresses, and retaining walls so tightly that the thinnest knife blade cannot be inserted between them. Withstanding the earthquakes of countless millennia, they are as permanent as the metamorphic strata from which they came, monuments of man for all earth's ages.[3]

Some display intricate carvings that present another enigma. According to A. Hyatt Verrill, "No living man, Indian or otherwise, could . . . duplicate the simplest of their stone carvings by means of the stone implements we find. It is not a question of skill, patience, time—it is a human impossibility."[4]

Stone implements would endure like the rocks themselves, but iron tools would have disintegrated after this lapse of time. Iron mines in the Lake Titicaca region were worked in antiquity, but given the same amount of exposure, iron, which is subject to rust, does not last as long as other metals. Tools made of other metals may have been used by the great-stone builders and subsequently lost.

Another puzzle is transportation. Great stones can be dragged by many men, usually with the aid of tree logs as rollers. Such a method, however, is simply not practical in the mountainous Andean terrain with its steep slopes, swift torrents and cliffs. Yet the stones were moved, and the distant quarries from which many came can be identified by their mineral composition.

How were the monoliths transported in such massive sizes and weights? Some have speculated that the ancients used a power or force unknown today. It is said this energy may have reacted with the gravitational field, applying a levitating force to every part of the stone simultaneously, inside and outside, thus eliminating the need for any external force applied to the surface only by pressure or harness.

Might such a force be limited in its application to minerals or to nonmagnetic materials? And might this partially explain why practically all relics of the very deep past are nonmetallic? Such a limitation too would have prevented the power's use in the development of a mechanized culture, such as our own. It should be noted that these mammoth stones appear only in the earliest constructions. Later cultures that inherited these megaliths built with stones of lesser and lesser weights until only large pebbles were used.

Was this energy available only temporarily due to certain gravitational-magnetic conditions existing at the time? Both at Baalbek and on Easter Island it appears the construction work was terminated suddenly. Baalbek's largest block was never moved, and a huge unfinished stone statue lies in the island quarry. There may or may not be a connection. Did disaster strike a people who could transport and raise rocks weighing hundreds and hundreds of tons, and was the power source they used lost thereafter? [5]

There are counter-gravitational forces that manifest themselves occasionally. Saints, mediums and East Indian fakirs have levitated themselves; counter-gravitational effects can occur during poltergeist phenomena. In *The Books of Charles Fort* there are accounts of hail and stones falling with "uncanny slowness," and of objects like baskets, bottles and clothing rising from the ground and drifting away in the windless atmosphere, sometimes to the accompaniment of sharp detonations. At Marbleton, Ulster County, New York, bewildered witnesses watched as stones slowly rose three or four feet above a field, then moved horizontally for thirty to sixty feet. Obviously there are forces in nature that man has yet to discover—or rediscover. [6]

It's possible that remains of the power grids used by megalithic peoples as a levitating agency still exist. Modern governments have sponsored efforts to overcome gravity with an electromagnetic method or some form of vibrational energy. While discoveries of grids like those that may have been used by the ancestors of the Amerinds as well as by early cultures elsewhere await future research, it is in Great Britain where we find what may be evidence now. Throughout the United Kingdom there are literally thousands of carefully-designed stone structures, as well as ancient cairns, barrows, mounds and temple sites.

Early in this century a man named Alfred Watkins, while riding across high hills near his English home, stopped to look out over the landscape below. Suddenly he realized that there was a network of absolutely straight lines connecting and intersecting the locations of stone monuments and other ancient sites, alignments that stood out "like glowing wires all over the surface of the country." Studies since then have confirmed the existence of these lines, or leys as they are now named. They are not roads or paths; they cross over lakes, bogs and up over mountains. They are from five to twenty miles or more in length and are marked by standing stones along the way or notches cut into the hillsides. At some places where the leys intersect the spots are of long traditional sanctity, and churches have been built on them within historical times.

Quite a number of amateur archeologists locate and study leys as a hobby, and they have their own monthly magazine, *The Ley Hunter*. To eliminate coincidence, ley hunters stipulate that an alignment which merits investigation must have at least five valid sites aligned within a fairly short distance, that is, ten rather than fifty miles. One student is Guy Underwood, who has used a dowsing rod in outlining the patterns of underground rivers and springs beneath the leys. He claims the patterns reveal an unnatural alignment that follows what he calls "geodetic forces."

These sites and stone constructions are not the crude works of ancient Britons who were ignorant, superstitious savages. There is computer evidence that Stonehenge was an observatory that predicted solstices, equinoxes, and eclipses of the sun and moon. The leading authority on the astronomical nature of Britain's stone monuments is Professor Alexander Thom. In his books *Lunar Observatories* and *Megalithic Sites in Britain* [7] he presents the results of an examination of 600 stone circles and detailed surveys of 300 of them. The circles provide an extremely accurate means of calculating the movements of sun, moon and major planets and stars during the year. He has discovered that the people who constructed these circles had a knowledge of mathematics that was only equalled thousands of years later in classical Greece. Quite likely they were the ones who erected the huge zodiac at Glastonbury.

At this point I can do no better than to quote from my friends Janet and Colin Bord, whose book *Mysterious Britain* is a masterwork of text and photographs:

Further research into leys, in the light of other unexplained mysteries such as dowsing, radiesthesia, ufology, terrestrial zodiacs like that at Glastonbury, folklore, all of which appear to have links with leys, suggests that there may be a subtle reason for their existence. It is now widely felt that the leys may in fact follow invisible lines of power criss-crossing the countryside, and that early man was aware of this power, which he harnessed for his own spiritual and physical benefit (and also for the benefit of nature and the earth) by erecting his "temples" at certain significant points along the power lines. Some people who seem to have a particular kind of sensitivity receive shocks, sometimes violent, when they touch certain ancient stones, but the stones don't seem to be "charged" with power all the time.[8]

The suggestion that the stones form a gigantic power network is advocated by John Williams who, as leader of a group of amateur archeologists, is the subject of a NZPA-Reuters news dispatch dated 23 September 1969. Over a seventeen-year period Williams has compared the positions on ordnance survey maps of more than 3,000 stone circles and individual standing stones, all aligned in a single huge geometrical pattern. In addition to the leys, he says each one is aligned to neighbors up to twenty miles away at an angle of 23½ degrees (the angle of inclination of the earth's axis), or a multiple.

Williams told the London reporter that he took thousands of photographs and a surprising number were "fogged." Once he and a friend photographed the same stone together and both came out with a fogged band across them in the same place. His own picture was in color and the fog band was a dark blue. This led him to surmise that a kind of ultraviolet light in the stones was spoiling his pictures.

"Since then I've had many more examples of the same phenomenon," Williams said. "Most, if not all, standing stones contain quartz, a crystal similar to that used with the cat's whisker in early wireless receivers. I believe most stones would show the fog effect if systematically photographed. I now think the stones form a gigantic power network, though I cannot guess for what purpose."

Williams observed that more than 200 of the stone sites are in north-south alignment and are named after King Arthur. "But Arthur," he said, "does not signify a Celtic warrior king. In Welsh the name means Great Bear, and this may be a clue that the power system was based on polar magnetism. Radio waves and X-rays have always been there, although modern man only recently discovered them. Is it possible that prehistoric man discovered something analogous which is still unknown to us?"

Do leys exist elsewhere? Most countries have ancient building sites, and it is more than likely that leys are a world-wide phenomenon. There are dragon lines in China which seem to have the same purpose. Alfred Watkins in his book *The Old Straight Track* mentions briefly similarities to certain ley features in Burma, India, Palestine, Egypt and Syria.[9] If leys formed power grids to transport stones, they will certainly be found eventually in Central and South America where the terrain is rugged compared with that in Great Britain.

Another mystery is how these massive, irregularly shaped stones were so closely fitted together without mortar. Despite the fact that some have as many as thirty angled planes, each plane surface fits tightly and exactly with the adjoining stones, including the inner surfaces. All of the stones interlock like the pieces of a jigsaw puzzle, which is probably why the walls are earthquake-proof. Considering their weights, they could hardly have been fitted into the wall by endlessly taking them out, cutting, replacing, cutting, and repeating until the fit was perfect. As far as is known, the pre-Incas had no precision stonecutting implements.

One theory holds that the ancients had discovered a method of softening stone, thus permitting it to be molded like fresh putty. This would explain both the tightly-fitted walls, the intricate carvings that could be imprints, and the bas-reliefs. The late Ivan T. Sanderson, discussing this subject in his book *Things*, points out that with a mixture of stone, sand, water and cement we can make concrete—comparable to hard, solid rock. And rock can be unmade by pulverization or heat. Certain chemical agents can dissolve at least one component of any rock that is a mixture of substances in crystalline form.

Sanderson writes:

In the Maya city of Chichen Itza, in Yucatan, Central America, you may look at a building called "The Nunnery." It's an eerie structure with bas-reliefs that sprawl all over it. After studying these bas-reliefs for half an hour or so I guarantee that you'll find it hard to remember that the men who built this had no metal tools, and there are no hard rocks within 200 miles. You may well begin to ask yourself how they executed these acres of intricate carvings, some of them not just bas-reliefs but very nearly in the complete round. Try chipping a thousand figures out of a block of limestone, with, presumably, another bit of limestone, from behind, with about an inch of space in which to do it. Did the Mayas really chip out these bas-reliefs with stone handaxes, picking away day after day? [10]

How much easier it would have been to soften the surface of the stone until it had the consistency of fresh putty and then mould and sculpture the decoration in an hour or so. As for the walls, soft surfaces of stones, like the concrete lowered underwater when building dams today, would naturally take on the appropriate contours of all the stones next to them.

An advocate of the soft stone theory who became a legend was Colonel P. H. Fawcett, who vanished along with a son and a companion in 1925 while searching for a lost city deep in the Amazon basin. An army officer and an explorer, he was commissioned by several South American countries to survey and define their political boundaries. He was awarded the Gold Medal of the Royal Geographical Society. And like his fellow British Army officers General Charles "Chinese" Gordon and Major Yeats-Brown, he was a mystic. Another son, Brian Fawcett, has published the colonel's diaries written during seven earlier South American expeditions.

There is a small bird resembling a kingfisher that is native to the upper forested regions of the Peruvian-Bolivian Andes. Living in flocks, their nests are circular holes in rock faces above rivers and streams, and these are the only locations where such holes are found. When Fawcett expressed surprise at nature's wisdom in creating the rock nests in such favorable spots, he was told by natives and resident Europeans that the birds *made* the holes.

The colonel decided that this was something to see. Sure enough, as he watched, the birds flew in, each with a plant leaf in its bill. They clung to the rock face like a swallow, rubbed the rock with the leaf in a circular motion until it crumbled, flew away, then returned with another leaf. Four or five leaves were applied, then the birds pecked away on the spots with their bills and, lo, the rock crumbled away until a circular hole was made. Moreover, the rocks varied, being sedimentary, metamorphic and nonsedimentary like granite. The colonel was unable to identify the plant.

Another account is of a man who walked about five miles through forested territory along the Pyrene River in Peru's Chuncho Province. The purpose of his hike was to recover his horse which had been crippled and left at a ranch. He was wearing large spurs. Upon arrival at the ranch he discovered that his spurs were almost totally corroded away. His excited host asked if he had walked through a dense patch of low, fleshy-leafed plants with red leaves. He said he had. "That's the plant," the rancher said, "that the ancient Incas used for shaping stones."

Fawcett's final report was received firsthand from an Englishman, a veteran executive of a mining camp at Cerro de Pasco, Peru. He had joined a group of men searching for relics in an ancient burial ground. A native had been taken along to do the digging. They found some undisturbed graves, and in one of them was a large earthenware jug that had been carefully sealed. Upon opening it, they discovered it contained a thick, black liquid.

When one of the men, somewhat intoxicated, tried to force the native to taste it, the native fled and the men boisterously chased him. Meanwhile, the jug, which was resting on a large rock, was knocked over and broken. When they returned a few minutes later, they discovered that the liquid was gone. In its place was a pool of claylike putty that had formerly been the surface of the rock. The rock beneath the broken jar had a doughlike substance that could be kneaded and shaped like warm wax.

Are there plant juices that can dissolve rocks? Sanderson points out that some rocks can be dissolved with dilute hydrochloric acid. And there are plants that produce acids (and alkalines) that are by no means diluted.

The most popular theory is that the irregular stones were ground to a perfect fit, *in situ*—they were above the adjoining stones and worked into place in their designated niches by pushing them back and forth, assisted by their own weight and gravity, plus, perhaps, water and sand.[11] Such a procedure, if performed by hand, would be extremely laborious and incredibly time-consuming, if not impossible.

An example is the Sacsahuaman Fortress mentioned in chapter 2, in the Peruvian High Andes above the pre-Inca city of Cuzco. The mammoth stones on the lower tiers dwarf a man on horseback standing beside them. Some are eighteen to twenty feet high, and about twelve feet square at the base. They are estimated to weigh about 200 tons each. Even modern engineering machinery would not be able to lift them up into position, shove them to and fro against terrific friction without loosening their snugly fitting neighbors, and fit tightly every angle and contour. The fortress walls are sixty feet high and the stones are dark basalt, as hard and rugged as granite.[12]

Perhaps the same titanic power that transported the stones was used to erect the walls. The megalithic peoples must have had a practical method of placing together with such accuracy the edges of stones weighing tons. Occasionally a latter day, less well-built stone wall is torn down, and the workmen are astonished to find behind it another wall showing the workmanship of the master masons of all time—an original true megalith. A true megalith can be seen at Hatun Runiyok in eastern Cuzco, Peru, and at Saksa-Waiman where it is partially covered by later, cruder masonry. At Ollantay-Tambo the joints in the polished walls are too fine to be seen by the naked eye, and a lens is necessary to make sure that there is really a seam. Comparing these with the monuments of early Egypt and elsewhere, it's clear that the finest of all megalithic workmanship was performed in South America.

Not only was their workmanship precise, but almost incredibly colossal. The airplane has made it possible in recent years to recognize certain apparent hills and mountain foothills as artificial structures, man-made pyramids or mounds. Many of these were constructed with adobe bricks which in time disintegrated into great earthen masses. A lack of strata, plus the dicovery of a strange beehivelike stone construction during excavations by treasure seekers, have caused speculation that Panecillo or "bread roll" mountain near Quito, Ecuador, is a stupendous artificial mound.

In 1947 an earthquake in Paraguay resulted in a mountain landslide. It disclosed an inner wall about 120 feet high and almost a mile long. And in Peru's Marcahuasi region giant mountain rocks have been carved into figures of animals and human faces, but they are only recognizable at the summer solstice and other times when the sun is in a position to reveal all their features.[13]

Although strictly speaking it is not megalithic, and its erection obviously covered a long period of time, the largest definitely known man-made monument ever constructed is the pyramid temple-platform at Cholula de Rivadahia in Mexico. A church crowns its top, but it is a pitiful symbol of any victory of Christianity over paganism. The massive edifice honors Quetzalcoatl, the mysterious white prophet represented by the plumed serpent

*Amen To a good Atheist

god of the Toltecs and Aztecs. At present it is 177 feet tall and its base covers twenty-five acres. Its total volume is estimated at 4,300,000 cubic yards, as compared with the 3,360,000 cubic yards of the Great Pyramid of Gizeh. Originally it covered a greater area and was over 200 feet tall. After partially destroying it, the Spanish conquerors finally gave up and covered it with earth to disguise it as a hill. Such a deception could not be successful, and the natives to this day regard it with reverence as a memorial to the greatness of their forefathers.[14]

Another great earthwork, not in mass or height but in extent, is the intriguing "Nazca Lines" of Peru, about 250 miles south of Lima. Here precisely drawn lines and figures cover the landscape over an area sixty miles long and five to ten miles wide. To fly over this immense pictorial panorama is an awe-inspiring, bewildering experience; one is inclined to agree with Erich Von Daniken and others that perhaps this was a guide and landing place for long ago extra-terrestrial visitors. Who made them—and why—is unknown. What shocks one into total bafflement is that the patterns cannot be observed from the ground. They were unknown until aircraft began flying over the region.

The lines and figures, thousands in number, are actually furrows. The color contrast that makes the huge patterns visible was achieved by removing the surface layer of dirt and bringing into view a paler substratum of less oxidized soil. The removed earth was placed along the edges to create sharp outlines. The furrows are from three to six feet deep, and while mostly only a few feet wide are sometimes as much as 300 feet. They were originally thought to be irrigation ditches.

What enigmatic message bridging millennia lies in this complexity of designs? There are triangles, rectangles, trapezoids and other geometrical shapes. There are huge figures of birds, turtles, spiders, a jaguar, a whale and a man. Long and absolutely straight directional lines that go on for miles testify to expert surveying over the uneven terrain; one line even passes over a mountain. The figures average around 150 yards in length and width.

Dr. Maria Reiche, a German scientist, has spent twenty-five years studying the pictorial maze. With the help of engineers, surveyors and cartographers, she made a detailed map of the area. She has not arrived at any definite conclusion as to who made the maze or why.

Dr. Paul Kosok, of Long Island University, after lengthy studies has discovered that many lines mark the solstices and equinoxes, while others appear to designate the paths of the moon, planets and certain fixed stars. He calls it "the largest astronomical picture book in the world, a giant astronomical calendar." [15]

By working out the annual deviation rates of key stars plus the carbon-14 dating of a wooden stick believed to have been used in surveying, Dr. Kosok has announced a tentative date of about 500 A.D. But if the makers of the expertly designed and polished pottery found in the region were the same people who created the maze, the Nazca lines are far, far older. Approximately 225,000 pots have been found, mostly in burial pits, and they are unlike those of other Peruvian cultures. The pots are decorated with beautiful, detailed polychrome paintings. When human faces are shown, they vary greatly in color and physiognomy.

Far more startling, however, are the clear representations of llamas. Today llamas have cloven hoofs or two toes. The llamas on Nazca pottery have five toes. Scientists say llamas once had five toes on each foot, but that was thousands of years ago in the early Stone Age when man supposedly was much too primitive to even make pottery. [16]

High in the Bolivian Andes, where the land meets the clouds in the tenuous crystal air, lie the ruins of Tiahuanaco, a city that has slumbered for countless millennia. Its Cyclopean walls, its huge statues gazing stonily from the centuried gloom of a dark antiquity—these are the herculean works of long vanished master builders. This was a capital of a megalithic culture, probably the oldest of them all.

Here the visitor does not feel the serenity experienced at Baalbek or Petra, but the profound awe of seeing the legacy of a mighty, alien race. One feels too a sadness, perhaps inspired by the carving of the god on the Gate of the Sun. Hewn from a single hard andesite slab, it is ten feet high and twelve feet wide. Once a part of a temple, today it is a portal opening onto open space. Bas-reliefs of curiously birdlike, eternally running men cover the lintel, and above them is the god—standing short and squat and squarish. His eyes look out from eons past, and below them are round teardrops forever descending.

Why does the god weep? What tragedy, what great loss inspires his grief? Is his sorrow in remembrance of things past, a longing for some home forever gone, perhaps a time lost in catastrophe?

Tiahuanaco in the Quichua (Incan) tongue means "Seats of the Mighty Ancients." It was here, said the Incas, where the sun first appeared, meaning it was the birthplace of the first empire of the sun. When the Spaniards reached this deserted city on this vast, desolate plateau, the oldest living Incas had no knowledge of who built it or when. "Long, long ago, when the mountains were hills and the deserts were green, it was built by giant gods," they said in bewilderment. But the greed-driven conquerors lost no time in breaking up many of the stone blocks in order to remove silver bars and tenons.

Ten miles distant is Lake Titicaca, the "wash basin of the gods," 138 miles long and thirty to forty miles wide. The plateau is 12,500 feet above sea level, thus making Titicaca the highest navigable lake in the world. It was sacred to the Incas, who believed the sun god sent down his son and daughter to Sun Island, the largest island in the lake, to become the parents of the royal family. A stone temple, the "House of the Incas," was erected on the island, and it became the most holy place in their empire. The ruins of the temple terraces are still there, rising like a gigantic flight of steps.

Much of Tiahuanaco has been destroyed. Stones and statues have been broken up and carted away to furnish a roadbed for a railroad and to erect other buildings, including much of the city of La Paz. Some walls have collapsed in violent earthquakes.

Still there are great halls, courts, platforms and underground chambers. There is a step pyramid, carved gateways, ornate decorations and massive sculptured figures staring into an infinity of time. From these and other geometrically true megalithic masterworks, the later Incas learned their architecture. But great as were their own accomplishments, they lived always in the shadow of their superior predecessors.

The cultural attributes of stones cannot be dated by any quality inherent in the stones themselves. Animal bones and other organic objects have been given widely different ages by the carbon-14 method. This is to be expected. Not only was the city occupied over a long period of time by its original builders, but parts of the city and the region around it were the later homes of the Colla, the Aruakians and other Amerind peoples. The deep antiquity of this place is indicated by unearthed pots with painted pictures of the toxodan, a large, hairy, short-legged animal supposedly extinct a million years ago.

At this great height of more than two miles above the sea, visitors from lower altitudes are stricken by *soroche*, a mountain sickness induced by thin air. Here corn and other crops will not ripen. Campfires produce little heat and candles have tiny flames. Aircraft engines lose a third of their rated horsepower, and some planes are forced to make two-mile runs to become airborne.

The local natives are small and sturdy and have adapted to the scarcity of oxygen by developing chests and lungs far larger than normal. Their bodies contain approximately a quart more blood than the average lowlander, which gives them a million more oxygen-bearing red corpuscles. Even with this equipment, however, they are unable to do sustained strenuous labor. They are a shy, almost melancholy people who live by fishing and barter.[17]

Spanish chroniclers wrote that the Amerinds they encountered during the conquest had no knowledge of the wheel. Certainly the technology and advanced scientific knowledge of the megalithic peoples would include knowing the principle of the wheel, so this would have been part of the knowledge lost in the decline of cultures. John Brown, leader of the 1950 British Andes Expedition, reports finding stone wheels with axle holes under heaps of debris in the Puma Gate ruins. Other wheeled objects have been found in Mexico in recent years.[18]

Nevertheless, in this hostile environment of thin air where practically no grains or vegetables grow, a huge city of immense stones was built. It is estimated that 100,000 citizens lived in Tiahuanaco in its prime. And food was grown here long ago, for around it are the remains of agricultural terraces. ·

Jacques Cousteau and his team discovered and photographed a man-made wall of massive stones on the lake bottom. It stood at right angles to the shore, pointing straight across the flat tableland southeast to Tiahuanaco. There is evidence that the city was once a Lake Titicaca port since there are traces of large canals that appear to have been docks for vessels. The lake's old strand line reveals that the water was once ninety feet higher than it is now. This strand line, however, is tilted and in places it is more than 360 feet above the present lake level.

The most likely solution to the Tiahuanaco enigma is startling and runs counter to orthodox geological and archeological theories. It is simply that the mountain had risen considerably after the city had been built. The conservative view is that mountain making is a slow, continuous process during hundreds of thousands of years. The idea that a large land mass can be raised thousands of feet in a short time, geologically speaking, is rejected. Tiahuanaco challenges this dogma.

On this altiplano, the elevated plain between the eastern and western cordilleras, the former agricultural terraces seem endless, and they obviously provided food for a huge population for many years. They rise to a height of 18,400 feet above sea level to the present eternal snow line atop Mount Illimani, forty miles from the city. Many are 2,500 feet above Tiahuanaco. Yet the plateau is inhospitable and practically sterile.

This is earthquake country, and there is abundant evidence of cataclysmic convulsion. H. P. Moon expresses wonder at "the freshness of many of the strand lines and the modern character of such fossils as occur." [19] Titicaca and other lakes on the plateau and several salt beds have chemical compositions similar to those in the ocean. A marine crustaceous fauna in Titicaca was discovered back in 1875 by Alexander Agassiz. In the sediment of a dry lake bed are certain mollusks, such as ancylus, revealing that it is of relatively recent geological origin.

Charles Darwin was impressed by beaches at Valparaiso, Chile, at the foot of the Andes, that had been raised 1,300 feet above the sea. The movement had been rapid since only a few intermediary surf lines were visible. What surprised him was the fact that sea shells on the surface at this height were still undecayed, clearly indicating a recent action. It appears too that it was not so much by compression of the strata that the Andes were raised, as by magna (molten rock) that invaded the strata and lifted them. There are a number of high and large volcanoes in these mountains as well as earthquake faults. [20]

At some period in the past the entire Titicaca plateau was at or below sea level with its lakes forming part of a sea gulf. At a later time, perhaps, a city was built and surrounded by farming terraces on the elevations around it. There was a final upheaval, and the plateau was raised to its present height, making the city uninhabitable.

Leonard Darwin, then president of the Royal Geographical Society, and Sir Clemens Markham in his book *The Incas of Peru*, may have been the first scientists to pose this theory, back in 1910. But in more recent years its greatest advocate has been the late Arthur Poznansky, called "Bolivia's greatest savant." He devoted his life to a study of Tiahuanaco, and no one knew more than he about this mysterious city. His series of books in Spanish, especially *Tiahuan-aco: The Cradle of the American Man*, are testimony to his many years of research.

Poznansky believed Tiahuanaco had been a seaport and in its prime about 14,000 B.C., dating from the last interglacial. Potsdam University studies of the sun temple led to the belief that it was intended to serve as a great sidereal clock, and was constructed for the star which was a pole star in 9550 B.C. But that date, Poznansky insists, was the time the city was finally abandoned since the temple was never completed. There are other indications in the ruins that point to a hasty abandonment.

But if Tiahuanaco went up, there was another mysterious city that went down. Off the coast of Callao, Peru, Dr. Robert J. Menzies of Duke University has found what he calls "the first indications of something needing further exploration." And he adds that this could be "one of the most exciting discoveries of this century insofar as ruins go." [21]

Dr. Menzies was in charge of an oceanographic expedition sponsored by the National Science Foundation in 1966 using the research vessel *Anton Brunn*. While exploring the Milne-Edward Deep, a depression nearly 19,000 feet deep in places, the underwater camera photographed some astonishing objects on a muddy plain at a 6,000-foot depth.

They were what appeared to be ornately carved rock columns. Some stood upright; others were half buried in the mud on the sea bottom. They displayed some sort of an inscription. Sonar depth recorders revealed other irregularities on the ocean floor in the same area which normally would be flat. They showed up as lumps on the bottom and may have been parts of structures. The seacoast in this region is still slowly sinking, but how long did it require for ancient monuments to drop over a mile and Tiahuanaco to be thrust upward for more than two miles? [22]

For about 5,000 years the story of man, despite the rise and fall of cultures, disasters and wars, migrations and colonizations, has been a recorded history. It has its mysteries, but there are known lines of succession back to the early civilizations of the Indus, Nile and Euphrates valleys.

Beyond that is the deep darkness of antiquity. There are the world-wide legends of mighty catastrophes, the dim racial memories of peoples and lands lost, of glacial winters that threatened human existence. Slowly, bit by bit, we are getting glimpses of a faraway time when mankind possessed advanced knowledge and noble works, when greatness dwelled on the earth.

Why did it all pass away into night? What titanic cataclysms returned the survivors to barbarism, to begin the upward struggle all over again? Is this why the god above the Gateway of the Sun weeps?

4

Tunnels of the Titans

WHERE WERE THE TUNNELS of the ancient mega-
lithic master builders? Where was the City of the Seven Caves?
Throughout all the Americas there are legends of archaic ave-
nues, racial memories of subterranean passages stretching for miles.
After a great cataclysm the ancestral Amerinds lived in the vast
cavern complex until it was safe to return to the upper world. The
story is spread through many tribes, from the kivas to the Pueblos
to the lodges of the Blackfeet, from the hogans of the west to the
campfires of the eastern woodland tribes before their dispersion.
To the Hopi this is the fourth world. Thrice the world on the
surface has been ravaged while the Hopi escaped by living with the
ant people (ant totem) in an underworld beneath the ground.[1]
The Mandans of the northwestern states, some of whom had
blue eyes and silky hair, were almost wiped out by smallpox in
1830 with the survivors being forcibly incorporated into the Rick-
aree tribe. Their legend was linked with the Great Deluge. They
said the first men to emerge from the tunnels were the *Histoppa* or
the "tattooed ones." Having left safety too soon, they perished.
The rest, who remained below, waited until a bright light dispelled
the darkness on the surface. They found that the destruction was
over, but the world above was uninhabited. Each spring the Mandans had a dance celebrating their deliverance from the flood.
The Apaches have a legend that their remote ancestors came
from a large island in the eastern sea where there were great buildings and ports for ships. The Fire Dragon arose, and their ances-

47

tors had to flee to mountains far to the south. Later they were forced to take refuge in immense and ancient tunnels through which they wandered for years, carrying seeds and fruit plants.

But it is in the south, in Central and especially South America, that the tales of underground passageways and caverns are the most widespread. Myths say that the Votans, who came from the east, were kings of the snake (totem) people, a people of the Great Cataclysm, who through tremendous Atlantean tunnels journeyed to Central America in a very remote time.[2]

"Before the time of the Great Flood," say the Zapotec sages of old Mexico, "we lived in cave-cities. Our forefathers came out of the caves of the Underworld where it was crowded. They came out by tribes, each led by the spirit of its own animal-totem."

"Our people long ago came through the places of the cavernous openings," said the quippos readers of the Incas.

It is in the south that we have the legend of Chichomoztoc, the City of the Seven Caves, but this city cannot be definitely identified with any known city or ruin. And there too are the legends that various ruined cities—Tiahuanaco, Campeche, Palenque and others—are far more extensively built underground than upon the surface.[3]

In the sixteenth century in Peru came Don Francisco Pizarro and his greed-crazed conquistadores. They seized Atahualpha, last of the Inca emperors of the sun, and promised to release him upon receiving a ransom—gold that would fill a room seventeen by twenty feet, and nine feet in height. It is estimated that this ransom consisted of 600 tons of gold and jewels. While awaiting this ransom the Spaniards busied themselves stripping the gold-plating and water pipes from the Cuzco Temple walls.

The gold flowed into the capital city, arriving by caravans from throughout the empire. Dazzled by the ever-growing display of boundless wealth, Pizarro demanded to know the source. Rumors reached him that the Incas possessed a secret and seemingly inexhaustible mine, or enormous depository, which lay in a vast subterranean tunnel, running many miles beneath the imperial dominions.

Soon gold filled the treasure room to the specified level, but Pizarro refused to release Atahualpha. He announced that if he were not given the secret of the gold's origin, he would take the emperor's life. Since Pizarro had broken his first promise, the Inca queen decided to consult the oracles of the priests of the sun. By this mystical means, she learned that whether the secret was given to Pizarro or not, the emperor was doomed. Orders were issued. Under the directions of the high priests, tunnel entrances were sealed and hidden from view.

Beneath the brilliant light of a great comet that gleamed in the southern skies, the empire of the sun came to its tragic end. Atahualpha was strangled and his queen committed suicide. As news of the emperor's death spread throughout the empire, caravans en route to Cuzco with treasure for their ruler's ransom stopped and quickly concealed their burdens. Today these lost Inca hoards lie in forests, on lake bottoms, beneath piles of earth and rocks in canyons below the high cordilleras. They are hidden in fortress vaults, under hills and sealed in caves.

But the greater treasure, the secret place that Pizarro vainly sought, according to legend, is in the strange subterranean tunnels, thousands of years old, that lie locked in the earth. Only a few decades after the conquest, Cieza de Leon wrote: "If, when the Spaniards entered Cuzco they had not . . . so soon executed their cruelty in putting Atahualpha to death, I do not know how many great ships would have been required to bring such treasures to old Spain, as is now lost in the bowels of the earth and will remain so because those who buried it are now dead." [4]

The Quichua Indians of today are the direct descendants of the Incas of old, a gentle, quiet people with melancholy eyes. Their traditions insist that in each generation a very dedicated few of their number, unknown to all the rest, possess the ancient secret. Shortly after the conquest they told the soldier-priest, Cieza de Leon, that "the treasure is so concealed that even we, ourselves, know not the hiding place."

Today the Quichuas, down-trodden and poverty-plagued, remember with fanatical devotion the grandeur of their ancestral past, and they dream of a tomorrow when the old glories shall return, when the wheel of time will come full circle, and when, with reincarnated leaders, the empire of the sun will again raise its shining banners beneath Andean skies. Against this day, they preserve their secrets, and dream . . .

With eternal vigilance they watch the treasure hunters. Any large-scale attempt to locate the tunnels would almost certainly start a revolution. It is to be regretted that the archaic tunnels were used as a depository for Inca wealth, for now, due to the brutality of the conquistadores, they are cut off from modern archeological investigation.[5]

Beneath the veneer of the white man's civilization with its education and religion, many Amerinds still cling to old beliefs and customs, and take pride in their cultural heritage. The Quichuas have quietly resisted as much as possible the influence of their Spanish-blooded neighbors. In Mexico the blood of the conquerors and the conquered have mixed. It is estimated that on the average the natives are about 20 percent Spanish and 80 percent Amerind.

Nevertheless, Mexico too apparently has a concealed cache of gold, its very existence known to only a few in each generation. Said to be hidden somewhere in the buried city below Mexico City, *La Ciudad Enterrada* awaits the reincarnation of the murdered Montezuma. From time to time, however, some of the gold has seemingly been used for special charitable purposes.

The Mexican's legacy from the past lies not in far away Castile, but in old America. Go to his so-called "Christian festivals" and you will see the elaborate headdresses, clowns, ritual dances, and other marks of a pre-Spanish America. In his music you will hear the guitarlike harp, the Aztec marimba, the ages-old gourd rattle, the lively tunes and haunting nocturnes that have survived the marching centuries. And you will see him eating the same foods, preparations of tortillas, beans, squash, and highly seasoned spices, that are portrayed upon the temple walls of old Yucatan.

In the southwestern United States among the Pueblos, Navajos, and Apaches, some tribesmen guard hidden gold mines—"gold for Montezuma when he comes back." That was the explanation given a hunter in the Sandia Mountains when the ground gave way and he fell into a mine and couldn't get out. A Sandia Pueblo found him, pulled him out, blindfolded him, led him to a trail, and warned him not to go back. He did go back but he never found the mine and he was certain he was being watched.

You will find that tale in *Apache Gold and Yaqui Silver*, a book written by J. Frank Dobie, the late and beloved "maverick professor" of the University of Texas who probably "knew more about Southwestern lore than any of his contemporaries." [6] And in this book you will learn of the tragic fates of Amerindians who tell white men the locations of mines. For whether Montezuma ever returns or not, the discovery of gold brings out the worst in the white man's nature and culture, including usurpation and despoliation of the land. The Amerind has a feel for Mother Earth, a love of his land equal to life itself. Why should he offer more wealth to the invaders who have driven him from his own soil, given him the most barren worthless land for his reservations, destroyed his forests, annihilated his buffalo herds and wild game, and polluted his rivers and streams?

The North American Indian has a lore, a tradition, a "deep knowing" that is kept secret from the white man and sometimes within the tribe. As we shall see later on, this lore and racial memory can contain astonishing insights into the mysteries of Amerind antiquity. The keepers of this wisdom are the sages, the elderly wise men with erudite eyes and weathered faces, who have received it from their fathers.

Occasionally they offer some of this knowledge to trusted scholars with the understanding that it is to be kept to themselves. Dr. David Banks Rogers, noted anthropologist and authority for early man on the California Channel Islands, received confidential information from a sage he considered one of the greatest among the red men. A careless fellow scientist published some of this information. The sage had betrayed his trust and he was slain by his fellow tribesmen. When a wise man is killed, it is science itself that is the loser.[7]

Greatest of Inca treasures, it is said, was the sun of purest gold which shone from the walls of Cuzco's Temple of the Sun. It blazed with yellow light, and its radiating scintillations burned the eyes of beholders. Upon its massive circular surface were human facial features, personifying the sun god and his pure, life-giving benisons of light and heat. Each morning as the sun rose above the Andean highlands, its rays fell upon this great disk in the temple, setting it aflame in a dazzling spectacular glow.

It was there when Pizarro and his conquistadores arrived to sack and destroy this ancient civilization, but bandit hands must not touch this most sacred symbol of the Inca god. While the Spaniards slept in their camp near the city, that glorious sun of gold vanished. And along with it into hiding went the golden life-size statue of the Inca Huayna Capac.

There was a smaller sun, a plate of gold known as the child of the greater sun. It was stolen by Don Marcio Serra de Leguisamo, who lost it while gambling the night after the day on which he had taken it. Said Fray Acosta, the monk, "He plays away the sun before the dawn."

Quite likely the greater sun, the statue and the royal mummies lie somewhere in the mysterious subterranean caverns. There were thirteen embalmed bodies of Inca kings sitting in gold chairs in the temple prior to the murder of Atahualpha. Twenty-six years after the conquest, the conquistador, Polo de Ondegardo, accidentally found three of them. After stripping the mummies of their jewelry, he destroyed them.

To the Incas gold was more an element for ornamentation than a medium of exchange. The yellow metal was used for rail roof gutters and water pipes. It plated temple walls and thin sheets of the beaten gold wallpapered their houses. So delicate in workmanship, so exquisite in artistic detail was some of the jewelry that even the brutish Pizarro refused to melt it into bars.

John Harris, writing his *Moral History of the Spanish West Indies* in 1705, noted that while debts were paid in wedges of gold, "no Spaniard troubled if a creditor got twice the amount of his debt. Nothing was so cheap, so common, so easy to be got as gold and silver . . . a sheet of paper went for ten Castilians of gold." [8]

Much of this wealth was taken to Spain in galleons. Divided among the conquistadores, each man received hundreds of pounds of gold and silver. Since this booty could not be easily transported, some of it was hidden and for one reason or another was never recovered. These lost caches are occasionally and quietly being found today.

Catari, a quippos-reading Incan historian, told Bartolome Cervantes, canon of Chuquisaca, that old records disclosed that Tiahuanaco was primarily an underground city, extending below the surface into vast caverns. There are legends around Lake Titicaca that Tiahuanaco and Cuzco are joined by an underground tunnel and that caverns extend clear through the Andes to the eastern slopes.

Beneath Cuzco are the entrances to three caverns, one being located under the Sun Temple. A number of adventurers during past centuries have entered these caverns but none returned. Finally one man came back carrying two bars of gold but with his mind gone. It was then that the Peruvian government ordered the entrances walled up. [9]

Alan Landsburg visited Tiahuanaco while producing the Jacques Cousteau television documentary on Lake Titicaca. He observed an artificial ridge around an enclosure approximately 4,000 square yards. "I hear that the Bolivian government plans to dig there," he writes. "It may find nothing, although there are said to be Incan legends of a honeycomb of tunnels at Tiahuanaco, and of great vertical shafts . . . Any subterranean chambers at Tiahuanaco may have long since collapsed, or filled with dirt. Still, the solid evidence of that four-thousand-yard earthworks seems meaningful." [10]

Another legend is that Tupac Amaru, the Inca leader, with several thousand soldiers and refugees, in 1533 escaped through tunnels east of Cuzco from Pizarro and his men, a route leading into the unexplored jungle territory of northern Bolivia.

After almost every earthquake in Peru puzzling sounds are heard. They are described as comparable to the sounds of huge boulders falling under the earth's surface as though dropping from the roofs of caves to the floors. The sounds frequently continue as long as twenty minutes after the quake itself, one dominant characteristic being a hollow booming noise with apparent echoes.

But reports of tunnels and caves are not limited to the Andean countries, but exist throughout the southern Americas. Many ancient ruins are above man-made burrows. Fifty miles south of Mexico City archeologists have found the remains of a Toltec pyramid that once covered a larger area than the Great Pyramid of Egypt. Beneath it are labyrinthine passages 1,100 yards long.

Fuentes, a Spanish historian who lived about 1685 A.D., wrote: "The marvelous structure of the tunnels (*subterranea*) of the pueblo of Puchuta, being of the most firm and solid cement, runs and continues through the interior of the land for the prolonged distance of nine leagues to the pueblo of Tecpan, Guatemala. It is a proof of the power of these ancient kings and their vassals." [11]

Yucatan, with its lost and silent temples in the green hell of the jungle, rests on a limestone strata honeycombed with caves. Some of these caves were apparently used as oracles; others are said to lead to carvings deep in the bowels of the earth. They were well-known to the Mayas who lived here millennia ago, but today are largely unexplored. Some have carved figures at their entrances and the natives refuse to enter them.

The greatest subterranean cave associated with ancient man that is known to definitely exist is the vast Loltún Cave complex in the Puuc Hills of central Yucatan. From the huge chamber inside the entrance, corridors lead off into various directions like the petals of a gargantuan flower, hence its name, Loltún—"Flower in Stone."

No one knows how far or how deep into the dark bowels of the earth these spacious passageways go, for they are still largely unexplored.

And as dark as earth's bowels is the antiquity of man's occupation of these caverns. From stalactities, stalagmites and rock pillars have been carved gigantic statues of animals, men and gods. Some are Mayan in origin, but there are strange older ones, along with puzzling petroglyphs, that in no way are similar to Mayan carvings. The men display luxuriant beards. One figure is a nine-foot giant with a full beard and wings that is reminiscent of early Assyrian sculpture. Its body is perforated with holes both vertically and horizontally.

But the most startling fact is one that reminds us of Tiahuanaco and confirms the astonishing antiquity of man in the Americas. Dr. Manson Valentine, the archeologist who has made the most intensive study of the cave complex, tells us that the older statues indicate the caves were under water after they were carved. They were water-eroded and there are water marks on the cavern walls. Moreover, divers exploring the nearby sacred wells have brought up oceanic marine growth from the bottoms.

Today this complex is several hundred feet above sea level. How long ago was it beneath the sea? What cataclysms caused this limestone strata to sink and later be raised above the ocean? And who were these people of a dim dawn era who emerged from an enigmatic eon and vanished into a limbo of the lost? Dr. Valentine writes:

The present-day Maya say that they [as a race] had nothing whatsoever to do with such carvings in Loltún and nearby caves. They say these things were placed there by the "first inhabitants" of Yucatan, the small, hunchbacked men they call "Púus." These men were supposed to have been completely destroyed by a catastrophe that swept Yucatan in remote times, destroying everything on the surface and leaving only the carvings in the caves as reminders that they had passed that way. The Maya say that later their ancestors, the first Maya, entered and found these strange remnants of the "Púus." [12]

While all the migrations of Amerinds will never be known, there is abundant evidence of a northern movement, of early relationships between the southern and northern Americas. The long, frigid winter of the ice age probably forced the northern peoples to the south, and quite likely some returned as the glaciers retreated.

The Andean country is a vast land of mountains and silences, of breathtaking vistas and melancholy ruins. It is a very ancient country that has known the passing of many peoples, from the mysterious "Old Ones" whose greatness survives in their megalithic monuments, to the sun emperors of old Incan Peru, to the cruel conquistadores and fanatical monks, and finally to today's impoverished Quichuas and the more prosperous Mestizos. And over it all is a haunting, mystical atmosphere, imbued with a venerable aura of men, conflicts and dreams during countless millennia.

In the Lake Titicaca region of these highlands the natives speak an Aruakian dialect. They have a legend that long, long ago enemies drove them from their capital on the lake. At first they fled to the south, but later, after many generations, they came far to the north, to a land of lakes and forests.

Years passed. Nima-Quiche, an orator and a dreamer, became the leader of the people, known as the Chichimecs (or Chees). He persuaded his followers to return to their legendary homeland. Either some were left behind to join Algonquin tribes or they adopted Algonquin words into their language. Nima-Quiche died before his people's migrations south came to an end, but in time they came to Lake Titicaca. On the bank of the sacred lake their sages held council, and they agreed that this was their original home, the place "where the first sun appeared."

Towering above the lake and hoary Tiahuanaco is Mount Illimani with its height of 21,184 feet. The name means "Sun God" in both the Aruakian and Michigan Algonquin Chippewa tongues. In Longfellow's Hiawatha the name "Kichee Manitu, the Mighty" was taken by the poet from Bishop Barraga's *Chippewa Language Dictionary*. The "tu" which the Chippewa adds to the name for euphony means "unparalleled splendor" in Aruakian. In Bolivia the tribe's name is spelled Quichna, but is pronounced "Cheepwa." Its old meaning is "Ancient Chee." Another astonishing similarity is in the ancient leader's name, "Nima-Quiche." In Chippewa, Nima means "ancestor" and Quiche is "illustrious."

Nor is this all. Tribal customs are shared by the Bolivian Quichna and the Algonquins of the northern forests. Both practice exposure of the dead followed by secondary burial; carry their infants in cradle-boards; specialize in bird decorations; divide the two sides of the face for painting; have similar costuming including feather robes; and make ceremonial use of tobacco in worship of the wind god. In this observance the tobacco is mixed with shavings of certain sacred woods, placed in stone pipes, and the smoke is blown in the four directions. Another identical practice is plucking out the hair of the eyebrows, a custom of the Iroquois and especially of the Senecas. [13]

If a migration from modern Bolivia and Peru to the northern forests of Michigan and Wisconsin seems improbable, consider the migrations from present Siberia and Alaska to Tierra del Fuego and Cape Horn advocated by many anthropologists. There is far greater evidence that the totems moved north, not south.

In the *American Heritage Book of Indians*, we learn that most experts agree that three-fourths of the population in all the Americas was concentrated in the Mexican and Andean areas at the time of the Spanish conquests. However the number of tribes and groups in the Americas "is all but immeasurable; estimates here really run wild." In North America there was a greater variety of languages than in all the Old World put together, and there was a greater variety in South America than in North America. "The most conservative guesses put the number of mutually unintelligible languages in North America at from 500 to 1,000 and in South America to at least twice that." [14]

In the migrations of peoples, smaller language groups are forced back to borderlines opposite the point of invasion. The indication is that the tide of migration was not from the northwest, but consisted of a series of repeated thrusts from the southeast, principally up the Mississippi River and then toward the west. Thus tribe was pushed against tribe until these smaller groups reached a point beyond which there was no retreat. As a result there are hundreds of tiny groups islanded along the Pacific coast.

The order in which they came from the south is largely guesswork even when the legends are studied. The fact is that many of the North American tribes frequently migrated over long distances. For example the Pawnee, of the Caddoan language stock, once lived beside Iroquois of different stock at the mouth of the Mississippi. The Pawnees moved to Nebraska and beyond; the Iroquois migrated north to New York and Canada. The Dacota were farmers in Virginia when the white man came and introduced the horse, which completely changed their lives. They gave up growing grain and traveled west to the plains and Black Hills where they found an easier living following the herds of buffalo.

The linguistic jigsaw puzzle map is only another Amerind mystery. Language, as Walt Whitman said, "is something arising out of the work, needs, ties, joys, affections, tastes, of long generations of humanity, and has its bases broad and low, close to the ground."

The myriad tongues testify to the countless environments of Amerind groups, to the many influences that came their way, especially after the fall of the southern empires and the dispersion of their peoples. Doubtless the diversity of languages was a cause of conflict. Inability to understand breeds suspicion and mistrust.

5

Totem Trails Northward

SURVIVALS OF A STRANGE southern heritage still exist in certain North American Indian tribes. They will be found among the peoples of the southwest who, somewhat more advanced in culture than their racial neighbors, continue the customs of their fathers and observe the old ways. Doubtless the origins of much of their symbolism have been forgotten although they possess a secret lore screened from the white man, but there are traditions almost incredibly remembered, passing from generation to generation from out of an awesome ancient past.

One such tribe is the Navaho, master weavers and silversmiths, creators of hauntingly beautiful sand paintings, worshipers of a rich pantheon of gods equal to that of Greece and Rome. Led by priestly singers, they chant sensitive poems in praise of nature and spirit. Navaho music contains thousands of exquisite melodies, hundreds of which must be used for a single rite only, and repeated exactly as they have come down from the past. Sings the Singer, in a song of the Talking God:

> Now I walk with Talking God . . .
> With goodness and beauty in all things around me I go;
> With goodness and beauty I follow immortality.
> Thus being I, I go.[1]

A god represented by a masked and horned man appears at initiation ceremonies for children. A fringe of red horsehair around his forehead resembles the Inca crown of "Son of the Sun." He is accompanied by his wife, who is painted white. She wears knitted stockings that are identical with those on the sculptured pottery of long-dead Chan-Chan in Peru. The Incas conquered and ruled Chan-Chan—known as the White City—before wiping out the original inhabitants.

The master metalsmiths of all time dwelled in Chan-Chan. Here the art of intricate plating reached an astonishing height, and the fact that trade with the north was carried on is indicated by the discovery of copper pendants plated with sheet gold in a mound in Georgia.

We can only guess about the movements of peoples, customs, and knowledge in prehistoric America. It is assumed the Navaho learned silversmithing from the Mexicans, who in turn learned it from their Toltec predecessors. Perhaps the Toltecs acquired their skill from Chan-Chan.

There are pueblo legends telling of large groups of strangers who came to the southwest with gold and silver jewelry and chests containing iridescent feather robes. They may have been the Toltecs. Old Mexico as well as Central and South America, however, had many a highly advanced nation overthrown by conquering armies. These victims of barbarism were forced to flee through the wilderness to the north where eventually they were adopted into various tribes. The Navahos probably had their share of these refugees.

Natchez is the name of a fascinating Mississippi River town of ante-bellum mansions built when cotton was king. Above the Father of Waters, called "Old Big-Strong" by the Amerinds, Natchez is perched on a high bluff, and its story is turbulent and fabulous. Once there were two towns. Below the bluff was Natchez-under-the-Hill, where depravity and garish iniquity made it the wildest sin spot in North America. Above it was Natchez proper, with its elegance and grace, the Old South perfumed with magnolias, of prosperous plantations and balls of a thousand candles. The homes remain, but the era of plantations, steamboats and hoopskirts has passed into history.

But before the planters and their slaves, before the sinners under the hill, the river men, the pioneers and bandits of the Natchez Trace, another people lived on this bluff overlooking the surging river. They were the Natchez Amerinds, a strange tribe destined for a tragic end. They were here when La Salle and his companions floated past in their search for the river's mouth; and they were here when the French founders of Louisiana chose the site for a permanent settlement.

In the beginning the Europeans and the Amerinds dwelled peacefully together. Then a French leader, a petty dictator, seized a sacred village for his own home and drove the natives away. The Natchez retaliated with a massacre. The end came when the French and their Choctaw allies, with superior numbers and arms, overwhelmed the Natchez. The French governor ordered the villages totally destroyed, picked a few men and women for public burning, and sentenced the rest of his prisoners to backbreaking slavery in Santo Domingo. The few who managed to escape joined other tribes—Chickasaw, Creeks and Cherokee—where they became medicine men and mystics.[2]

The Natchez had an organization more fitted for cities than for a life in the forest. They had a caste system, hereditary aristocracy and lineage of rulership. Their king and high priest, believed to be a descendant of the sun, was called the Great Sun. His relatives (with the exception of his children) were Little Suns. His mother or sister was the principal woman sun, and when the Great Sun died she chose his successor from among her sons and brothers.

Below the Suns in importance was a class of nobles, and below them was a class of Honored Men and Women. Lowest of all were the commoners, known as Stinkards. A Stinkard by piety or exceptional service in war could become an Honored Man or Woman. There were two languages in use among them, a common or "vulgar" and a "court" language.

When the first French arrived there were about 4,000 tribal members living in nine villages, two of which were the homes of refugees from Chickasaw aggression whom they had taken under their protection. Most of the villages were on the east side of the present town of Natchez. Their homes were log cabins featuring built-in beds and mattresses and other furniture. They were expert gardeners, and their fruit and nut trees gave evidence of long cultivation. Quite likely they represented the last surviving temple mound culture in North America.

The flat-topped earthen pyramid mound was about ten feet high, although earlier ones were much larger, seventy or eighty or even 100 feet high and covering acres of ground. It resembled the pyramids of Middle America. The Temple of the Sun which stood on its top was built of long logs with plaster chinking. It had a large entrance decorated with satyrlike figures carved from wood and painted in brilliant colors.

Within the temple's inner sanctum was the sacred eternal fire attended continually by priests, a custom similar to that of the Incas and Romans. Here too was kept the "Boat of the Sun" which the priests carried in war parties. Is it significant that a "Boat of the Sun" was an important part of sun-worship ritual in both the temples of the Incas and those of Egypt?

And in the temple were kept the records of the past carved and painted in hieroglyphic script on large slabs of wood. These priceless records were lost during the final bloody battle with the French and the traitorous Choctaws, when the temple was destroyed by fire.

The Natchez and the earlier Mound Builders representing the temple mound culture were southerners. The *American Heritage Book of Indians* points out that there "are so many points in common, even to some specific pottery styles, with the Maya and other early civilizations of Mexico and Central America and even of South America that there must have been contacts . . . it would seem the connections must have been by sea, across the Gulf, possibly from the Yucatan peninsula, possibly from Toltec ports along the Mexican east coast. A few archeologists suspect there may have been migrations of people themselves, not only ideas and fashions, from Middle America." [3] We shall see that one man, called the "best of the Natchez reporters" by the Heritage book editors, did learn something about the tribe's traditions, and that there was a great migration.

He was Le Page du Pratz, a French traveler and scholar, who came to the Natchez villages when relationships between the French and the tribe were still friendly. Du Pratz was startled by the evidences of former greatness which he observed around him. The natives even made their clothing by weaving fibers from a variety of hemp. Where had they acquired all their advanced skills, their urban-style customs? One night while he was being entertained by the Natchez chief he inquired about the tribe's past. It was a strange but illuminating story.

Long ago the Natchez and their fellow Muskhogean tribes lived in a land far to the south. They had come as invaders and they conquered the original inhabitants, the Chichimecs, who dwelt in cities. The Chichimecs fled from the aggressive armies and eventually went into the land of the northern forests. There they rested and multiplied. After some generations a great leader arose among them. He persuaded his people to return to their motherland and in time led them back into the southland to recover their lost cities.

Meanwhile, the ancestors of the Natchez and their brother tribes had prospered. They carried their Sacred Fire from city to city. Over each city was a "Great Sun"—a ruler whose kingly title was similar to that of "Pharaoh" or "Inca." As millennia of moons passed, the Natchez lived in peace, expanding their cities, developing their civilization, cultivating and improving their trees and plants.

Then came retribution as the forces of the Chichimecs attacked. One after another the wealthy city-states of the Great Suns fell as the days were grim with bloodshed and the nights were bright with flame. Like their conquerors now, the Natchez Suns and their people fled into the mountains while the Chichimecs again established their former reign. And once again it was the futility of man against himself, the seesaw of successions, the victor becoming the vanquished, causing the rivers of blood and tears to flow senselessly through time.

It was the turn of the Natchez and their fellow tribesmen to endure the privations of wilderness life, to wander homeless. When game became scarce and their survival was threatened, a great council was held. The Great Suns, the priests and the chiefs were frustrated in their efforts to reach a practical solution. Then a wise old man asked to speak.

"We cannot all stay here, my children," he said in effect. "Our enemies went north and recovered their strength in a far land. We can do the same. We can multiply our numbers and return to recover our cities and our heritage."

A debate among the leaders followed. They wondered what dangers they might face in an unknown country. Perhaps they were better off where they were.

Then a Great Sun spoke: "My own people will go north, my brothers," he announced. "Other tribes may join us. Those remaining here will have more food. If you do not hear from us, that will mean we have met with disaster. It will be a warning. But if we discover a fair land with friendly people and abundant game, we will send messengers back to you and you can join us."

All of the tribes joined in assisting the migrating people in preparing for their great adventure. Huge trees were felled and the logs trimmed and hollowed to create ocean-going dugouts or canoes. Each vessel was large enough to carry between fifty and a hundred rowers. Along with other provisions, they were loaded with nuts, dried fruits and seeds of their domestic plants. With shouts of encouragement and farewell, the flotilla set out across the Southern Sea (undoubtedly the Gulf of Mexico) and dropped below the far horizon.

Time passed and one year, during the Moon of the Falling Leaves, the messengers appeared paddling their dugout canoe. Up a large river that flowed into the Southern Sea, they had found a new home. Natives were living there, but they were friendly and the land was not crowded. Game was plentiful and fish thronged the great river and its tributaries. The messengers urged more of the Great Suns and their peoples to join them.

So a second migration took place. Again the others helped the migrating people to build their long canoes. Provisions were taken aboard and the fleet of dugouts sailed away to the north, leaving behind the Great Sun and the tribe that would later be known as the Natchez.

Centuries passed, timed by seasons and circling stars. At first the population decline made game abundant in the mountains, but after a time their own increasing numbers made hunting difficult. Land suitable for crops became more scarce. In addition, their enemies were harassing them by making occasional raids into their territory.

So they decided to follow their tribal brothers to the land to the north. The long canoes were built and provisioned, and bearing the Sacred Fire they crossed the Southern Sea without difficulty, and found the mouth of the wide river which had been so carefully described by the messengers and remembered. They made their way up the river until they came to the high bluff on the east bank that is still the landmark of Natchez, Mississippi. And here they settled.

They learned that their tribe brothers had long before spread far into the forest, mingling and intermarrying with the natives. In this dispersion they had given up the ways of their fathers, they had allowed their Sacred Fires to die. Now the Natchez, as the latest arrivals, were the keepers of the ancient flame.

Did both the conquered and the conquerors of an archaic struggle find their way to territory now a part of the United States of America? Did the Chichimecs whose descendants now live in the Lake Titicaca highlands flee from their enemies to find refuge in the far northern forests today designated Michigan, Wisconsin and Minnesota? Did they, after a time, return to "where the first sun appeared" and drive out their former conquerors and restore their city-states? And then was it the turn of the Natchez and their fellow Muskhogean tribes to become wanderers and finally reach the southeastern United States?

We know so little about the movements of peoples during former millennia that we cannot afford to ignore any clues. The abyss of the past yawns dark and deep. Our ignorance is deepened by man's bellicoseness and vandalism. No one will ever know how much knowledge was lost in the destruction of the libraries at Alexandria and elsewhere. The full story of the Natchez and their remarkable heritage died when the last "Great Sun" was slain, and when the hieroglyphic scripts were consumed in the flames of the Temple of the Sun.[4]

Southern and eastern New Mexico was the home of Apacheria, the home of the Mescalero Apaches. Their name came from the Apache custom of roasting mescal (agave) to make a nutritious and popular dessert. Despite centuries of living on the frontiers of Pueblo civilization and European settlement, they remained completely independent, a record unequaled by any other Indian people on the continent.

This was the Apache's home, and he fought as few men have to keep it. The white man humbled and degraded him, but he has never lost his personal pride. The reservation Apache is harmless, but he remembers his triumphs in the days of Cochise and Geronimo. Even today, the less he has to do with the white man the better. Time will never efface his mark upon this land.

Since they speak the Athapascan language, Amerind ethnologists have classified the Apaches as "Dene" or Athapascans. But use of the same or related languages does not necessarily mean that the people who use them are related. This is true of the Apache.

Perhaps it is their stern haughtiness and exclusiveness that made it possible for them to retain customs, symbols and traditions that have survived for untold thousands of years, perhaps reaching back before the great catastrophe cast a dark curtain across an archaic past.

They have the Crown Dance, called "Devil Dance" by their enemies and the ignorant, and, startlingly, it is the most perfect example of the old Egyptian figure of Ammon-Ra existing in modern times. Girls who are to be initiated into the tribe have been praying and fasting for several days. Now they dress in white, beaded deerskin garments and await the coming of "The Men of the Mountains." They and the blanket-clothed spectators stand beneath the stars in the glow of the sacred fire as they listen to the crescendo of the tom-toms.

From over a hill to the east comes the first dancer, wearing his trident headdress and carrying a snake-marked spear in either hand. He is followed by the others, similarly attired, trotting in a column. Chanting, they approach the sacred fire and worship it by bowing and backing up four times from the east, then from the south, then the west, then the north, and finally back to the east once more. Other chants and dances follow throughout the night, ending with the light of dawn.

Lucille Taylor Hansen is a most remarkable person, a lifelong student of Amerind lore and the possessor of a tremendous knowledge of the inner meanings of signs and symbols. Much of this knowledge has been gained by direct contacts with shamans and inheritors of the ancient traditions. As a woman, she has inspired trust and been permitted to witness ceremonies usually closed to Caucasians. Thus she was allowed to be present at a Mescalero Apache Crown Dance. Moreover, she came prepared to question the principal chanter or ceremonial leader, who wore the most elaborate costume. No one else would be expected to possess all his knowledge, as he would be the keeper of the ancestral wisdom.

As her first act, Ms. Hansen showed the frowning shaman some paintings of Yama, the Tibetan ruler of hell with his trident and skullcap whose scarlet fringe is so similar to the crown of the Incas. After a quick glance, he turned away with a "No-savvy" while several young men took the pictures and began commenting in Apache. The shaman became interested in spite of himself and examined the pictures carefully.

Lucille Hansen explained that the figure was from Central Asia and pointed out the headdress with its triple horns. Next she exhibited some photographs of Egyptian temple wall paintings. One of these suddenly caused startled exclamations and shouts for other tribesmen to come and look. It was a painting of Ammon-Ra, the horned ram god.

"What tribe painted this picture?" the ceremonial leader asked, bewilderment clouding his previously mask-frozen face.

She explained that it was a temple painting from ancient Egypt, and she indicated the similarities between it and the fire god in the Crown Dance. "Could you tell me the name of your god so I can compare the names?" she inquired.

"I cannot do so," the shaman replied. "We are forbidden to name him aloud. It reduces his power when we need his help and it brings bad luck."

"Very well. If I tell you the name of the Egyptian god, will you tell me if it's close to your own name?"

The shaman nodded his head.

"The Egyptian god is Ammon-Ra."

There was a simultaneous gasp from the Apaches, and they stared at each other in a startled, even frightened, manner. "The name is identical," said the shaman. Across what mysterious void of millennia, what unknown interrelationships of cultures, could this name of a god link the antique land of the Pharaohs to this reservation in New Mexico's Sacramento Mountains? Adding to the enigma is the fact that the Apaches are an Athapascan-speaking tribe, with the origin of the language believed to be Asian.

In the Apache legend as told by the shaman, Ammon-Ra is the good and mighty ruler of the Men-of-the-Mountains. Long ago he came with his Men-of-the-Mountains from the east, out of the Fire-Land which was in the midst of the waters. Then they went south where they built cities on the tops of mountains and worshipped the sacred fire. They were cities built with huge stones.

Once again in North American Indian lore and legend, as in the megalithic cities of the south, appears the fire god, the sacred fire. These were Caribbean traditions, too. One might have expected such statements from a member of the Iroquois or Muskogean groups, but Caribs speaking Athapascan! Then Ms. Hansen recalled conversations she had had with the Athapascan Chippewayans in Canada. Their wise men too told of a fire god in the south who came out of the sunrise sea when the world was young, but he was a powerful devil whom they had conquered.

The ceremonial chief touched two mirrors that flashed, one over each breast, in the dawn light. "In those great days so long ago," he said, "our people had the strength of the stars. Once we were People-of-the-Stars, and the Twin-Stars were on the horns of our crown."

Could this be the ghost of the Venus calendar emerging from out of a fog-shrouded past? She observed that there were thirteen points across the top of his cap. Below it were eight and between them a horned and lightning-arrowed circle. The Venus calendar was once used by the Mayans and the Caribs, and it is considered by some scholars as a possible inheritance from a lost motherland that existed before the most ancient of nations.

Venus, circling on an inside orbit, makes thirteen revolutions around the sun to eight terrestial revolutions. This is the basis for the Venus-sun calendar. The Mayans, however, with mathematical precision and astronomical expertise, adopted other calendars. The *Tzolkin*, or Book of the Days, was a ceremonial round of 260 days probably based originally on the planting, growing and harvesting of crops. Their solar calendar used nineteen months and turned through a cycle of fifty-two years between recurring conjunctions. Their lunar calendar was brought into a fixed relation with the day count (with an error of less than five minutes a year). They "created whole galaxies of cycles, wheels within wheels, all turning like the perpetual works of an infinite clock, and the emphasis was always on that marvelous repetition of time." [5]

"What do the mirrors represent?" asked Ms. Hansen.

"The twin stars, the stars of the dawn and the twilight. In the white man's school they say Venus is both the morning and evening star, but we regard them as twins."

"And the numbers sacred to them are eight and thirteen."

"That is true," the shaman agreed. "But how could you know that?"

"They are the numbers of the Venus calendar."

After telling the leader and the interested tribesmen that had gathered around them about this ancient American calendar, she observed that there were thirteen appendages in the horned circle on the shaman's headdress. Moreover, she was told, the Men-of-the-Mountain are decorated with twenty-six painted pyramids on their bodies, that is, thirteen for each of the twin stars. The tribe's most sacred number is 104, which is eight thirteens.

"Doesn't this mean that our forefathers observed the stars long enough to form a calendar, that they possessed great knowledge?" inquired one bystander.

"That's right," she said, and the glow of pride appeared in his eyes.

"It is our tradition that we once lived in cities far to the south," the leader declared. "The white teachers laugh at this and tell us we are a primitive people who came here from Asia not so long ago." The muscles around his lips grew taut with bitterness.

Lucille Hansen recalled the shaman's remark that his ancestors had built cities with huge stones on mountain tops, and she thought of Tiahuanaco and the god figure on the great gateway. She opened her photograph file case and found a picture of the figure which she handed to the shaman. He gasped, then began talking to the bystanders in excited Apache. Turning to the four directions, he shouted, and tribal members came running from everywhere to join the group. The picture was almost pulled to pieces as it was passed around.

"This must be the city of our traditions," the leader declared. "It is the secret sign of recognition. The god is holding two swords, one in each hand, and the points of the swords are upward meaning friendship. Then they are held at right angles to the upper arm, thus forming with the head a trident. It is our sign."

(The trident, the three-pronged spear of Poseidon or Neptune in classic mythology, is an ancient symbol that may have survived the catastrophe. South of Lima, Peru, on a huge rocky slope above the Bay of Pisco, is the pictograph of a trident, at least 300 feet high, and visible only from the air, coming in from the sea. It is not far from the vast, mysterious Nazca figures on the Atacama Desert, and it points southeast toward Tiahuanaco.)

"Where is this city?" the shaman asked.

"Far to the south," she answered. "It is in the Andes and has been in ruins from long before Inca times. But this is fantastic. First Egypt and now Tiahuanaco!"

After the excitement had subsided, Ms. Hansen pointed out that the figure could have been an accident, a duplicate, perhaps, of a similar figure elsewhere.

"That is true," said the sage. "Let us council further. Was this city in the mountains on a large lake, a lake with islands?"

She nodded.

"The islands were our sacred places," the shaman continued. "Tell me, were there great caves under this city?"

"Quite likely. There is a legend among the local Indians that the caves in that region held most of the real city and that very little of it was built above the ground."

The leader smiled. "That's the way our cities were built. It is our tradition that has come down to us from our ancient ancestors. Tell me, did they terrace the land to grow crops?"

"Yes they did, from the snow line to the base, through many climates."

"I suppose water was brought from the snow at the peaks."

"That is true, through tunnels no longer known."

"And was there one city built right on the top of a range?"

"That would be Machu Picchu. Like Tiahuanaco, it was built by the Megaliths, the great stone-builders whose cities and monuments defy time."

The shaman turned and looked at the misty New Mexican mountains in the distance, now coming into view below the sun of dawn. He shook his head. "They were our forefathers," he said sadly. "Our people once knew greatness."

"Would you please tell me of the Old Land, of the long ago time?" she asked.

"White men laugh when we speak of those times."

"Well, here's a white woman who isn't going to laugh. I ask because I wish to know of things beyond the power of our histories to teach."

The Apaches, men, women and children, gathered around the sage, keeper of traditions, blankets over their shoulders. Upon the faces of the crown dancers were the horizontal paint marks of the Caribs. Once again they were eager to hear the old, but ever new, story of their fathers.

"We lived in the Old Red Fire Land before the Great Flood," he began. "It was to the east, in the Sunrise Sea. We lived in a capital city, a great seaport, the heart of the world then. The land was not wide, but it had high mountains. Beneath the land in giant caves dwelt the fire-god whose name we never speak.

"There were the Twin Stars. The Navaho remembers them as the Sparkling-Star-Which-Lies-As-Two. There were four mountains. We were the Men-of-the-Mountains. And among our totems we had the Horned Mountain Sheep. When the fire-god crawled through his caverns, all the land shook like jelly. He became angry and left the caves and came up through the mountains, raining fire and death upon the people, destroying the Old Land. Then came the Great Flood.

"We with the other people came west over the water and came to a new land. We went south along the ridges of the high mountains where we built our cities of the great caves. When enemies drove us out of them, we left by the caverns and wandered through them in darkness. Years passed and finally our fathers came to this land."

This was basically the same story told in the *Chilam Balaam*, the destruction of a land mass in the Atlantic by volcanic eruptions followed by a flood, of the flight of survivors to what is now Central and South America, and the beginnings of the great southern civilizations of the pre-Incas, the Megaliths.[6]

"Once the tale was more complete," the sage continued, "and there are parts of it I do not understand. Much is being forgotten because our young people are told by their white teachers that these traditions are fairy tales. The white man's world overwhelms us and the old memories and the ways of our fathers are disappearing."

Carib and Sioux medicine men say a Carib tribe shaman can be recognized by the white neck feathers of the condor worn above the forehead as ordered by the fire god to his children. In South America it is called the Bird-of-the-Lightnings, and it may be the Thunder Bird of the north. Ms. Hansen observed that above the ceremonial leader's headdress, the cap with the thirteen and eight pyramids, and below the horns of the Twin Stars, was a top-knot of white feathers.

"Con" is the native Andean name for the fire god, and the condor is an ancient totem. Cuzco, the Incan capital, was built in the shape of the condor, its streets representing feathers. The fortress of Sachsahuaman, with the immense stone blocks, forms a condor's head when viewed from the air.

What is the meaning of the word "Carib" (or Cariao)? Braghine, in his book *The Shadow of Atlantis*, suggests that the "K" sound may be defined as "people" as it was in the Pueblo, Aztecan, Muskhogean and other languages where it retains its root sound, and "A. R." stood for Ammon-Ra, the god whose name is kept secret and who is still worshiped. It would appear that the Apaches were originally a Carib people, but later adopted the Athapascan language.

It seems clear that some of the North American Indian tribes are the descendants of ancient South and Central American peoples, who in turn were refugees from a great catastrophe. They developed their cultures and built their great cities, but some of these early Southerners became conquerors and conquered, victims of man's everlasting strife; forced to migrate north, they began their new lives in the forests and on the plains. But some have remembered their forefathers' greatness in legend and myth passed on generation after generation, century after century. It is a part of the Amerind enigma, the mystery of man and his true beginnings in a remote dawn era.

6

Early Old World Contacts

THE BELIEF that the Americas were isolated from the Old World until the appearance of Christopher Columbus is rapidly giving way as evidence accumulates that there was a pre-Columbian melting pot. Diffusionism is the concept that more and more scientists are accepting today. This means that many of the puzzling artifacts and ancient constructions spread from culture to culture, perhaps from a single world-wide culture, rather than being developed by each culture independently.

The honor of discovering America has been claimed for Vikings, Phoenicians, Egyptians, Negroes, Polynesians, the Chinese and Japanese, Irish monks and others. It's a cloudy business of myths, legends, ancient scrolls and maps, as well as definite artifacts and monuments that are thorns in the sides of establishment anthropology. The subject has grown amazingly vast in recent years, with more research and discoveries, and we can only skim it here. But as an Amerind spokesman once said, "The Americas were not discovered by anyone from the past because they were never lost. We were already here, and it just took the Europeans a long time to find out about it."

The principal objection of those who cling to the notion of only late contacts is that it would have been impossible for early peoples to have crossed either the Atlantic or Pacific oceans. The Polynesians, however, traveled almost incredible distances over water. The Late Bronze Age vessels, in fact, were far larger than any of Columbus's ships and, as previously said, the oceans have been

71

crossed by twelve-foot-long boats little larger than bathtubs. More-over, if a northern route is followed, you can circle the globe and hardly ever be out of sight of land.

The fact is that diffusionism has been going on for a very long time. Anthropologist James Bailey's monumental book *The God-Kings and the Titans* gives ample evidence that there was regular transoceanic contact between the Old and New Worlds before the time of Christ, going back nearly 8,000 years before the present.[1]

Cyrus Gordon, the famous Brandeis University scholar, in his book *Before Columbus: Links Between the Old World and Ancient America*, presents evidence for a civilization that antedated what we call the classical civilizations (including the Egyptian) and shows that the science and technology of the classical cultures were inherited from an earlier civilization of which we at present know practically nothing.[2]

What apparently happened is that "before the continental con-cept of the classical world, there was a maritime view of the world based on the oceanic voyages of ancients such as the Minoans and Phoenicians in the Bronze and Early Iron ages. By Roman times the geographical horizons of mankind were shrinking back to the continental view, which persisted to the time of Columbus."[3]

Dr. Gordon tells us that the achievements of civilized man in preliterate times, prior to the building of the first cities in Neolithic antiquity, included a high development of the exact sciences. "No-where," he writes, "is the interdependence of the Old and New Worlds clearer than in the domain of science. Astronomy, mathe-matics and chronology bridge the two worlds so inextricably that it is impossible to understand the history of science in the one with-out the other."[4]

There was not only an inheritance of scientific knowledge from an archaic civilization but also a movement of cultural customs throughout much of the world. This was probably due to the voyages and settlements of various sea peoples that occurred prior to known history.

Dr. G. Elliot Smith, in his *Migrations of Early Culture*, found similar customs among the peoples who were living in various con-tinents at the dawn of that land's civilization. Many of these cus-toms characterized the early inhabitants of Central and South America.

They built immense megalithic monuments and pyramids whose four sides faced the cardinal points, worshiped the sun, adopted a serpent totem, mummified their dead, terraced hillsides and used irrigation canals and large underground storage systems in their agriculture. They wore clothes of cotton cloth which for the men consisted of a short skirt fastened by a long belt whose fringed ends hung in front, while those of the women were draped in such a fashion that one shoulder was left bare.

They practiced ear-piercing and tattooing. To give the profile the appearance of being a continuation of the nose line, they artificially flattened the forehead of their infants. Deluge legends were universal. They had sacred fires attended by virgins, symbolized the sun by a red pyramid and water by a serpent, and held spring and fall festivals. Certain outer garments and a tall hat were the ceremonial clothes worn by their priests. Even their square or zigzag pottery designs were similar, with black on white being a favorite color theme.

Dr. Smith lists many more similarities, and he states there must be a limit to coincidence. There is a point at which the law of probability conflicts with the number of possible accidents. After this point has been reached in the comparison of two cultures, we are forced to accept some kind of interchange.[5]

The meanings of words used by widely separated peoples may indicate former contacts. In an interview in 1956 the late Dr. Vilhjalmur Stefansson, noted Arctic explorer and scholar, expressed his bewilderment at learning that the natives of Alaska, Greenland and Brazil have used for a very long time the same word for chewing gum. Years ago while exploring in Alaska he heard the Eskimos call spruce gum "kutsuk." In a dictionary of the Eskimo language published in Greenland in 1871 the same word is defined as meaning "resin, gum." And early explorers of Brazil and elsewhere in South America found natives calling a chewing gum of various plants "gutteux."

Furthermore, Stefansson said, the natives of Alaska have always used a word for fire which is very similar to the word for fire of the ancient Romans. The Eskimo word is "ignirk" and the Romans said "ignis," a word derived from Sanskrit. Is this coincidence or could there be a connection? "A connection," he said, "from the Sanskrit to the Latin to the Eskimo. That is something to stagger your imagination. Especially when you remember that Sanskrit was the language of an India that pre-dated the ancient Latin empire of Rome—and the Eskimos of Alaska are a long way in both time and space from either." [6]

In 1962 Jack Cohane, a former newsman and amateur archeologist, entered the British Council Library in Rome to look up the origin of the word "Thames." He came out wondering whether he had stumbled onto the key to much of prehistory. His studies have led him through the labyrinths of linguistics ever since.

If his theories are right, there were two dispersions of people from the Mediterranean over the world thousands of years before Columbus. Certain key words and names brought out from the Mediterranean in prehistoric times link together the Homeric cultures of Mycenae and Crete, the British ruins of Stonehenge, the Aztec and Mayan civilizations of the Americas and ancient monuments in the Far East. There are, he says, word links of approximately 20 percent between the Mayan and Aztec dialects on the one hand and Hebrew on the other.

Cohane believes he has compiled abundant evidence of oceanic contacts between the Old and New Worlds going back to the Bronze Age—contacts which had been under way a long time by 1500 B.C. Names and words which are identifiable as the same in the spoken and written languages of widely separated peoples permit the charting of the routes of these contacts.

What Cohane discovered when he was at the British Council Library was that "Thames" is a cognate of the Sanskrit Tamasa, the name of a tributary of the Ganges in India. Tamasa means dark, thus the Thames is "the dark river." [7]

In 1607 a monk, Fray Gregorio Garcia, wrote a book entitled *The Origin of the Indians of the New World,* in which he claimed, "The Indians proceeded neither from one . . . part alone of the Old World, or by the same road, or at the same time; some have probably descended from the Carthaginians, others from the lost Atlantis, from the Greeks, from the Phoenicians, and still others from the Chinese, Tartars and other groups." [8]

Now comes Alexander von Wuthenau, an internationally known art expert and lecturer at the University of the Americas in Mexico City. In his book *The Art of Terra-cotta Pottery in Pre-Columbian Central and South America* are pictured figurines with characteristic and unmistakable head and facial features of the Chinese, Japanese, Tartars, Negroes and Semitic types, with or without beards. They came from the west and they came from the east; they all "discovered" America. It would appear that the early Americas had a racial melting pot. [9]

Let us first deal briefly with trans-Pacific contacts. A Reuters

News dispatch (17 July 1970) reports from Moscow that two Leningrad specialists in Oriental antiquity have found evidence that ancient Asian geographers knew of the existence of the Americas at least before 1500 B.C. Lev Gumilev and Bronislav Kuznetsov state they have deciphered ancient maps of the world in old Tibetan books that were earlier thought to be charts of imaginary lands of Buddhist fantasy. The arrangement of continents and countries conformed with the knowledge of the world by the ancient Sumerians and Chaldeans. In addition, they interpret a reference to a "green land lying far across the Eastern Sea" as meaning America.

There was occasional chance and some purposeful contact across the Pacific in ancient times. Typhoons have driven Japanese fishing vessels and Chinese junks to American shores. Between 1782 and 1875 more than forty junks drifted to the California west coast. But there is also evidence of sea trade routes.

In 1961 Emileo Estrada, an amateur archeologist, found incised pottery at Valdivia, Ecuador, that has no New World pedigree. Betty J. Meggers and Clifford Evans, of the Smithsonian Institution's division of cultural anthropology, discovered that the pottery site carbon dated to at least 2500 B.C. The reddish pottery had decorations and an oddly marked protuberant rim that identified it as contemporary at the time with the Jomom culture in Japan. The Smithsonian scientists point out that this Valdivian-style pottery occurred in Japan earlier than in Ecuador where it appeared suddenly; and the design is esthetic and not functional—it had no purpose other than decoration.[10]

Back in the 1920s Dr. G. Elliot Smith compared motifs found in the Mayan area with those in Cambodia, Indochina, India and throughout southeastern Asia. On certain Mayan temples the builders had sculptured elephant heads. He wrote that the Mayans could not have known what an elephant looks like unless it had been described to them by travelers who had come across the Pacific. On Stela B at Copan there are not only elephants but mahouts. Opponents of the cultural diffusion theory argued that they might be representations of the American tapir. Dr. Smith pointed out that the Mayan animal heads had tusks. The Asiatic elephant has tusks while the American tapir does not. Moreover, he said that the proboscis was closer in appearance to an elephant's trunk than to the snout of a tapir.

There is controversy too about the so-called Elephant Slab dug up by a small boy about 1910 near Flora Vista, New Mexico. It is now in the Arizona State Museum. It was found in Indian ruins dated at about 1200 A.D. by archeologist Charles A. Amsden. The quartzitic sandstone is exceedingly hard, six by six inches, yet the unknown petroglypher meticulously chiseled fifty-five pictures and symbols, among them an elephant.[11]

There is no question about Polynesian contacts with the Americas. And the fact that Easter Island was populated when discovered is testimony to their navigational skill. The island is 1,600 miles from Polynesian Mangareva, the nearest land, and 2,200 miles from the South American coast. It is only ten by thirteen miles in size, a mere dot in the vast Pacific.

Thor Heyerdahl, who proved that a native balsa raft could span the Pacific from Peru to the Polynesian islands, believes he was following an ancient sea route, that there was a movement of peoples from the New World to the islands. Frank C. Hibben agrees, since ocean currents and winds favor a westward movement. The sweet potato, native to America, was found growing in the islands and in Hawaii when the first Europeans arrived. In Tahiti the potato was known by its Quichuan name. It appears terraced pyramids are an indigenous American development, so the terraced hilltops in the islands and in Asia may have been conceptions carried westward.

On the other hand, migrants from the islands and southeastern Asia could have brought to America art motifs, including the elephant, megalithic stone carvings and even the idea of building in stone. "The Andean coast," Hibben writes, "seems a curious place for one of the high civilizations of the New World to have begun. If the original germs of this civilization came from the other side of the Pacific, however, the Andean location would be satisfactorily explained." [12]

Hibben adds that dancing figures, headdresses and other motifs appearing on Mayan temples seem exactly to parallel sculptural details on Buddhist monuments of southeastern Asia. And the distinctive sword clubs, the *patu*, of the South Pacific have been found in Peruvian graves.

Heyerdahl theorizes that in pre-Inca times a superior race from Peru, including blonde and bearded leaders, sailed their log rafts to Easter Island and Polynesia. He thinks that the basic Malayan stock sailed north from the Malaya region instead of west and rode the Japanese current to America. Some stayed there as the Northwest American Indian tribes, who amazed early white men with their great war canoes. Others followed the currents once more to

Hawaii and thence to the islands of Polynesia and New Zealand.[13]

There is excellent evidence that the Chinese had early contact with the New World. In addition to the Valdivian pottery previously mentioned, there is another site in Ecuador where archeologists have found proof of the presence of other Asians. They are believed to be Chinese from the early Han dynasty, dating from about 220 B.C. Only recently Peking scholars have reported finding evidence that around 450 A.D. five Chinese led by a Buddhist monk landed in Mexico. They say the newcomers influenced the coinage and mythology of the Aztecs. At any rate, there are remarkable similarities in decorative styles in pottery between those of the Tajin culture of Veracruz in Mexico and the late Chou period of 700–200 B.C. in China.

There is the famous "Fu Sang" legend that has appeared in many Chinese writings over the last several centuries and is presented in the opening chapter of *A History of the Chinese in California.*[14] The tale has been traced back to the sixth century A.D. in China when it was presented to the ruling court.

The story is of a Buddhist monk, Hwei Sham (or Hui Shen), who with his companions had their ship blown far off course during a severe storm. The time has been estimated as about 500 A.D. The vessel eventually reached the shores of a strange new land which the monk said was around 20,000 li, or 6,000 miles, to the east of China. Hwei Sham remained in this land for about forty years, calling it Fu Sang after a bamboolike tree that grows in China. This reference could be to the tules of the northwest coast.

In his report the monk said the natives lived in wood frame houses, the custom of certain northwest Amerind tribes. They drew pictures on bark, another similarity with the tribes of that region. The inhabitants showed no appreciation of gold or silver, were men of peace "possessing neither arms nor armor, and do not make war." Some of the plants he described resemble those of the northwestern United States; and he referred to strange animals with "ten horns" which may have been antelope, elk or moose.

The Japanese current which flows northward and eastward in a great arc would carry vessels to the northwest coast of North America. Hibben says the first explorers of this region found the natives using Chinese bronze dangles and coins for ornaments.

Amerinds do not usually have hair on their faces, but the northwest coast natives have ornamented wooden dance masks with a large mustache. This implies contact with the hairy Ainu of the northern Japanese island of Hokkaido. Other similarities with the Ainu are decorated blankets or capes with similar designs, ceremonial hats, and ceremonies eulogizing the bear.

Henriette Mertz, author of *Pale Ink*, writes that the *Shan hai Jing*, or "Mountain Sea Classic," comprising sixteen historical books in ancient Chinese, refers to a voyage to America about 2000 B.C.[15] The work also includes an account of the journey of the monk Hwei Sham. Some of these travelers may have left artifacts.[16]

Near Hemet, California, is the Maze Stone, an intricate, perfectly formed labyrinth symbol, unlike any figures left by the Amerinds in the West. It has been a subject of controversy for years. Oriental experts have said the symbol is very similar to Buddhist ones in China and Tibet, and it has been suggested that the Buddhist monks who came in 450 A.D. may have landed here rather than in Mexico. Greeted by friendly natives, they may have traveled inland. Unlike most Amerind-marked boulders, no other petroglyphs (figures pecked into the stone) or pictographs (painted figures) are on the large boulder.

According to Robert Marx, writing in *Oceans* magazine, a cache of Chinese brass coins dating around 1200 B.C. has been discovered in British Columbia.[17]

Along the shore of Lake Pend Oreille, about five miles west of Hope, Idaho, there is a large exposed rock surface with carvings or petroglyphs, incised deeply and obviously very old. While their origin may be Amerindian, they do closely resemble one of the most sacred symbols of the Buddhists—"the Feet of Buddha." The petroglyphs are large footprints enclosing symbols. In the Orient this symbol of the foot may enclose the entire sixty-five signs of Buddhism. These carvings are not so detailed, but are similar and resemble the early and more primitive representations of Buddha's feet. It is reported that similar petroglyphs are located on two islands in the lake, and along the Alcan Highway in Alaska.[18]

A well-digger's dynamite blast near Luther, Oklahoma, in the late 1940s unearthed a Chinese statuette. The eight-inch-high figure has been identified as Shu Sing Lao, an ancient deity representing happiness and prosperity. Since ancient times the god has been depicted seated on the back of a faun, with the animal's head turned back to face him. An expert on wood carving told the owner that the statue was carved from a material as hard as ebony, and that he believed the tree it came from must now be extinct. It had been slightly scorched by fire and its once polished surface is covered by a maze of tiny cracks. There is no doubt about its identity; there are others in museums. It was found at a depth of fifteen feet, but the site appears likely to have been a creek bed where such a depth of soil could have been deposited in a century or two.[19]

Most startling is the recent discovery of very ancient Chinese anchors off the California coast. In May 1973, the USGS *Bartlett*, while making a scientific study for the U.S. Geological Survey off Cape Mendocino, north of San Francisco, dredged up an anchor. Dr. Roland von Huene, who was in charge of the study, notified Dr. James Moriarity, an archeologist at the University of San Diego and an expert on ancient anchors.

Moriarity's investigation of the large circular stone anchor showed that it bore striking resemblances to those used by Chinese ships off the southeastern coast of China in times before the birth of Christ. "It's so archaic I can't believe it," he said during an interview with Bob Corbett, San Diego *Evening Tribune* science editor.

The anchor is comprised mainly of some type of consolidated sandstone. It is roughly doughnut-shaped, about three feet in diameter. There is a hole in the center that is obviously man-made. The hole consists of two conical drillings that were started from both sides. Its weight is about 120 pounds. The stone disk is covered with a relatively thick coating of manganese, an average of about three millimeters over the entire stone. Moriarity said a rule of thumb is that it would take 1,000 years to lay down a millimeter of manganese. This would make the anchor 3,000 years old, but the rate of manganese deposition varies from place to place, and the stone anchor may not actually be that old. It was taken to the U.S. Geological Survey laboratories at Woods Hole, Massachusetts, where tests will be made by Dr. C. C. Woo in an effort to approximate its age. In addition to radioisotopic methods to gauge the rate of deposition of the manganese, Dr. Woo will make an effort to locate the place where the dolomitic sandstone was quarried. He believes it was quarried in southern China.

This is not a case of a single ship reaching a North American shore. Dr. Moriarity said that since he started his investigation of the Cape Mendocino anchor, he had learned of four other stone anchor finds involving two different sites. He refused to pinpoint the locations for fear the sites will be pillaged by amateur divers. They are, however, off the coast of the northwest United States. Should the anchors, especially the Cape Mendocino one, prove to be of ancient origin, he said it will go a long way toward confirming hints in literature that contact between Asia and North America had been made in the dim past.[20]

We do not, of course, know when the Chinese first came to North America. Pierre Honore, in his book *In Quest of the White Gods*, states that coastal Peru was reached by the Chinese between 500 and 400 B.C. He presents evidence that in the fourth century B.C. this contact was taken over by people of the Dongson culture of Tongking and Annam and that their influence extended as far south as Chile and Argentina.[21]

There is a saying that nothing is more impossible to predict than the past. Archeological studies in Mesoamerica and South America are currently in a fluid state. We cannot be dogmatic. James Bailey points out that comparatively little archeological work has been done in Peru and Ecuador, where the southern peak of New World civilization was reached in the Copper and Bronze Ages. Much of what work has been done is postwar, and much of the new data applies to cultures that were completely unknown prior to 1940.

There is a widespread cultural trail going back to ancient India. As liberal-thinking archeologists and anthropologists probe the shadows of a forgotten world, evidence increases that the Aryan conquest of India, a time between the first and fourth millennia B.C., overthrew a great maritime power. These sea peoples may have left their language traces in Japan, the Philippines and elsewhere. On land they may have been a megalithic people, as witnessed by the megalithic graves in southern India. There is a southern Indian tradition of lineal descent from Heracles, a hero personifying an ancient sea people.

In the Caroline Islands there are megalithic remains, including the huge and enigmatic city of Nan Motal built by an unknown people at an unknown time. Here delicate rose pink beads have been found, exactly like beads found recently in the ruins of Mitla in Central America, and like the wampum of shell-bead money of the North American Indians. And on one of the islands is a syllabic script. Regarding it, Prof. J. Macmillan Brown, author of *The Riddle of the Pacific*, has written: "This Oleai script is manifestly the product of long ages for the use of the organisers of a highly organised community of considerable size. In other words, it must have belonged to the ruling class of an empire of some extent, that needed a constant record of the facts of intercourse and organisation." [22]

The Carolines were important to the ancient seamen, since their geographical position was at the beginning of the Pacific counter-current for which Ecuador is the American landfall. And in India itself there is the memory of these master mariners. In the Hippolyte Fauche translation of *The Ramayana* there is a reference to a former people whose "fleets passed from the eastern to the western oceans and from the southern to northern seas in ages so remote that the sun had not yet risen." Does this mean before the first sun-empire?

There is the trail of the raven. According to *The Ramayana*, Prince Rama, the father of India, was attacked by the power of the Raven, who carried off Rama's beautiful wife, Sita, in a great flying chariot. In the northwest among the Alaskan tribes, totem poles prominently display the raven. Carved wearing a tall hat, the raven is not only reminiscent of the South Seas, but thus also of pre-Aryan India. A totem pole of the Thlinget Indians on Cat Island in southeastern Alaska bears a man in a squatting position wearing a tall hat strikingly similar to the Easter Island statues. When first seen by Europeans, the giant figures on Easter Island all wore tall hats.

The ancient ceramics of India, writes Alexander von Wuthenau, "are full of interesting parallels with the ones produced in Meso-America, and anyone acquainted with Mexican pieces also feels 'at home' with pieces from Siam." [23]

Other cultural trails will be found in books entirely devoted to early Old and New World contacts. There is the diffusion of plants. The banana and the breadfruit, both tropical plants that must be cultivated by hand from small shoots, were hardly carried by Arctic tribes across the frigid Aleutians. The banana has been here long enough to gain much variety. The Asian rice plant too has required a long period of time to become the vastly different variety still gathered today by the Chippewas.

George F. Carter, writing in *American Antiquity*, gives diffusion examples of the coconut palm found by the Spaniards in western Central America, the bottle gourd and cotton. We have already referred to the migration of the sweet potato to Polynesia. Maize, of unknown ancestry, may have been carried either way across the Pacific. Grain amaranths, native to Mexico and Peru, appeared in China and Hawaii long before Columbus. Carter suspects the common bean, the sword bean and the lotus as part of the diffusion. He tells of a breed of chicken found both in Peru and pre-Columbian Japan that lays blue eggs.[24]

Languages and plants testify to the great antiquity of cultured man. There are links between cultures throughout the globe—between Asian countries, Africa and hoary Egypt, America, and the early nations of the Mediterranean. From all the continents sea peoples set forth and braved the oceans and transmitted artifacts and knowledge that we are only beginning to discover. Human history and culture are not recent things. They drop back into a dark, deep maelstrom of confusion and bafflement.

It is unlikely that all the pieces of the jigsaw puzzle of voyages and migrations and cultural relationships will ever be assembled. Nor is it likely that we will ever be able to answer that greater question—"Where was the Motherland?"

7
Columbus Was Late

INSTEAD OF BEING HAILED as the first discoverer of the Americas, Christopher Columbus should be credited for renewing interest in it. Many scholars now hold that he was well aware of the existence of the New World. As Robert Graves has said, quite likely he had a map.

The evidence that early Mediterranean sailors reached the Americas has recently grown, thanks to the research of Dr. Cyrus H. Gordon, Brandeis University scholar and expert on ancient Mediterranean culture and languages. He is the author of some thirteen books and is especially known in the academic world as an authority on Semitic languages.

In 1872 slaves found an inscribed stone on a plantation at Pouso Alto near Parahyba, Brazil. The owner copied the text and sent it to the Historical Institute in Rio de Janeiro. In 1966—ninety-four years later—Dr. Jules Piccus, professor of Romance languages at the University of Massachusetts, came across a transcription of the markings. He sent the copy to Dr. Gordon.

In comparing the inscription with the latest work on Phoenician writings, he noticed that the peculiarities of this text found in Brazil and written in a language very closely related to Hebrew and Phoenician referred to events between 534 and 531 B.C.

"I realized this had to be genuine because it contained words, grammatical forms and expressions that were not known in the 19th century, but were only authenticated in the 20th century. This is important, because if one of these inscriptions turned up in

1973, there would be no way of knowing if it were genuine or fake. The reason is a forger can know everything I do, or anyone else. But a forger cannot know what's going to be discovered in the next century." [1]

Gordon translated the script as follows:

We are Sidonian Canaanites from the city of the Mercantile King. We were cast up on this distant shore, a land of mountains. We sacrificed a youth to the celestial gods and goddesses in the nineteenth year of our mighty King Hiram and embarked from Ezion-geber into the Red Sea. We voyaged with ten ships and were at sea together for two years around Africa. Then we were separated by the hand of Baal and were no longer with our companions. So we have come here, twelve men and three women, into New Shore. Am I, the Admiral, a man who would flee? Nay! May the celestial gods and goddesses favor us well!

If the Parahyba stone is authentic and if Gordon's translation is correct, Canaanites from the Near East reached the Americas 2,000 years before Columbus and some 1,500 years before the Norse.

The term "Canaanites," as a proper noun, was given to inhabitants of the Near East who are related by language. These include Phoenicians, Hebrews, Moabites, Edomites and others. As a common noun it means "merchants." Gordon believes the crew of the ship that sailed from the Red Sea port of Ezion-geber to Brazil could have been any mixture of these nationalities, as all of them had men who were skilled sailors. Crews were chosen because they were able seamen and not because of their national or religious backgrounds.

"By the hand of Baal" means the same as saying "by an act of God." The reference to Baal and human sacrifice does not eliminate the possibility that some crewmen were Hebrews, as the Bible states that groups of Hebrews at times turned to pagan religions. The language of the inscription, according to Gordon, "is more akin to Judean Hebrew than to Sidonian Phoenician." [2] At any rate, a seafaring trade partnership between the Israelites and Phoenicians was established almost a thousand years before Christ by King Solomon and Hiram I.

"In the nineteenth year of our mighty King Hiram" indicates that the ruler must have been Hiram III who reigned from 553 to 533 B.C. If so, Dr. Gordon sets 531 B.C. as the year the Near East vessel made its Brazilian landfall. But this was not a solitary voyage. There were other Canaanites, perhaps many, who reached the Americas.

In 1885 Smithsonian Institution archeologists opened an undisturbed burial mound along Bat Creek near Loudon, Tennessee. They found nine human skeletons. Beneath one of the skulls was an inscribed stone. It was called a Cherokee tablet, and in 1894 in a Smithsonian Bureau of Ethnology Report it appeared in a photograph printed upside down. Since then it has been lying unnoticed in the museum's vaults.

In 1970 Dr. Joseph Mahan, curator of the Columbus Museum of Arts and Crafts in Columbus, Georgia, noticed the picture during his search in archeological literature for inscriptions that might be of Old World origin. He directed Dr. Gordon's attention to it.

The Bat Creek Stone, as it is called, is a piece of slatelike ironstone measuring about 4½ inches long and two inches wide. The inscription reads from right to left as "DWHYL'QS," or in the order of our writing "SQ'LYHWD." Gordon is not certain of the meaning of the first two Hebraic letters, but thinks the first may be a "sade" or "S" and the second a "qof" or "Q."

But the last five letters can be translated definitely as "for Judah." The "L" means "for" and the "YHWD" stands for "yehud" or "Judah." "Neither I, nor anyone else," says Gordon, "can say it was possibly a forgery." [3] It appears to be the first Mediterranean text found in the New World in its original site and with the original objects connected with it.

The well-carved letters represent Hebrew of the Roman period, roughly 100 A.D. They suggest a migration of Jews, possibly to escape the disastrous Jewish defeats at the hands of the Romans in 70 and 135 A.D.

Their descendants may still be living in eastern Tennessee about sixty miles northeast of the Bat Creek burial mound. They are the Melungeons. They are neither Indian nor Negro. They are Caucasian, but not Anglo-Saxon, and are best described as a dark-complexioned, straight-haired, Mediterranean-type people. When the first white men reached Tennessee they were here, and they have been here for a long time.

The Melungeons live in the communities of Vardy and Snake Hollow, near Sneedville in Hancock County. Only in the past fifty years have both communities been reachable by narrow dirt mountain roads; before that the only communication was by horseback. Originally they occupied the rich bottomlands, but greedy white settlers forced them out of the valleys and into the mountain ridges. This isolation was one of several factors that led to discrimination against them. They were strange: their physical features were different from those of other people in the area. They kept to themselves. Superstitious mountain folk whispered that they drank blood and dabbled in witchcraft.

Today only about 200 Melungeons live in the Tennessee mountains. Claude Collins, a Melungeon and county school official, says intermarriage with others has made a "pure" Melungeon hard to find. He doubts if any full-blooded Melungeons still exist, although their unique physical features are still evident. The story of their struggle to attain freedom and equality is presented during July and August at Sneedville in an outdoor drama, "Walk Toward the Sunset." The Hancock County Drama Association introduced the play in 1969 as a means of lifting the economic level of the county, the eighth poorest in the United States.

The origin of the word Melungeon is a mystery. Some theorists speculate that it comes from the French "melange," meaning mixture. Others refer to the Portuguese word "melango" for shipmate.

But it is the greater mystery of their origin that has been pondered by scholars and historians. A prominent theory is that they were originally a band of Portuguese sailors who were shipwrecked on the North Carolina coast and wandered inland, married Amerind girls and lived undisturbed until the settlers drove westward. Another is that they are descendants of the ill-fated Roanoke Island Colony of Englishmen who disappeared about 1590. Other theories are that they are descendants of dissident Welshmen led by Prince Madoc in the twelfth century, or of deserters from Hernando de Soto's Spanish expedition in 1540. The most intriguing theory is that involving Phoenician sailors who came to the New World some 2,000 years before Columbus.[4]

But the Bat Creek Stone causes Dr. Gordon to suggest that the Melungeons were of Mediterranean and possibly Hebrew origin who came to the western world almost 2,000 years ago, moved inland over the mountains and settled in Tennessee's Clinch Valley.

In the relationships between peoples once considered properly situated in time and space on their respective continents, we have more recent discoveries that leave progressive scholars breathless. We find that the Melungeons may have had Canaanite brothers in an adjoining state who even now practice rites that were already ancient in the time of Christ.

Another ingredient in the Amerind racial melting pot was discovered in 1966. Manfred Metcalf, an amateur archeologist, was collecting rocks at the U.S. military reservation at Fort Benning, Georgia, in order to construct an outdoor fireplace for his patio. In a rubbish pile at the site of an old gristmill he found a red sandstone slab with symbols cut into it. He took the stone to Dr. Joseph B. Mahan at the Columbus Museum of Arts and Crafts, the same man who was to call Dr. Gordon's attention to the Bat Creek Stone later.

Mahan is an expert on Amerind ethnology and archeology. He is a specialist on the Yuchis, a tribe that once inhabited what is now Georgia, but was resettled in Oklahoma in 1836. He believes the Yuchis may have originally come from the Old World, and he thought the stone's inscription might add evidence to his theory.

He sent a cast replica to Dr. Gordon. Gordon, famous for establishing a common background for ancient Greek and Hebrew civilizations and his Mediterranean language studies, noticed that the markings were very old and it was unlikely that the inscription was a hoax. In an article in *Manuscripts*, a quarterly published by the Manuscript Society, he wrote: "After studying the inscription, it was apparent to me that the affinities of the script were with the Aegean syllabary, whose two best known forms are Minoan Linear A and Mycenaean Linear B. The double-axe in the lower left corner is, of course, reminiscent of Minoan civilization . . ."

He concluded: "We therefore have American inscriptional contacts with the Aegean of the Bronze Age, near the south, west, and north shores of the Gulf of Mexico. This can hardly be accidental; ancient Aegean writing near three different sectors of the Gulf reflects Bronze Age transatlantic communication between the Mediterranean and the New World around the middle of the second millennium B.C."

He makes the rather startling suggestion that "the Aegean analogues to Mayan writing, to the Aztec glyphs, and to the Metcalf Stone inspire the hope that the deciphered scripts of the Mediterranean may provide keys for unlocking the forgotten systems of writing in the New World. A generation capable of landing men on the moon may also be able to place pre-Columbian America within the framework of world history." [5]

After lengthy study, Gordon believes the Metcalf Stone text is an inventory, with some symbols representing objects and others representing numbers. Three of the other characters resemble the Greek letters theta, pi and delta. A bow-tie-shaped symbol had both a phonetic and symbolic value in the Minoan language. Some marks are duplicated in Linear B and follow counted items in certain lists. Like the Latin alphabet, the Aegean writing may have been used for different languages.

A problem is presented by the time lag between the early Old World inscriptions and the later New World inscriptions. Gordon suggests the explanation may be "conservatism in transmission." Or as Mahan says, "There's no chance of an accidental duplication by a primitive people of these ancient symbols. What this means is that somebody in this area, hundreds of years later than this writing was in use in Europe, retained this writing system and carved this on a Georgia rock." [6]

There is an emerging "New World pattern into which the Metcalf Stone fits," Gordon writes. [7] He refers to the striking similarities between the Phaistos Disc from Crete and the Aztec glyphs that were matched by Svein-Magnus Grodys, a Norwegian scholar. And he cites the comparison of Minoan Linear A and Mayan writing as pointed out by Pierre Honoré in his book *In Quest of the White God.*

Based upon their religion and customs, Mahan believes the Yuchis came from the Mediterranean during the Bronze Age, that is, around the middle of the second millennium B.C. when the Minoans ruled the seas, and that they are the descendants of an ancient Minoan people. Apparently they broke away from the parent stem "about the time writing in stone was in vogue." [8]

Yuchi tradition is that their ancestors came from the east in boats after a natural catastrophe. Their new homeland was to the south (probably Central or northern South America), and they lived there for a long time before migrating north, perhaps across the Gulf of Mexico.

A chief interviewed by Mahan said his tribe came to the southeastern United States about 1,000 years before the appearance of the explorer DeSoto. White settlers drove them out of Georgia. Today about 1,700 Yuchis live in Oklahoma where they maintain their traditional ways and their ancient religion.

It is their agricultural festival that is so amazing, for it is described in detail in the Bible—in the twenty-third chapter of Leviticus. Mahan points out that there are far too many resemblances for this to be accident or sheer coincidence. This is the Feast of Booths (Tabernacles or Succoth) which includes (1) an eight-day festival (2) that starts on the fifteenth day or full moon of the holy harvest month, (3) living in "booths" throughout the festival (4) at the religious center for the tribe and (5) maintaining a sacred fire. The first three of these same observances are carried on by some Jews to this very day.

The Yuchis make a pilgrimage to their religious center on the fifteenth day of their harvest month. During the eight-day festival they live in "booths" that have open spaces in the roofs and are covered with foliage and tree branches. There is a sacred area in which a fire is kept burning, and they celebrate by walking around the fire in a circle. Two large decorated branches are carried by two men during the circling walk, and other men during other parts of the observance shake similar branches.

During identical time periods, Jews today who celebrate this festival dwell in booths open to the sky, but covered with fruits, vegetables and foliage. They take circular walks or "circumambulations" and plants tied together into a staff are used for ceremonial shaking. Although the Jewish celebration of Tabernacles no longer has the sacred fire, it is referred to in Leviticus 23:37.

Neither Gordon nor Mahan believe the Yuchis to be one of the legendary lost ten tribes of Israel. "The implication," writes Dr. Gordon, "is rather that the Yuchi and biblical feast of booths are both rooted in the ancient Mediterranean and constitute reflexes of the same international synthesis that was already old by 1500 B.C.—long before we can speak of historical Hebrews, let alone historic Yuchis." [9] In other words, both peoples share certain cultural features inherited from the ancient East and Mediterranean of the Bronze Age. Gordon says agricultural ceremonies are slow to die in a culture, and the Hebrews perpetuated many of those inherited from their Canaanite predecessors.

In his doctoral dissertation at the University of North Carolina, entitled *Identification of the Tsoyaha Waeno, Builders of Temple Mounds*, Mahan offers additional evidence.

We see certain artistic designs in the Yuchi pottery and architecture—particularly the mounds—that are identical to religious symbols and art forms from the Bronze Age, prior to 1500 B.C., in the eastern Mediterranean area. Most striking of these [similarities of design on Mississippian temple mound-builder pottery and Minoan pottery] is the famous spiral and the various sun circles associated with hands and eyes. There are also many pottery shapes which are related including "stirrup vessels" and human foot and human head or face effigies.[10]

Gordon and Dr. Alexander von Wuthenau, the art historian, agree that people from not only the Mediterranean, but Africa, Asia and the Middle East populated the Americas along with the Amerinds before 300 A.D., and that the Central and South American civilizations may have reached their heights as a result of this cultural enrichment. While primarily Amerind, these monumental relics of ancient America between Peru and Mexico could have been stimulated by transoceanic contacts from the east and west.

Several years ago Von Wuthenau, on a visit to the National Museum of Mexico, noticed on a six-foot stela uncovered near Campeche a Star of David design engraved in the earring of a Mayan dignitary. The figure also had a hat seemingly patterned after the reed boats of ancient Egypt along with horizontal lines that might well mean water. When he investigated reproductions of rock drawings in the Jewish necropolis of Beit-Shearim, he was surprised to find a very similar figure featuring an interlaced six-pointed Star of David and an authentic ancient reed boat.[11]

If these ancient Old World and New World contacts occurred, why are they not a part of known history? Much historical knowledge has been lost as cultures rose and fell, advanced and retreated. Quite likely there were no large migrations to the Americas. At best there may have been small colonies that made their cultural contributions, then intermarried and were absorbed by the Amerinds, thus creating the "white Indians."

Again, Old World seafarers in ancient times were secretive about their trade routes. Competition from other traders and piracy would have been invited if they advertised their ports of call. And whenever a seafaring nation or a particular group of seamen stopped coming to New World ports, these ports eventually were forgotten. This is what happened much more recently in historical terms to the Vinland of the Norse.

There were, however, maps that survived. Maps are important. They can mean life or death on the vast stretches of the seas. Thus we have the Piri Re'is and other old maps, which were copied from still older charts, showing parts of the eastern Americas. Where the shorelines charted by the ancient mapmakers have receded into the sea, underwater sounding has proved their accuracy. The evidence is that long ago seafarers sailed over much of the earth and constructed reliable maps. Fragments and copies of these maps survived into the Middle Ages and were copied again, although their significance had been long lost to most scholars.

These ancient mariners were a hardy breed, able to take two-year voyages. Prof. Armundo Cortesao, of the University of Coimbra in Portugal, insists that ancient navigators in pre-Christian times attained a competency that Europeans did not duplicate until the last quarter of the fifteenth century. And these early sailors had excellent ships, far superior to those of Europeans prior to the fifteenth century.

The notion that ancient vessels were too small for transoceanic travel is erroneous. By 2500 B.C. the Egyptians had built merchant ships well over 100 feet long. The Greeks were building grain freighters of 1,900 tons burden in the third century B.C., ten times the size of Columbus' *Santa Maria* and twice the size of the largest galleon used by the Spaniards in their voyages to the New World.

These seafaring peoples roamed the world. In 3000 B.C. the Babylonians had established regular sea trade with India. It is known that by 1200 B.C. the Phoenicians were making frequent voyages to the Azores, and in the seventh century B.C. they circumnavigated Africa. They sailed north to Scandinavia where the Vikings later copied their ship design. Their invention of the keel made it possible for them to control their vessels under sail and to construct seaworthy ships over 100 feet in length.[12]

During those pre-Christian years there were writers who mentioned lands far out in the Atlantic. Theopomus, a Greek writer in the fourth century B.C., referred to an enormous "continent" outside the Old World, inhabited by peoples with strange life styles. Diodorus of Sicily, who lived in the first century B.C., wrote: "For there lies out in the deep off Libya [Africa] an island of considerable size, and situated as it is in the ocean, it is distant from Libya a voyage of a number of days to the west. Its land is fruitful, much of it being mountainous, and not a little being a level plain of surpassing beauty. Through it flow navigable waters . . ." There is no island with these features unless he was referring to the West Indies or the Western Hemisphere. He adds that "In ancient times this island remained undiscovered because of its distance," and he tells of Phoenician ships that were driven to this island by storms.[13]

Seneca, Plato, Plutarch, Aristotle, Homer, Strabo and many other ancient writers referred to lands far to the west.

Of all the ancient maritime peoples, it appears the Phoenicians, especially the Carthaginians, roamed the farthest, leaving evidence of their presence not only along the seashores but occasionally inland. In fact, they may have established colonies. In Spanish archives there is a manuscript written by a bishop who visited Yucatan around 1550. While in the village of Mani, near Merida, he observed a number of unusual buildings that closely resembled the ruins of buildings he had seen in the Holy Land and the Near East. They had stone roofs supported by iron rods, yet iron was supposed to have been unknown in the New World prior to the arrival of the Spaniards. The structures were obviously centuries old.

The village elders told the bishop that the buildings had been erected by a band of white men who had come from a place called Carthage. The Romans destroyed Carthage in 146 B.C. Could these Carthaginians have been shipwrecked sailors, or were they immigrants coming to the New World to avoid being vassals under the Romans? [14]

Alexander von Wuthenau reports finding a terra cotta head from Guerro, Mexico, remarkably similar to the god Bes of the Phoenicians and Egyptians. Similar images of this peculiar deity are found at almost all Phoenician excavation sites around the Mediterranean. Terra cotta heads of *Urweisse* or "ancient Whites" have also been discovered in the Guerro district. He has found evidence that Mediterranean peoples dwelt around Acapulco. Female figurines from the district have small mouths, delicate eyebrows, opulent coiffures and are markedly Caucasian.

Art objects with long curved noses, narrow faces and beards (the Amerinds had no beards) were found by him in the region of Mexico City. The female figures had delicate profiles, fine straight noses, sometimes with a slight upturn common in the white race. The Spaniards might have failed in their conquest of Mexico if the Aztecs had not believed them to be the returning "bearded white gods" who, according to legend, had visited their land in the past. Their heroic god Quetzalcoatl was a white, bearded deity. The conquistadors commented on Montezuma's unusually light skin.

In Aztec mythology, Quetzalcoatl came from the east, dispensed his knowledge, then left with the promise that someday he would return. The Incas had a white god called Vuracocha, and the Mayans had a similar one named Kukulcan.

Clay and stone figurines found near Miguel de Allende, Mexico, display a Mediterranean influence. Some look like mermaids, legendary beings derived from the Phoenician god Dagon, while others feature stringed musical instruments, chairs and beasts of burden pulling chariotlike vehicles, all unknown to Amerinds before the Spaniards came.[15]

There are a number of rock inscriptions in eastern South America, particularly in Brazil in the Amazon basin, believed to be Phoenician, but it appears they came to North America too. According to Charles M. Boland in his book *They All Discovered America*, Phoenician relics have been found in Pennsylvania and New Hampshire.[16]

If Professor Barry Fell, a Harvard University linguist, has read stone inscriptions correctly, a Phoenician seafarer-king named Hanno came to New England almost 2,500 years ago. Fell and James Whittall, chief archeologist for the Early Sites Research Society of Danielson, Connecticut, made a study of the stone in the spring of 1975. The stone, measuring forty-five inches by five inches by fifteen inches, was found by New England settlers in 1658 and until recently had been used as a doorstop at an Amerind mission. Fell's translation of the two-line inscription: "Proclamation of annexation. Do not deface. Hanno of this takes possession." He believes the last sentence means Hanno takes possession of this place.

Hanno was a Phoenician seafarer. Early in the fifth century B.C. he explored and colonized the west coast of Africa, establishing seven cities and a trading post. An account of this voyage, written in the Temple of Baal in Carthage, survives in a Greek manuscript dating back to the tenth century A.D., and is believed to be a translation from the ancient Punic language.

Fell believes the inscription on the stone "is one more of the same series, evidently belonging to a second voyage that Hanno made of which the Greek account has been lost. But the Greeks remembered that he did make such a voyage, that is to say they remembered he had circumnavigated the northern ocean. This stone comes from that voyage which, according to our Greek sources, dates from approximately 480 or 475 B.C."

There is evidence that Hanno was not only a navigator from Carthage, but also a king of southern Spain with Cadiz his principal port. He sailed from Cadiz and probably returned there. The inscription was written in a southern Iberian alphabet. "It was deciphered by Spanish scientists," Fell said. "So it's not just a case of one crackpot Harvard professor alleging that it's this. I have plenty of authorities to support me." [17] The Phoenicians founded the city of Cadiz.

To explain the inscription on a certain basalt rock in New Mexico, you are asked to believe that a Mormon wandering far south of the Mormon trail to Utah came to a remote desert area. Here he laboriously chiseled the Ten Commandments in a combination of Phoenician, Hebrew and Greek on the tipped underside of a large boulder while lying on his back. Or perhaps a desert drifter who was an expert on ancient languages cut the hieroglyphics as a hoax that he never thought worth disclosing. This, in effect, was the suggestion of Smithsonian Institution scientists when they were confronted with this enigma.

The rock lies in one of the most desolate regions of the state—a bluff along the now-dry Rio Puerco River. The nearest town is Los Lunas. The characters are worn and are obviously very old, cut into the hard basalt centuries before the Mormons came west. Also obvious is the fact that the inscription was made when the rock face was perpendicular to the mesa, but years later the soil supporting it on the bluff had eroded, causing it to topple.

The translation originally was made by Dr. Robert Pfeiffer of Harvard University. A startling feature is that the hieroglyphics are similar to those inscribed on the sarcophagus of the King of Sidon, which dates from about 572 B.C., even to the same combination of the three languages. If Phoenician seamen had sailed around Florida and into the Gulf of Mexico, then up the Rio Grande River and the Rio Puerco, the rock's location would have been where the voyage ended, as from this point on up the river would not have been navigable. [18]

The Phoenicians were a secretive people, believing that a secret can best be kept if it is not written down. Our knowledge of them comes from the Greeks who recorded all they could learn about them. In fact, the Greeks took their alphabet from the Phoenicians, and this is the same basic alphabet we use today. The thriving commerce of the Phoenicians took them to all parts of the ancient world. As a result, their culture was eclectic. It included elements of other contemporary cultures, Egyptian, Babylonian, Sumerian and Hittite.

Constance Irwin, in her fascinating book *Fair Gods and Stone Faces*, says that once voyages began in the open Atlantic, prevailing winds and currents almost compelled the discovery of Central America. If the Phoenicians established settlements there as they did in Europe and Africa, we might well find traces and artifacts of all the Old World cultures with which they were in contact.[19]

Thus we find pyramids in Central and South America comparable to ziggurats erected in Sumeria, Babylonia and at least one known part of Phoenicia. Both were oriented to the four compass points, terraced and topped by temples. Then too there is a dark side to the striking parallels of religious observances. In the temples burnt offerings were made and infants sacrificed to grim gods. Some of the New World priests wore artificial beards in the manner of Egyptian pharaohs.

The Olmecs were the most enigmatic of all preconquest Amerinds. In Mexico, at ancient archaeological sites mostly Olmec, have been found figurines or carved reliefs of bearded men with Semitic features, in one instance wearing shoes with pointed upturned toes similar to shoes worn by the Phoenicians and Hittites. Other discoveries are urn figures apparently depicting the Egyptian bird-headed god Ra and a sphinx; small wheeled chariots similar to those found in Phoenician tombs; reliefs of Negroid dancers in Assyrian style; and huge basalt heads with Negroid features. Some of these massive heads weigh over ten tons.[20]

During his third voyage Columbus recorded that when he reached Haiti the inhabitants told him that black men from the south and southeast had preceded him to the island. And in 1513 Vasco Nuñez de Balboa reported finding a colony of Negroes living at a place called Quareque on the Caribbean coast of Colombia. It is known that the Carthaginians not only traded for gold along the African coast, but also for slaves. Were they the survivors of wrecked slave ships?

The Negroid sculptures and reliefs, however, indicate that black people came to America as free men. Some must have arrived at a very early time. Only recently, no less than seven Pygmy graveyards have been discovered in Venezuela, the skeletons definitely identified as African Pygmies.[21]

Other groups came later. Spanish explorers found a Negro settlement on the coast of Central America—where there are many black settlements today—and they were supposedly survivors of a ship launched by the Sultan of Guinea, in Africa, in 1300 A.D. to look for land across the South Atlantic.

8

The European Wanderers

WE WILL PROBABLY NEVER KNOW who the first Europeans were who came to the New World. There is a prehistory that has faded into a limbo of the lost, and there is a history still dotted with enigmas.

On Labor Day 1975, at a meeting in Cambridge, Massachusetts, members of the Epigraphic Society reported that they had found evidence that Celtic Europeans had been in New England 2,500 years ago. The claim was based on inscriptions found on stone structures in New Hampshire and Vermont. These inscriptions were part of an ancient language called Ogam (or Ogham) that was used by the Celtic peoples, who ranged from southwestern Germany to Spain and north to the British Isles. Dr. Barry Fell of Harvard said the inscriptions found in North Salem, New Hampshire, and at the foothills of the Green Mountains in central Vermont have been tentatively dated from about 800 B.C. to the third century B.C.[1]

Ogam too is the inscription on a large boulder in an isolated cove on Newfoundland's northern tip. Dr. Robert McGhee, professor of archeology at Newfoundland's Memorial University, and a colleague were being guided along the rocky coast by a local fisherman when he asked if the professors would like to see a rock with writing on it. That's how the inscription was discovered.

If the Ogam Stone is a hoax, it's an old one. The markings are covered with lichen moss that is a minimum of 100 to 200 years old. Dr. McGhee is excited but cautious about his discovery. "I record what I see," he said. He found the script was probably Ogam when he observed that it wasn't the runic writing of the Vikings nor was it at all similar to Indian rock carvings.[2]

Apparently associated with the New Hampshire Ogam inscription near New Salem is "Mystery Hill," a megalithic monument now owned by Robert Stone, president of the New England Antiquities Research Association. It consists of a strange complex of twenty-two low and underground chambers cut into a bare granite outcropping and provided with drains. The chambers contained stones that have been moved around or removed altogether for building materials. Vandals have wreaked their havoc through the years. Colonial farmers seem to have used them for storing vegetables, for making maple syrup or as root cellars. Nevertheless, the basic structures are there to bewilder the visitor.

Robert Stone invited professional archeologists to visit the site and conduct excavations. One, James P. Whittall, Jr., unearthed materials that gave valid radiocarbon datings of 1000 B.C., plus or minus a small overlap. Tools and pottery found at the dig indicate the structures were built by a culture similar to those which inhabited the Mediterranean from about 3000 B.C. to 500 B.C. It is Whittall's theory that the chambers and shaping of the stones are strikingly similar to the megalithic culture known to have existed on the Iberian Peninsula. Some experts even feel they may be of Phoenician origin, or perhaps were occupied by Phoenicians after they were built. They claim that sea currents and prevailing winds could have enabled Bronze Age sea adventurers of that time to cross the Atlantic Ocean in a southwesterly direction and then go up the American east coast.[3]

In the *Newsletter and Proceedings* of the Society for Early Historic Archaeology, Dr. Ross T. Christensen writes:

A number of theories have been proposed to explain the origin of this strange complex of "maverick" archeology. The constructions were plainly not built by New England Indians or their ancestors of any known variety. They clearly do not fit into the pattern of prehistoric cultural development usually assigned to the Eastern Woodlands area by professional archeologists. The latter as a rule consider the "caves" to be stables or root cellars of early New England farmers . . . and indeed they probably were used as such at a later time . . .

William B. Goodwin was persuaded that the constructions at Mystery Hill were built by a band of Irish monks fleeing from the Vikings. . . . Charles M. Boland believes that Irish monks were later occupants of the

site, but that it was the Phoenicians who built it in the first place . . .
Frank Glynn, a prominent amateur archeologist of Clinton, Connecticut,
developed a theory that the New England complex is related to the Bronze
Age "Megalithic" culture of Malta and western Mediterranean lands of
1500 B.C. . . .

The evidence so far argues in favor of a transatlantic crossing. But apparently those who came were not Indian hunters, Yankee farmers, Irish
monks, nor Phoenician mariners; they were a nameless people of the late
Bronze Age of the western Mediterranean area, perhaps from Portugal.[4]

Near the chambers are some rock carvings. One is of a gazelle.
Andrew E. Rothovius, historian and editor of the New England
Antiquities Research Association's *Newsletter*, points out that another carving is the Minoan labrys, or double axe, "a point of considerable importance." This is almost identical to one of the carvings on the Metcalf Stone (see chapter 8).

What influences Old World arrivals had on New World cultures
is only now beginning to come to light, but we can assume that
some of those who stayed were in time assimilated by the Amerindians. This may explain the so-called "white Indians." Columbus
himself during his second voyage, after discovering the wreckage of
a European ship on Guadeloupe, was sailing off the coast of Venezuela when his small fleet of ships was approached by a large
wooden canoe containing about eighty men. He described them as
"of stout build, white-skinned, with long blond hair and beards."

There are the white Indians of Brazil and Colombia. The light-
skinned Indians in the San Blas region of Panama are reported to
have Norse and French words with identical meanings in their vo-
cabulary.[5] There are other scattered groups of white Indians in
Central and South America.

In North America there were the Mandans, a strange tribe now
long gone, wiped out in the smallpox epidemic that swept across
the Great Plains in 1837. In two Mandan towns with a population
of 1,600, there were only thirty-one individuals left alive. The few
survivors were assimilated into other tribes, and the Mandans were
no more.

In 1738 Pierre de la Verendrye was the first white man of record
to penetrate to what is now western North Dakota. In his journal
he wrote: "Their towns are fortified. Within are streets and
squares. Our Frenchmen would often lose their way in going about
. . . The fort is built on an elevation in mid-prairie, with a ditch
over 15 feet deep, and from 15 to 18 feet wide. . . . This tribe is of

mixed blood. The women are rather handsome, particularly the light colored ones; they have an abundance of fair hair." [6]

The Mandans had fair complexions, blue eyes and blond hair. Some of the women had gray eyes. The men had beards, while the Amerinds who surrounded them were beardless. They erected European-type fortifications. In the rich bottom land along the upper Missouri River they raised bumper crops and sold the surplus to other tribes. Their ornamented leather work was outstanding, and they made the region's only pottery. In time, as middlemen of the northern plains, they carried on a profitable trade in European goods.

The Lewis and Clark expedition in 1803–1805 noted the blue eyes and silky hair of some of the Mandans. In 1832, five years before their tragic end, George Catlin, noted artist and ethnologist, arrived to spend considerable time among the Mandans. He penned his observations:

> So forcibly have I been struck by the peculiar ease and elegance of these people . . . the singularity of their language, and their peculiar and unaccountable customs, that I am fully convinced that they have sprung from some other origin than that of the other North American tribes, or that they are an amalgam of natives with some other civilized race.
>
> A stranger in the Mandan village is first struck with the different shades of complexion . . . and is almost at once disposed to exclaim that "they are not Indians." There are a great many whose complexions appear as light as half-breeds; and amongst the women particularly, there are many whose skins are almost white, with the most pleasing symmetry and proportion of features; with hazel, with gray and blue eyes, with mildness and sweetness of expression which renders them exceedingly pleasing and beautiful. [7]

What were the ancestral origins of the Mandans? In their own traditions they said they were descendants from the First Men who survived a great flood in a huge ark. They had a model of this ark, and each spring they danced around it to celebrate the survival of their ancestors. The dance lasted for forty days. Here again we have an ancient Old World legend appearing almost intact in America.

George Catlin wrote that the Mandans spoke fifty words of pure Welsh and about 130 words of near-Welsh. The word *Mandan* suggests the Welsh *madder* for red, and Catlin thought the name came about because of their red-dyed porcupine quills. He also noted that they made Welsh blue beads, had circles of stone for their hearths in Welsh fashion, and navigated the Missouri River in willow and rawhide coracles.

The Mandan flood legend was so close to the biblical version that it had a dove being sent from the ark and returning with a willow slip in its beak. The old Welsh Cwmry tradition, however, had several men escaping in an open boat, but there were also two arks called Nwydd Nav and Neivion.

John Paul Marana, who wrote *The Turkish Spy* back in 1734, said that in British Canada there were native tribes called the "Tuscoards" (Tuscarora Indians), and the Doegs, who spoke Welsh, and were believed to have descended from them.[8]

It is unlikely that the Mandans have any connection with the alleged Welsh expedition to North America within historical times. Such a late origin would have been prominent in their traditions, and they probably would have retained some cultural features identifiable with that period. It seems more likely that the Mandans and the historical Welsh people shared an early cultural origin.

In 1167 A.D. Owen Gwyneth, Prince of Wales, died, and contention arose among his sons about who should succeed him. It is said that one son, Madoc, withdrew from the conflict and decided to seek his fortune elsewhere. He gathered together a company of about 200 men and women and sailed westward. A colony was established on the Gulf of Mexico.

The legend, fairly well substantiated in Welsh histories, relates that Madoc returned to Wales for more settlers, but when he returned he was unable to locate the colony. It has been suggested that during Madoc's absence the colonists, for some reason, decided to relocate and moved up the Mississippi River.

Hakluyt, in his book *Divers Voyages Touching the Discovery of America*, written in 1582, mentioned the Welsh. Captain John Smith, in one of his accounts, made a curious reference to white Indians who spoke almost pure Welsh.

There are two locations in the United States with traditions of Welshmen. On the Ohio River near Jeffersonville, Indiana, there is a fortress formed by high natural rock walls that are joined by artificial embankments of earth and stones. Archeologists attribute this stone fort to the Mound Builders. An unreliable tradition maintains it was built by twelfth-century Welshmen. Several early writers believed the fort was used as a defense against Indians by Madoc's colony, which eventually came up the Mississippi and Ohio Rivers. Chief Tobacco's son told George Rogers Clark that there had once been a great battle between the Indians and a "strange race" at the nearby falls of the Ohio at Louisville.

According to *Indiana: A Guide to the Hoosier State* (American Guide Series), there is an account, taken seriously by some local historians, of Welsh armor being found on the river bank near Jeffersonville in 1799. It is described as being of brass, bearing a Latin inscription meaning "Virtuous deeds merit their just reward," and displaying a Welsh coat-of-arms, the "Mermaid and the Harp." The tale still persists that early settlers discovered a tombstone bearing the date 1186.[9]

The other location is in northern Georgia, near the Tennessee border. This once was the land of the Cherokee. Tribal legends tell of the "moon-eyed people who came from afar." They had blue eyes and the Amerinds believed they could see better at night than during the day, hence the moon eyes. Some Georgia citizens of today link the moon-eyed people with Madoc's colonists, who purportedly landed in the vicinity of present Mobile, Alabama.

Nine miles east of Chatsworth, Georgia, is 2,838-foot-high Fort Mountain. On its top is a so-called fortress, the remains of a rock wall some 885 feet long, built for an unknown purpose by an unknown people. It is composed of small, rather flat stones, and at present is about three feet high. It has a base, however, twelve feet wide, indicating it was much higher originally. The stones are carefully fitted together without mortar.

Twisting its sinuous way, the wall extends from one steep precipice to another, taking advantage of the rough terrain. It darts down and back up at one place, forming an acute angle like the bastion of a medieval castle. There are pits at fairly regular intervals, now around three feet deep but probably deeper when the wall was built. At two places there are the ruins of what originally must have been towers. At another location there are the remains of a large gate or entrance. Four hundred yards from the gate, now closed by fallen stones, and outside the walled area is a spring. While the wall protects the only accessible side of the mountain, it may not have been a fort at all. If so, there would have been no water supply within the alleged fortification. It may have been an Amerind religious center, erected by a people preceding the Cherokees.

Max Hunn, in an article in *Grit*, writes:

Cherokee legend says the Welsh settlers were driven northward by the Indians and built the stone wall atop Fort Mountain in a desperate effort to

defend themselves. Eventually they were either annihilated by the Cherokees, disappeared through intermarriage, or were persuaded to leave several centuries after Madoc first landed.

But it appears doubtful that the wall was built as part of a fortress
whether by "moon-eyed" Welsh, Indians or Spaniards. If it had been built
by Indians, some evidence would have been found. However, excavations
in the vicinity have disclosed no arrowheads, war axes, or other weapons.
The Indian fort theory is also weak. The Indians did not fight from fixed
positions. Finally, it seems poor strategy to build a fort where the enemy
could cut off your food and water. . . . Some day the answer may be
known, but more likely the rocks will continue to guard their secrets.[10]

Then there were the Romans. In 62 B.C. the Roman Consul Ma-
tellus Celer was officiating in Gaul when the king of a neighboring
province came to his court. The king brought with him several
strange people with red skins and black hair. He told the Roman
the strangers had been blown across the Atlantic in a large wooden
canoe. But it appears that the Romans themselves followed the
westering sea lanes and came to the New World.

In the 1880s near Veracruz in the Gulf of Mexico a Greco-
Roman torso of Venus was found. Conceivably it could have arrived in the New World after Columbus, but that is not true of
other artifacts discovered in more recent years. Greco-Roman oil
lamps of classical design have been found by the dozen in pre-Inca
tombs in northern Peru. A Roman terra-cotta sculptured head of
the third century A.D. was discovered in association with a twelfth
century A.D. tomb in Mexico. And the pineapple, of New World
origin, is depicted in murals in the uncovered Roman city of Pom-
peii.

In 1961 Dr. Garcia Payon, of the University of Jalapa, found a
large hoard of Roman jewelry in six graves near Mexico City. They
were identified as Roman dating from about 150 B.C. by Dr. Robert Heine-Geldern, of the University of Vienna, and Professor
Hans Boehringer, of the German Institute of Archeology. Carbon
dating of the bones and other material discovered with the jewelry
indicates that the burials took place no later than 100 B.C.

Near York, Maine, a rock on a beach has been known since the
days of the first settlers in the region. It bears a Latin inscription,
and nearby a Roman coin dated 237 A.D. has been found.[11]

Roman coins have been found in several places in North
America, some in mounds. One found in Cass County, Illinois, in
1882 was identified by Professor F. F. Hilder of St. Louis as a coin

of Antiochus IV, one of the kings of Syria who reigned from 175 B.C. to 164 B.C. Another, found in an Illinois mound, was identified as of "the rare mintage of Domitius Domitianus." A hoaxer would hardly have used a rare coin when a common Roman one would have been as satisfactory. Some of these coins, but not necessarily all, may have been brought to this continent after Columbus.[12]

The Roman crosses of Tucson, Arizona, have been a subject of controversy in recent years. The story began in 1924 along Silverbell Road northwest of Tucson. Charles Manier and a visiting relative were climbing a steep road embankment to examine the ruins of an old brick kiln at the top when they noticed something metallic protruding from the soil near the top of the bank. They obtained a trench shovel and small pickaxe from their parked car and dug out the object. It turned out to be a large religious cross made of lead and heavily encrusted with tough caliche. It was heavy and later was found to weigh sixty-two pounds. The discovery was made on land owned by Thomas Bent, an attorney, and Manier gave him the cross.

The find was not at first considered startling. After all, Spanish conquistadores and Jesuit missionaries had passed this way many times. Manier and Bent did wonder, however, why the cross was made of heavy lead. Together they cleaned it and found it consisted of two crosses held together with lead rivets. When pried apart, they discovered the flat inner sides were coated with a wax-like substance that covered writing cut into the soft metal on both the vertical and horizontal sections. They took the cross to the University of Arizona where Dr. Frank H. Fowler identified the language as a form of Latin which included some words in Hebrew.

When Karl Ruppert, of the Arizona State Museum, heard about the discovery, he examined the double cross and studied the translations with increasing bewilderment. Then he accompanied Manier and Bent back to the site and the trio found another object. After chipping away the heavy coating of caliche, they discovered they had a circular piece of metal upon which a Roman head had been engraved.

Dr. Byron Cummings, at this time associated with the University of Arizona and one of America's most prominent archeologists, admitted he was puzzled after examining the cross and Roman head. He immediately organized a dig at the site, with Bent paying the wages of the workers. During the next few months twenty-seven objects were discovered. They included additional lead crosses, a crescent-shaped cross, a labarum, nine swords of ancient Latin design, spears, batons, daggers and a "something" that looked like a giant pancake turner but is far too thick. Many bore Latin-Hebraic inscriptions from which the dates 560 A.D. to 800 A.D. were translated.

If it was a hoax, whoever perpetrated it went to a lot of trouble and lived a long time ago. Caliche exists in most desert soils and is a hard mineral deposit similar to concrete. It forms on objects only after centuries of water percolation through the mineral-bearing soil and consists of a hard, crustlike coating. It required many hours to remove it from each artifact, plainly indicating the passage of a great amount of time and that the artifacts were very old indeed.

Analyses and assays of the metal revealed they were composed of a natural alloy of local origin. Tests for radioactivity were negative, indicating great age. Microscopic tests also indicated antiquity. Being inorganic, they could not be dated by carbon-14 tests, and no organic matter contemporary with the objects was found at the site.

On the labarum there was a patriarch's cap and cross with double bars, a Roman temple with pillars, drawn swords and a serpent. The Latin was a type used for records and religious inscriptions up to the eighth century, but it also included Hebrew ecclesiastical phrases and symbols. These phrases may indicate a possible religious integration. The Latin included such statements as "Nothing except peace was sought," and "We are carried forward on the sea to an unknown land."

When in July 1925 news of the discoveries were made public, it was a controversial sensation. There were very few scholars who could believe an early Roman settlement in Arizona was possible. As usual, the most vocal of the critics were the ones who knew the least about it. Bent and Manier were accused of engineering an elaborate hoax, while other critics placed the blame on Mormons and Jesuits.

Brad Williams and Choral Pepper in *The Mysterious West* write:

Dr. Cummings, whose integrity could not be challenged and whose position in archeological circles was most secure, called a press conference to answer the critics. All of the relics, he said, had been found encased in a solid, undisturbed strata of tough caliche, some as much as six feet below the surface of the ground. This alone precluded any possibility of a hoax, unless it had been concocted prior to the arrival of Christopher Columbus. . . . Whether or not they were as ancient as A.D. 900, the date indicated on the labarum—the imperial standard of the later Roman emperors—he would not say, but he added that they had been in their graves for many, many years before the arrival of the Spanish conquistadores. The evidence of this was irrefutable, he said, not only because of the undisturbed condition of the caliche, but also because of the discovery in the same area and depth from the surface of a pueblo culture at least eight hundred years old.[13]

Dean G. M. Butler, of the College of Mines and Engineering at the University of Arizona, made a study of the relics and joined the believers. "The objects," he announced, "were introduced into the caliche before cementation with the calcium carbonate occurred. Accumulation comes as a result of a very slow process. There is no chance that the objects were introduced into the caliche formation during the time Americans had occupied this section of the country."[14]

A study of the inscriptions reveals the following story. Approximately 700 Roman men and women in the year 775 A.D. sailed from Rome with Theodorus the Renowned their leader. After passing through the Straits of Hercules the fleet of ships encountered severe storms that sank some of the vessels and drove the other ships far from land. After the storms the ships sailed together for many weeks and finally reached land.

The survivors left their ships and traveled northwest for many weeks, finally reaching a warm desert where there was an ample water supply. Here they built a city named Terra Calalus. They captured natives known as Toltezus and forced them into slavery. Fourteen years after their arrival the natives revolted, destroying the city and killing Theodorus.

The city was rebuilt by the survivors under the leadership of a man named Jacobus. Again the Toltezus were enslaved. Jacobus was followed in leadership by Israel, who was followed by seven more leaders with the same name who ruled for 125 years. When more trouble with the natives began, it was Israel VII who had the story of Terra Calalus inscribed.

Thomas Bent has never tried to commercialize any of the finds. Quite the contrary, he invested his money and time in trying to further a scientific investigation of the relics. In 1964 he published a 400-page monograph covering all the then known facts about the artifacts. Copies were hopefully sent to institutions and individuals, but there was no response. As one writer puts it, the matter has been "relegated to that special limbo reserved for such disturbing finds." [15]

Occasionally an authoritative voice is heard. In 1966 a spokesman for the Archeological Society of Brigham Young University at Provo, Utah, wrote:

What seems to have happened, if the artifacts are genuine—and I see no reason to suppose they are not—is that some group, perhaps from the Mediterranean area, with a knowledge of both Christianity and Hebrew, intruded itself into the American Southwest somewhere around 700 to 800 A.D. The fact that the Latin inscriptions do not make much sense could indicate that generations had passed by and that the colony was rapidly losing its knowledge of how to write. . . . What is needed, it seems to me, is further carefully controlled field investigations by trained archeologists with sufficient funds and facilities and a genuine interest in the problem. [16]

Dr. Cummings, who was later director of the Arizona State Museum, said there was a possibility that the discovery site was not the location of Terra Calalus. The artifacts, he said, may have been brought to the place where they were found by the victorious Amerinds, then later abandoned as they lost interest in their spoils of war. Cummings died in 1954 at the age of ninety-six.

Time has passed since those exciting days in the 1920s. The relics were recovered from an area of eighty by 100 feet. There may be others still buried, but the site is fenced and there is a sign warning trespassers. The last information I have regarding Thomas Bent is that he was seventy-three years old and living in retirement in San Diego, California. That was in 1970.

Bill Mack, in an article in *Argosy* magazine, links the Tucson artifacts to the Inscription Rock, as it is known, at Los Lunas, New Mexico, which bears the Ten Commandments in Phoenician. He made his investigation with John Wagner, formerly with the Stanford Research Institute and now an archeological illustrator.

Mack reports that a young couple found a cache of ancient coins while exploring a cave in the Cook Mountains near Deming, New Mexico. They showed the coins to Mrs. A. W. Marshall, a Deming librarian, and they were subsequently identified as Roman.

"It is our conviction," Mack writes, "that a ship carrying the Romans, most probably crewed by Phoenicians, entered the Rio

Grande from the Gulf of Mexico, sailed up that long river until it reached the tributary Rio Puerco, sailing up that then navigable stream by intent or accident, and then for reasons unknown, abandoned the ship." [17] The Phoenicians carved the inscription on the Los Lunas rock, and the Romans in their wanderings and eventual settlement deposited the coins and Tucson artifacts. [18]

If anything like this occurred, it should be a part of local Amerind traditions. Several Arizona tribes declare that a band of tall white men, fierce fighters carrying spears and battle-axes and protected by metal shirts, long ago invaded their lands. They enslaved the Amerinds and forced them to work in mines in the vicinity of Red Rock, northeast of Tucson. These men came from a ship on a river to the west. After they had acquired sufficient metal, they started across the land to return to their ship. But they had killed and wounded many of the red men, and the chiefs met in council.

"Our warriors were instructed to act like wolves," say the Pima medicine men. "They were told to circle the white men and slay them one at a time. Many were killed. Those who survived fled toward their ship to the west. They never returned to the land of our forefathers."

Or perhaps the survivors or the Romans intermarried with the Amerindians. Herman Ehrenberg, an early western explorer whose name has been given to a town on the Colorado River in Arizona, reported discovering some Indians in western Arizona that had blue eyes and lighter skin tones than the other tribes. Some had red hair. He tried to trace their origin.

The chief of a Cahuilla tribe in nearby California told Ehrenberg that according to his forefathers two great ships came into the ancient sea in the Salton Sink. The white men and their women, dressed in strange clothing, left the vessels and began traveling overland. They were attacked by a hostile tribe. The men were killed, but some of the women were adopted into the tribe. [19]

Red hair enters into a tribal tradition of the Seri Amerinds, although the strangers who appeared were not Romans but more likely Vikings. Their arrival could have been comparatively late. During the tenth and eleventh centuries A.D., the northern hemisphere experienced its second warmest period since the last ice age. During this time, technically called the Secondary Thermal Maximum, the Arctic ice was so greatly diminished that sailing vessels

could have made their way through the Northwest Passage north
of Canada, where the prevailing winds are from the east, and then
on down the Pacific coast.

The Seris are a dying people. Once the largest ruling tribe of the
eastern (Mexican mainland) coast of the Gulf of California south of
Arizona, today only a few hundred members survive on Tiburon
Island in the gulf. Despite their decline they take pride in remembering their time of glory and in passing on to new generations
their ancient tales and legends.

Long ago when "God was a boy," goes the story, the "Come-
From-Afar-Men" came. Tall fair men, white-bearded and white-
haired, with their red-haired women, landed on Tiburon from a
"long boat with a head like a snake." The strangers hunted the
whales that were then abundant in the gulf, cutting up the huge
carcasses and cooking the meat on shore. Then they packed the
meat in baskets which the red-headed women made from reeds that
grew on the island. Finally, fully provisioned, they set sail down
the coast to the south. They had gone only a short distance when
their vessel ran aground and was ripped apart by the breakers.

Swimming ashore, the survivors were adopted into the Mayo
tribe of the Seris. They intermarried, and to this day each generation of Mayos produces some individuals with blue eyes, blonde or
red hair, or both. These characteristics, say the Seris, are the heritage of the "Come-From-Afar-Men," and in order to preserve these
traits the Mayos, until the 1920s, expelled from the tribe all who
married outside of it. The legend is told in detail by D. and M. R.
Coolidge in their book *Last of the Seris*.[20]

Then there are the red-haired alleged people-eaters. About
twenty-two miles southwest of Lovelock, Nevada, there is an exceptionally dry, smoke-coated cave. From this cave over the years
scores of red-headed mummies, averaging 6½ to seven feet tall, and
thousands of artifacts have been taken. Piute Indians living in the
vicinity state that the redheads were cannibals who preyed on the
Piutes. After a series of skirmishes, the last members of this can-
nibal tribe were driven into this cave and were suffocated by enormous fires built at the entrance. Annie Bill, an elderly Piute and a
lifelong resident of Lovelock, said, "All members of the tribe who
were exterminated had red hair. I have some of their hair which
has been handed down from father to son. I have a dress which has
been in our family a great many years, trimmed with this reddish
hair. Old Piutes called the redheads Siwash Indians, but many of

my people really wondered if the redheads were Indians at all."
Mrs. Bill said her grandparents told her that their grandparents had
described the redheads as having long faces and light skin "like
white man." [21]

A book entitled *Life Among the Piutes* was written by Sarah Winnemucca, daughter of the chief, Old Winnemucca, and published
in 1883. She told the story of the redheads and said the last of the
cannibals were slain by her people earlier in the nineteenth century. The Piutes were never cave dwellers, and recent carbon-14
dating tests indicate the cave was occupied as late as 1800–1850.
The earliest occupation is dated as somewhere between 2000 and
3000 B.C., but it was not occupied continuously up to 1800 A.D.

The mummies, some 5,000 human coprolites (fossilized excre-
ment) and the artifacts are currently being studied. These consist
of baskets, nets, duck decoys, stone tools and arrowheads. One artifact, however, is truly remarkable and may be seen in Clarence
Stoker's Museum in Winnemucca. It is a calendar stone marked
with fifty-two dots on the inside and 365 on the outside! [22]

There are others who some believe came to America within historic times ahead of Columbus. There were the Irish. St. Brendan,
patron saint of County Kerry, is said to have voyaged with Irish
monks across the Atlantic in the sixth century. In fact, he made
two voyages, one allegedly to Florida and the Bahamas where in
both places he found Irish monks who had preceded him.

The saint is referred to in several medieval chronicles, but principally the tenth century *Navigatic Brendani.* Those Europeans who
could read in the Middle Ages were so fascinated by an Irish
monk's account of the voyages that it was translated into a dozen
languages. St. Brendan's landfalls resemble identifiable regions of
the Scottish Hebrides, the Faroe Islands and volcanic Iceland, and
they even describe fog in the area of Newfoundland's Grand
Banks.

The voyages were made in curraghs, described by Roman geographers as the principal ocean boats of the British Isles. They were
made of tanned oxhides stretched over oak frames, the joints being
sealed with tar. They had sails as well as oars, and some were large
enough to carry twenty men. They were practically unsinkable and
would have been capable of crossing the ocean even in stormy
weather.

Dr. Carl O. Sauer, of the University of California, says that
when Norse explorers arrived in Iceland and Greenland they found

in both places traces of earlier Irish religious colonies. He believes it was the coming of the Vikings that drove the Irish farther west and into North America where they settled at Belle Isle, between Newfoundland and Labrador, and along the St. Lawrence River, "eventually merging into the culture of the Algonquin Indians."

Sauer writes: "Christian Ireland from its beginnings lived in a special awareness of the sea, not a sea to be feared, but which stirred the imagination and drew men to seek what lay beyond the far horizon." [23]

The Scotch and the Venetians too have their pre-Columbian discoverers. They were Henry Sinclair, a Scottish lord who became Earl of the Orkney Islands, and his Venetian navigator, Antonio Zeno, who may have landed in North America in 1398 A.D., ninety-four years before Columbus. A descendant of the navigator found the story of the voyage among his ancestor's papers, and the *Zeno Narrative* was published by Niccolo Zeno at Venice in 1558. The narrative is accompanied by the Zeno Map which has been found in recent years by scholars to be fundamentally correct.

Added evidence for the voyage was found in 1953 on a rocky moss-covered ledge near Westford, Massachusetts. Cold-punched into the rock is what appears to be a sword and the armorial heraldic emblems of the Sinclair family. It may mark the furthest point south that he traveled. His landfall seems to have been what is now Nova Scotia. There in Micmac Amerind traditions he may be Glooskap, the hero from "beyond the sea." [24]

If advanced civilizations existed prior to historic times, it is reasonable to suppose they used the resources of the earth. In various parts of the world, notably Africa, there are very ancient mines. Some are still being worked; others were abandoned long ago.

At the Lion Coal Company mine near Wattis, Utah, is a mystery. In 1953 miners were working an eight-foot seam when they broke into two mining tunnels of great antiquity inside the mountain. According to an account in the trade publication *Coal Age*, the tunnels were about six feet in height and width, and rooms had been mined off from both sides of the shafts.

Erosion had erased all evidence of the outside openings on the mountain slope, and the tunnels were 450 feet from the nearest outside point. The coal around the shafts was worthless from oxidation. In 1953 University of Utah professors examined the tunnels. According to John E. Willson, of the Department of Engineering, there is no doubt the shafts were man-made. "Though no evidence was found at the outcrop," he said, "the tunnels were driven some 450 feet from the outside to the point where the present workings broke into them . . . There is no visible basis for dating the tunnels." [25]

Professor J. D. Jennings, an anthropologist, said he doubted they were the work of any Amerinds of whom we have any archeological record. He pointed out that "such works would have required immediate and local need for coal," adding that there was no reported extensive burning of coal by aboriginals in the region.[26]

Those few tribes, such as the Hopi of northern Arizona, that did any mining at all employed only primitive surface stripping methods. This brings up the possibility that the coal was mined for and transported to a distant advanced culture.

Perhaps as puzzling are the prehistoric copper mines located in the Keweenaw Peninsula and on Isle Royale in Lake Superior. The mining was done a long time ago. When discovered by early settlers many of the pits and trenches were filled up, or nearly so, with soil and leaves. Huge trees had grown over the area and fallen to decay, other generations of trees springing up afterwards.

Modern carbon dating tests by Professor Roy Drier of the Michigan College of Mining and Technology have confirmed their great age. A piece of charcoal was found to be 3,000 years old, and part of a tree limb found in the bottom of a pit was 3,800 years old. Earlier work at the University of Chicago yielded an age of 5,000 B.C.

The Amerinds had copper implements, but they were not common. They probably obtained it from rich bedrock seams by building big fires in the pits, then dousing the flames with water. The rapid change in temperature would crack the rock. Then with stone tools they could free the copper.

The mystery of the Michigan mines lies in their almost incredible extent. There are thousands and thousands of pits. It is estimated that two million pounds of the metal were mined on Isle Royale alone. A writer in the *American Antiquarian* in 1889 states that the pits "extend along the whole range from the extremity of Keweenaw Point to and beyond the northwestern end of Gogebic Lake, a distance of fully 120 miles, and they are not confined to the central range alone, but are found on the ranges both to the north and to the south. It may be further stated that ancient pits are found along the copper range in northern Wisconsin and also in the region northwest of Lake Superior, both in Minnesota and on the Canadian side of the International Boundary line." [27]

In one place the excavation was about fifty feet deep, and in another deep pit a mass of copper weighing forty-six tons was found. In one pit eighteen feet deep a copper mass weighing over six tons had been raised about five feet from the seam on the bottom and secured on heavy oaken props.[28]

All these facts indicate that some ancient people developed a vast mining empire. The work quite likely went on for centuries. They may have taught the historic Amerindians the use of the metal, but the amount of copper possessed by the natives doesn't compare with the tremendous tonnage that was taken from the pits. Who were these archaic miners? How and to where did they transport this metal?

Finally, southern Ohio appears to have had an ancient iron age. Scattered over this part of the state are a number of well-built clay-brick-lined mounds which contain what appear to be bog-iron smelting furnaces. Inside them are bog iron ore, glazed stones, slag, charcoal, red clay and bog marl lime. Iron knives, daggers, shovels, plates, swords and bars were found.

They are natural draft furnaces of a type invented by the Hittites around 2000 B.C. and which went out of use in Europe about 1300 A.D. It would appear that this method of smelting was imported from the Old World. It may have been taught to the Mound Builders. These Europeans could have intermarried with the natives, and their recessive genetic traits and culture as well been swallowed up after a few generations.

The man who has led the investigation of this puzzle is Captain Arlington Mallery, whose name is anathema among most professional archeologists. In his book *Lost America* he presents his theory that the Vikings came down from their St. Lawrence settlements and, using Amerind workers, exploited the bog iron resources of southern Ohio. They created a vigorous mixed race later known as the Mound Builders by intermarriage with the Amerinds. They were wiped out by the Black Plague brought from Europe by traders. However, the evidence is that the Mound Builder cultures are far older than the arrival of the Vikings.[29]

Moreover, there are other European candidates who might have shown the Mound Builders how to smelt bog iron ore. It appears the Amerinds had many Old World visitors, and that the New World was indeed a racial melting pot.

9

The Lost Colony Enigma

FOR TWO MONTHS each summer the residents of little Roanoke Island on the North Carolina coast lead double lives—one in the twentieth century and the other in the sixteenth century. During the days they live their contemporary lives, but at night they are temporary colonists, soldiers and Amerinds. They are performers in Pulitzer-prize playright Paul Green's classic drama that recreates one of America's strangest mysteries—the disappearance of the first English settlers in the New World.

It is the oldest of the nation's outdoor historical plays. Since its premiere in 1937 it has been held annually except for three years during World War II. The Waterside Theatre at the edge of Roanoke Sound has rows of seats totaling 3,000 ranging up a hillside. A high palisade forms the backdrop. Log cabins with open sides toward the audience are on the stage. And the amphitheatre is on the very spot where the colony once existed. Surrounding it is the Fort Raleigh National Historical Site where the embankments of the earthen fort and the dwellings have been restored.

Under floodlights and starlight beside the restless sea, the spectacular drama reenacts authenticated events in Elizabethan England and on the island. There are court scenes with Queen Bess, ministers, ladies-in-waiting, heralds and pages. In contrast is displayed the pioneer life of the colonists with its hardships, simple pleasures and the birth of the first white child in the New World, Virginia Dare. Produced by a nonprofit association, the principal direction and leading roles are provided by the famed Carolina Players and

114

the University of North Carolina's Department of Dramatic Art, Chapel Hill. Andy Griffith is one of the Broadway and Hollywood stars who have appeared in the Roanoke production.

But most members of the cast of more than 100 are local folk—housewives, business men and vacationing children, aged six to sixty. Some have been members for many years. Annie Laurie Kee literally grew up with the play. During the first season, at the age of six months, she posed as Virginia Dare and, with the first actress to play the part of Eleanore Dare, the mother, became the face of a special commemorative silver dollar. Since then she has had a number of roles including a flower girl, a page and milkmaid.

What happened to the island colonists? It is still an enigma after nearly four centuries. Playright Green does not attempt to solve the mystery, but as we shall see, there is strong evidence that their fate was indeed a strange one.

Sir Walter Raleigh, with the blessing of Queen Elizabeth, sent two ships from England to explore the North American coast and determine a good location for establishing a colony of settlers. It was the first act in creating a British empire in America. After an eleven week voyage across the Atlantic, the explorers landed on the North Carolina coast in July 1584, climbed to the top of some dunes, and discovered they were on a barrier island just off the mainland.

At the northern end of the island now known as Roanoke they were greeted by friendly Indians living in a palisaded village. After excursions up and down the coast, they decided that the island was the best place for a settlement, and they returned to England with two of the Indians. The Queen honored Sir Walter for his ambitious project, and the territory was named Virginia to memorialize the Virgin Queen.

The following April Sir Walter sent out the pioneer expedition of 108 persons. It sailed from Plymouth in seven vessels. All male members had been carefully chosen for their skills, with the exception of the two Indians who were being returned to their native land. The first port of call was Puerto Rico where breeding livestock and other supplies were purchased, and then they landed on what is now Ocracoke Island.

Moving north past Cape Hatteras, they explored the coastal islands and adjacent mainland. At one Indian village they encountered, a silver cup was stolen. In retaliation and to teach the natives that white men were to be feared, they burned the village. This stupid brutality was to have hideous consequences. Four weeks after their arrival, they anchored off Roanoke Island and the colony was begun. The ships returned to England.

Ralph Lane was made governor. His first act was to have an earthen fort built near the shore on the east side of the island beside a creek. Trees were felled and cabins and furnishings built. Bricks were made, and up to the time of the Civil War pieces of these bricks could still be found.

As the months passed, their troubles increased. The ships that had gone to England were delayed in returning with badly needed supplies. The hostility of the Indians had reached a dangerous level. Then, near the end of the first year, Sir Francis Drake with a fleet of twenty-three ships anchored off the coast. He offered to take the colonists back to England or to leave one ship with some men and supplies.

Governor Lane at first decided to stay, but before supplies could be unloaded a severe storm swept out of the north and damaged some of the colony's structures and Sir Francis's vessels. Damp and discouraged, the colonists voted to return to England. On June 18, 1586, nine days after the fleet had arrived, they sailed away.

Several weeks later the supply ships from England arrived at Roanoke and found the settlement deserted. Sir Richard Grenville, the commanding officer, not wishing to lose possession of the land for England, left fifteen men on the island with provisions for two years.

Another expedition was organized by Sir Walter Raleigh the following year. The 150 colonists that sailed from Plymouth May 8, 1587, in three ships included some who had been members of the first expedition. One was Governor John White, the artist of the first colony, who was now in charge. Upon arrival at Roanoke they found that the fifteen men left by Sir Richard were gone. Nearby the bones of one man, apparently killed by Indians, were lying near the beach.

New cabins were built and the older ones cleared of overgrown vines and repaired. On August 18 Governor White's daughter Eleanore, wife of Ananias Dare, gave birth to a daughter. As the first child of English parentage to be born in the New World, she was named Virginia. Several weeks later another child was born to Dyonis and Margery Harvie.

It was too late in the summer for crops, and fall and winter were on the way. Additional supplies would be needed. On August 27, only nine days after the birth of his granddaughter, Governor White left for England with the three ships, planning to return as quickly as possible. Since there had been some consideration given to moving inland where more farming acreage would be available, it was agreed that if they moved before the governor returned, a message indicating their new location would be left in a prominent place.

Then war broke out with Spain. The vessels that had been scheduled to sail to Virginia were ordered into service against the Spanish Armada. The crews were assigned to defense duties. Roanoke would have to wait. In March 1589, Sir Walter Raleigh deeded his interest in the New World colony to Governor White, nine other men then on Roanoke Island including Ananias Dare, and a group of London merchants.

Months passed. Frustration and worry aged the governor. He was deeply concerned about the welfare of his daughter, grand-daughter and son-in-law, and about all the colonists who quite likely were suffering privations. They would get no help from the resentful Indians; in fact, there was a possibility they might attack the settlement. The London merchants were unable to find the ships for a relief expedition.

Finally, in the spring of 1591 the governor set sail for America with an expedition headed by Master John Wattes of London. He had no authority or supplies, simply Wattes's promise to visit Roanoke. After several ports of call in the West Indies, the ship anchored off the island early one evening. The date was August 15, only twelve days short of four years since he had left.

Smoke could be seen rising from the island, giving encouragement to his hope that all was well. The following morning the smoke from the island had ceased, but another column was towering north of Roanoke near what is now the Nags Head Dunes. With a small company of men in two boats, Governor White decided to investigate the smoke and see if the colony had moved to a new location. After hours of hard rowing, they landed only to find that the smoke was coming from a brush fire. When they arrived back at the ship it was dusk.

The next day the men headed for Roanoke. As they entered a treacherous inlet, one of the boats capsized. Seven men were drowned. After the tragedy the other boat was carried by a strong current about a quarter mile past the colony site. By the time they were able to row back, it was dark and too dangerous to risk landing. Anchoring nearby, they repeatedly blew a trumpet and sang English songs, but there was no response from the shore.

The governor and his company landed with the light of dawn and walked up over a sandy bank to the settlement. There they were greeted by a scene of desolation. The buildings were in ruins and overgrown with vines. Tall weeds covered the ground inside the log palisade. It was obvious that the place had been abandoned for some time. The only sounds were the hum of a swarm of insects above a discarded rusty pot and the growing whistle of the wind. There were dark clouds in the southeast. A storm was brewing.

Then Governor White noticed that one of the tree trunks forming the palisade and peeled of bark had, carved into the bare wood, the single word "Croatoan." And on a doorpost were the letters "Cro," as if the carver had been interrupted before he could complete the word. But there was no Maltese cross with the inscriptions, the sign of distress agreed upon when White sailed for England. Had the colony, then, gone to Croatan Island? He remembered that Manteo, one of the two Indians taken to England by the first expedition, had been from Croatan and the Indians there were friendly to the English.

They returned to the ship and Master Wattes agreed to go to Croatan Island the next day to look for the colonists. Then the storm struck and the weather would not permit it. With no safe landing possible and their supply of fresh water low, they returned to the West Indies where another storm blew the ship north toward the Azores. From there they went home to England.

Neither White nor Sir Walter could finance another expedition to America. In his last recorded words written in 1593, the governor "wished to God" he had the wealth to make the search for his loved ones and fellow colonists. Raleigh sought information about his lost colony from later expeditions that traded with the coastal Indians, with no results. After 1607 the Virginia colonists at Jamestown tried unsuccessfully to learn the fate of their missing countrymen.[1]

More colonies followed Jamestown in settling on the southeastern coast. The Europeans had come to stay. Time passed, and the now-white Americans began noticing some unusual characteristics in one tribe. In 1709 French Huguenots migrating to North Carolina found among the "Croatoan" or "Croatan" Indians some with light skin and gray eyes. Moreover, there were English words in their dialect, and they bore some strange un-Indian names like Locklear and Oxendine.[2]

It is reasonable to assume that the word "Croatoan" meant what it implied: that the colonists, in view of the hostility of the mainland Indians, had decided to go to Croatan Island to the south. There they would have been welcomed by Chief Manteo. The present town on Roanoke Island is named after the chief.

In 1864 the chief of a group of mixed-blood Indians in Robeson County made a protest regarding the murder of one of his band. The band was regarded as a medley of several tribes, chiefly the Cherokee, intermingled with non-Indian stocks. The chief, however, made a proud reference to the lineage of the group to which he and the murdered man belonged. His statement, says the *Encyclopedia Americana,* "led to an investigation which instilled a belief that they are the descendants of the Croatan tribe and the colonists." [3] As a result, the state of North Carolina officially recognized the band as "Croatan Indians."

The Croatans were in the news in January 1958 when about a thousand of them, shooting carefully and well, routed a cross-burning conclave of the Ku Klux Klan near Pembroke in Robeson County. The late Robert C. Ruark in his syndicated news column of February 1, 1958, following this incident, said he was raised in this region and knew the Croatans well. There are around 30,000 of them in Robeson County, he wrote, about a third of the population. They are farmers, businessmen and civic leaders. Ruark said "they have some white blood and some black blood, but the original Redskin remains intact."

But there is more to this mystery. In September 1937, a casual tourist walking through some weeds in an isolated area on the east bank of the Chowan River in Chowan County, North Carolina, found a quartz stone. It was fourteen inches long, ten inches wide and three inches thick, weighing twenty-one pounds.

On one side was a Latin Cross and beneath it an inscription: "Ananias and Virginia Dare went hence to Heaven 1591." Below this was the legend: "Anye Englishman shew John Wite Govr Via." On the reverse side were seventeen lines explaining the fate of the colony and signed with the initials E. W. D., presumably Eleanore White Dare.

The account alleged that soon after the governor left for England, the colonists decided to move inland to the Chowan region, approximately fifty miles northwest of Roanoke Island. There they suffered misery and conflict with the Amerinds for four years until they were reduced to twenty-four survivors. At that time (1591) the natives told them that a ship had come to Roanoke, but had left soon after arrival. A few weeks after this report, the natives attacked the colony and killed all but seven of the victims. The massacred colonists had been buried four miles east of the river upon a small hill on which a rock had been placed bearing their names. The message ended with an offer of a reward to anyone who would inform Governor White of the colony's fate and take him to the surviving colonists.[4]

If authentic (and the wording conformed to Elizabethan usage and spelling), it meant that the colonists did not go to Croatan Island. If so, why was the word left on the tree trunk? Did they change their minds? Were the seven survivors "adopted" into a tribe, thus accounting for the later light skins, gray eyes and English words? A number of eastern woodland tribes did adopt Caucasians, and if the survivors wanted to continue to live, they had no choice.

So the fate of the colonists and America's first white child remains a mystery. In 1948 archeological surveys by the U.S. National Park Service located the outlines of the fort on Roanoke Island. You can visit the site today and during the summer witness the historical drama. But time has cast a shroud over the story's ending, and when George Washington was chosen president, already two centuries had passed.

Part Two

THE
MYSTICAL
MYSTERIES

From the riddles of dark antiquity and more recent history, we turn to another group of mysteries that to some extent have existed in all cultures, past and present. What the North American Indian calls medicine *includes much of the phenomena that characterizes psychic phenomena or parapsychology. In medicine there are prophets whose prophecies prove true; wizards who can transmit messages over great distances instantaneously; shamans who are rain makers. With the physical realm merging with that of the psychical, is it possible that some of the puzzles of the past can be explained by paraphysical or parapsychological powers? In psychokinesis physical objects are moved by some form of psychical energy. Could it be that on a vast and united scale a similar energy, applied in a manner long forgotten, transported or teleported the multi-tonned stone blocks of Tiahuanaco and Sacsahuaman?*

10
Mystery of the Shaking Tent

OF ALL AMERINDIAN MYSTERIES, the shaking tent is one of the most baffling. Once it was an important part of the cultural life of the Woodland Algonquin tribes of the United States and Canada. Today it is said to be rarely performed on remote reservations by aging shamans.

When the first Europeans arrived in historic times they found in what is now southeastern Canada and northern New England a branch of the Algonquian language group that lived by hunting. They were divided into several tribes. Along the Ottawa River were the Algonquin proper, who gave their name to the entire stock. In Quebec lived the Montagnais and Naskapi. A loose confederacy of four tribes known as the Abnaki occupied northern New England and the Canadian Maritime Provinces. Under frequent attack by the Iroquois to the south, these people fought a constant battle with starvation in the trackless wastes of their rugged, inhospitable land.

During the severe winters they tracked moose through the big woods or followed caribou out onto the barren plateaus. The shaman or medicine man in his shaking, bending tent called forth spirits who told the tribesmen where enemy war parties were located and made prophecies as to where game would be found.

In 1609 Samuel de Champlain, the early French explorer was in the Quebec wilderness. He joined a war party of Algonquin and Montagnais Amerinds striking back at their hereditary foe, the Iroquois. In his diary he noted that even after entering enemy terri-

123

tory his companions failed to post sentries around their nightly camps. An ambush could have wiped them out.

This carelessness was due to their faith in their medicine man. Every night the medicine man was called upon to foretell the future and give warning if any danger was at hand. When the party reached Sorel Rapids, Champlain witnessed the divination ceremony.

A small tent or wigwam was made by staking pinewood saplings into the ground and covering the frame with beaver robes. Into this structure the medicine man entered naked. Soon he could be heard mumbling a call to the spirits, then his voice became louder and as he worked himself up into a frenzy, the tent bent and swayed back and forth as he screamed and shouted in a variety of voices. Champlain was told this shaking was caused by the spirits who were communicating with the medicine man.

Champlain's brief and somewhat superficial observation left him unimpressed, but this was not true of many later witnesses who made detailed studies of the phenomenon. One was Father Paul LeJeune. He arrived in Quebec in 1632 to head the Jesuit mission to the Huron Amerinds. A dedicated missionary, he learned to speak Algonquin and lived intimately with the natives, roaming the forest with them in search of game, crouching at night in their overcrowded, smoky wigwams. He and his colleagues conducted a thorough investigation of the occult claims of the medicine men who were the chief obstacles to their efforts to convert the natives to Christianity.

It was the purpose of this study to expose the shamans as charlatans. The Jesuits did find fraud and deception. They also found exhibitions of powers they could not explain and which they attributed to satanic agencies, in keeping with their theology. In his book *Relations* in 1634, Father LeJeune gave his first eyewitness account of a shaking tent. He was invited to the performance by a young Indian named Manitou-Chat-Ché who had been converted to Christianity, but had lapsed back into paganism. The youth wanted to convince the priest that the medicine men did possess magical abilities. LeJeune wrote:

Towards nightfall, when I was resting, some young men erected a tent in the middle of our cabin. They planted six poles deep in the ground in the form of a circle. To the top of these poles they fastened a large ring which encircled them. This done, they enclosed the edifice with blankets, leaving the top of the tent open. It was all a tall man could do to reach to the top of this round tower, capable of holding five or six men standing upright.

The tent completed, all fires in the cabin were put out in order that the flames should not frighten away the *khichi-gouai* (spirits). A young juggler crawled in under the blanket covering and closed the opening behind him, for there must be no means of entrance or exit save the opening at the top. He began to moan plaintively and the tent began to quiver, at first gently but with growing vehemence until I feared he would break everything to pieces.

He commenced to whistle in a hollow tone, and as if it came from afar; then to talk as if in a bottle; to cry like the owls of these countries; then to howl and sing constantly varying the tones. I was astonished at a man having so much strength; for after he had once begun to shake it, he did not stop it until the consultation was over, which lasted about three hours.

When the missionary began to make some remark, Manitou-Chat-Ché shook his head. "Be quiet, Black Robe!" he said. "The soul of our medicine man has now left his body, and has risen to the top of the wigwam. It is waiting there to welcome the spirits."

Suddenly the assembled natives called out with a loud cry, at the same time pointing to the top of the tent where sparks could be seen issuing from the vent hole. Manitou-Chat-Ché explained that a spirit had arrived, and the Amerinds shouted to the sorcerer in the tent, "*Tepouchai!*" (Call the others!)

The medicine man responded in a hoarse strident voice. One of his assistants outside began to beat a drum, whereupon several of the younger Indians leaped to their feet and danced excitedly around the tent. Again fiery sparks appeared floating above the vent. Now the spirits were consulted, and according to the sorcerer they forecast a mild winter with little snow, and that game—that is, elk and moose—were at a distance, but would appear later in the season.

After the exhibition, Father LeJeune had an opportunity to talk with the medicine man. He accused him of making the sparks by blowing on the tobacco in his pipe.

"But," the medicine man replied, "I took no pipe in with me. How could I? I went in naked, did I not?"

"But it was you who shook the tent."

"How could I?" the shaman answered. "You yourself tested the poles. You found them solid as rocks. Later you saw how the tent swayed, even bent over at the top where neither I nor anyone else could reach it."

"So what caused the tent to sway and shake?" the missionary asked.

"The power of the spirits," the medicine man assured him.[1]

In his *Relations* of 1637 Father LeJeune concluded that while some performers were impostors, there were others who had "communication with demons." He wrote that "in all probability the Devil communicates visibly with those poor savages who need help badly, both temporal and spiritual, to bring them up out of the slavery which oppresses them." [2]

In *Travels and Adventures in the Years 1760–1776* by Alexander Henry, the Elder, is an account of a tent ceremony that reveals how the Amerinds used it to obtain important knowledge. In 1764 Canada had passed from French to British control, and the Indians under Pontiac were in rebellion against the conquerors. Under these circumstances Henry, who was a trader, found himself isolated at Sault Sainte Marie and virtually a prisoner of the Ojibwa.

One day a canoe arrived from the east. It carried messengers from Sir William Johnson, the British government's chief Indian agent in North America, who presented to the Chief of the Ojibwas an invitation to him and his counselors to feast with him at Fort Niagara and discuss a peace treaty. If Henry could travel with the group to the fort it would help him to return to Montreal, and he urged the Chief to accept the invitation. But the Chief hesitated.

"We do not know if this offer is a trap or not," he told the trader. "We shall let Mikinak the Great Turtle decide for us."

"The Great Turtle?"

"Yes, he is our master spirit. Our medicine man will build a wigwam and ask him to come into it and tell us the truth about the British."

The following day an unusually large wigwam was erected, and inside it a smaller tent. The latter tent had a diameter of about four feet, and consisted of five poles set two feet deep into the earth. Each pole was about ten feet in length and eight inches in diameter. They were tied together at the top with a hoop. This framework was then covered with moose skins bound tightly to the poles with hide thongs. As night fell, the medicine man appeared clad only in a loincloth.

Henry's account continues: "His head was scarcely inside when the edifice, massy as it has been described, began to shake; and the skins were no sooner let fall than the sound of numerous voices were heard, and beneath them, some yelling, some barking like dogs, some howling like wolves; and in this horrible concert were mingled screams and sobs, as of despair, anguish and the sharpest pain. Articulate speech was also uttered, as if from human lips, but in a tongue unknown to any of the audience."

This pandemonium was said to be the cries and voices of evil spirits. It was followed by a dead silence broken only by what Henry called "a low and feeble voice, resembling the cry of a young puppy." The spectators applauded, for this was the voice of the Great Turtle. Now the shaman spoke in his own voice. "Mikinak is here," he said, "and he is willing to answer questions."

The Chief arose, approached the tent and made an offering of tobacco. "O, Great Turtle, are the English preparing to make war on the Ojibwas?" he asked. "Are there many Redcoats at Fort Niagara?"

Instantly, Henry states, "the tent shook, and for some seconds after, it continued to rock so violently that I expected to see it leveled with the ground." Then came a piercing cry, followed by a quarter of an hour of silence. During this silent period the Great Turtle was thought to have crossed Lake Huron to Fort Niagara and then to have visited Montreal.

Finally the medicine man was ready to announce the results of Mikinak's psychic journey. There were only a few Redcoats at Fort Niagara, although there were a large number of them at Montreal.

Again the Chief arose. "If the Ojibwas go to visit Sir William Johnson, will he receive us as friends?" he asked.

"Yes," the shaman answered. "The Great Turtle says that your canoes will be filled with presents and quantities of rum. Every man will return home safely to his family."

The ceremony continued until nearly midnight, the oracle answering the questions of individuals about their personal affairs, especially about sick relatives and absent friends. Henry was assured he would accompany the party to Fort Niagara and eventually reach Montreal in safety. He concludes his account: "I was on the watch through the scene I have described to detect the particular contrivances by which the fraud was carried out. But such was the skill displayed in the performance or such my deficiency of penetration, that I made no discoveries, but came away as I went, with no more than those general surmises which will naturally be entertained by every reader." [3]

During the centuries that have followed these earlier accounts, thousands of white men have witnessed performances of the shaking tent. Some have been obviously fraudulent exhibitions. Others have been so totally enigmatic that they can only be explained in terms of psychic phenomena.

In some instances the medicine men are securely tied hand and foot, and are still so bound at the end of the performance—or perhaps seance is a better word. Despite the fact that the poles or wooden framework of the tent are driven so far into the ground as to be immovable by the average man, the top of the tent is sometimes bent down until it almost touches the ground. Usually the shaman is inside the tent when it shakes and rocks, but in some accounts he is observed lying on the ground with his limbs extended and even protruding under a flap of the tent.

The sounds too can present a puzzle. Different voices and cries, both human and animal, can be distinguished, and they seem to come from different parts of the tent, high and low. The fiery sparks above the open top of the tent reported in some accounts have a mysterious origin.

The answers to questions asked by the spectators are sometimes ambiguous, but at other times are so exact as to indicate clairvoyance. The tent is sometimes used in healing the sick. Most remarkable of all are the "apports"—lost objects that are recovered from sometimes irretrievable locations such as the bottoms of lakes and rivers.

Some paranormal phenomena occurred during a relatively recent performance in July 1929. The witness was A. K. Black, an official of the Hudson's Bay Company, then stationed at White Sands, Northwest Territories. The medicine man, whose name was August, was famous among the Northwest tribes, and along with other Amerinds had come to the trading post to receive payments due them under a treaty. Black's account was published in the company's magazine, *The Beaver*. [4]

Willow poles were driven fast into the ground and secured with two willow hoops, one in the center, the other tapering the poles at the top. The poles were tested and found immovable. Birch bark was fastened around the outside, and a can of shot was tied to the top of the poles. The wigwam commenced to shake and the can of shot began to rattle as soon as the shaman entered the structure. The scene was an eerie one beneath a full moon high in the sky. The medicine man began singing and humming a haunting kind of tune. The account continues:

A small disturbance took place, and a strange voice was heard. The medicine man's voice could be heard at the base of the wigwam, while the strange voice came from the top. The voices were decidedly different. After having conversed with the strange voice for some time, August told his silent watchers that he could answer any of their questions, but they had first to place a plug of chewing tobacco under the teepee. He was soon showered with questions, many of them being of the type, "How many fish will I gather in the morning?" and "What luck will I have in trapping this year?"

Never once did the tent stop shaking. After all questions had been answered, August announced that he was going to call the spirit of a bear into the wigwam and show how he could kill it with his hands. Amid great excitement and encouraging shouts from the spectators, the fight began. "This was where I received my great surprise," wrote Black.

The top of the wigwam bent until it nearly touched the ground during the fight . . . Eventually the bear spirit was killed, and August repeated the feat with the spirit of a lynx, which brought yells of excitement from the gathering.

Daylight was breaking when August emerged from the wigwam with beads of perspiration covering his face. The bark was immediately removed from the wigwam, and we examined the poles and were surprised to find them as solid as they had been at first. I have been informed, although I have not witnessed it, that August can make a teepee shake by merely throwing his hat into it.[5]

An even more remarkable observation displaying parapsychological aspects was recorded by Paul Kane, a young artist who in 1848 accompanied a Hudson's Bay Company's fur brigade in western Canada. The performance was on the Behring River, near Winnipeg, where the party had stopped for the night.

At dusk the party's native guides and paddlemen constructed the medicine lodge. The tent, as usual, was formed by about ten stout poles driven into the ground, thus enclosing an area about three feet in diameter. The poles were covered by a large boat sail. And, as usual, the tent began to shake as soon as the shaman entered carrying his ceremonial rattle.

Kane wrote:

Being unable to sleep on account of the discordant noises, I wrapped a blanket around me and went out into the woods, where they were holding their midnight orgies, and lay down among those on the outside of the medicine lodge to witness the proceedings. I had no sooner done so than the incantations ceased, and the performer exclaimed that a white man was present. How he ascertained this fact I am at a loss to surmise, as it was pitch dark at the time, and he was enclosed in a narrow tent, without any apparent opening through which he could espy me, even had it been light enough to distinguish one person from another.

The medicine man predicted excellent sailing weather for the party's five boats the following day. Then after receiving the usual gifts of tobacco he answered the questions of the Amerinds, some inquiring after the health of their families at home, whom they had not seen for many months.

Paul Kane had a question of his own:

I asked about my baggage which I had left at Norway House (for want of room in our boats), to be brought on by the canoes which had taken up Sir John Richardson on their return. The medicine man told me that he saw the party with my baggage encamped on a sandy point which we ourselves had passed only about two days before.

However singular the coincidence may appear, it is a fact that, on the next day we had a fair wind, for which the medicine man of course took all the credit; and it is no less true, that the canoes with my baggage were on the sandy point on the day stated, for I inquired particularly of them when they came up to us.[6]

What is the secret of the shaking tent? Obviously, some conjurors consciously and deliberately shake the tent for prestige and tobacco. They are a minority. Even so, the actual mechanics of the shaking remains obscure. The performance still requires almost incredible vigor and skill. The shamans are often elderly men. The performances last for several hours at a time and the tent is in motion constantly. At the same time, the performer talks, chants and sings in different voices, acts dramatically as in fights with animal spirits, answers questions and predicts future events. Thus his skill is supernormal, even if his powers are not.

But the secret of the tent is not that simple. The anthropologist who has made the most intensive study of the phenomenon is A. Irving Hallowell. In his monograph *The Role of Conjuring in Saulteaux Society*, he points out that the ceremony or seance is part of a cultural tradition that must be understood in the light of the beliefs and behavior patterns of the people. The medicine man is playing a role that was established by his culture. He has dreamed the appropriate dreams that he believes have given him supernormal powers. We must assume that he unconsciously invests his seances with an emotional aura.

"The successful conjuror," Professor Hallowell writes, "thoroughly identifies himself with his role. The approved means are part of the total situation and inseparable from it. When, as outsiders, we raise questions about insincerity and fraud, therefore, it simply indicates that we find it impossible to penetrate and understand the behavioral world in which these Indians lived."

What Hallowell suggests is that the medicine man does shake the tent by his own physical means, though he genuinely believes it is done for him by the spirits. "Unless," he continues, "we believe in the possibility of supernatural forces ourselves, it must be assumed that the Salteaux conjuror must integrate the material means employed in manipulating the lodge with his personal inspiration and beliefs."

Whether using "supernatural forces" or not, it is the testimony of former medicine men that they were in a trancelike state, their actions subconsciously motivated. "Currents of air swirl inside like a whirlpool. But I never moved the tent. There I spoke to spirits which revealed to my mind the knowledge which I in turn gave you," reported one shaman.[7]

Hallowell quotes the declarations of converted conjurors he has collected from a number of sources. Some were made on their deathbeds when they were asked to explain their magic. One ex-shaman declared:

I have become a Christian. I am old, I am sick. I cannot live much longer, and I can do no other than speak the truth. Believe me, I did not deceive you at that time. I did not move the lodge. It was shaken by the power of the spirits. Nor did I speak with a double tongue. I only repeated to you what the spirits said to me. I heard their voices. The top of the lodge was filled with them, and before me the sky and wide lands lay expanded. I could see a great distance around me, and believed I could recognize the most distant objects.

Another Amerind said: "I possessed a power which I cannot explain or describe to you. I held communication with supernatural beings, or thinking minds, or spirits which acted upon my mind, or soul, and revealed to me such knowledge as I have described to you . . ." [8]

While in some instances the shaman may physically shake the tent while in his semitrance mental state, there is abundant evidence that the shaking can be a psychokinetic phenomenon. The Anglican Bishop of Montreal, the Right Reverend C. J. Mountain, witnessed the ceremony a number of times while on visits to missionary outposts in the 1820s. In all the cases he recorded the medicine man's hands and feet were tightly bound with cords before he was lifted into the tent.

His account states: "While he is lying in the tent it becomes violently agitated, the top swinging rapidly backward and forward in view of the spectators on the outside, who also hear a variety of strange sounds and voices unlike the voice of man . . . During the process going on in the conjuring lodge . . . he catches glimpses, on the same level with the topmost hoop, of a number of objects like little stars." [9]

Hallowell has witnessed the ceremony four times while making cultural studies of the Saulteaux Amerinds in Manitoba. In addition he has collected numerous reports by witnesses and had access to the unpublished material of other ethnologists. In one case there was a one-armed conjuror who remained in a shaking tent for six hours at a stretch. Although Hallowell did not see it, there are instances reported of tents shaking without an occupant, sometimes with part of the clothing of the shaman inside. In this way a shaman was said to set three or four lodges in motion.

Probably the most astonishing experience with a shaking tent was that of Sir Cecil E. Denny, at the time an inspector with the Northwest Mounted Police, later an executive in the Canadian Department of Indian Affairs and the Alberta Province archivist. He may have been the only white man to be inside the tent while the phenomena were taking place, watching the silent and motionless medicine man. His account, published many years ago, follows:

I happened to be camped on the Red Deer River in 1879 close to a large Blackfoot encampment. One moonlight night I walked over to the camp with my interpreter, Billy Gladstone. We intended visiting the lodge of the medicine man which was pitched a little distance from the main camp. We entered his lodge which had only a small fire in the center. The medicine man was seated wrapped in his buffalo robe at the side of the teepee smoking one of their long medicine pipes. He paid no attention to us. We sat down near him, and also proceeded to smoke quietly. He still gave no sign of recognition of our presence.

Everything was still, while outside from the main camp sounded beating drums where dances were being held. We had sat this way for quite a time when I was startled by the ringing of a bell above the top of the lodge. I could see nothing, and the medicine man made no move. Presently the teepee began to rock, even lifting off the ground about a foot. When it is remembered that such a tent as this consists of a dozen long poles crossed at the top, wide apart at the bottom and covered with heavy buffalo robes making it impossible to lift one side, as I now witnessed, for these teepees are so built that no ordinary wind could blow them over. And remember the Indian did not touch the tent!

After some time the rocking motion ceased. I hurried outside to see if anyone had been playing tricks. Not a human being was in sight near us; the moon was clear and you could see a long distance. I returned, resumed my seat. The tent began again to rock, this time so violently that it sometimes lifted several feet on one side so that both myself and the interpreter could plainly see outside. My interpreter was thoroughly frightened by this time, and I was not much better; yet the Indian never stirred. We had seen enough and left, returning to the camp thoroughly mystified.[10]

A number of writers have commented on the striking similarities between the ceremonial tent and spiritualistic seances. The tent is comparable to the medium's cabinet; the medicine man uses a drum and chants to induce ecstasy, while hymns aid the medium to enter trance. The Amerinds say the force that shakes the tent is a mighty wind inside it. It is the "Masters" of the winds who are responsible. In spiritualist seances cold breezes are often reported as coming out of the cabinet. Although shaking of the cabinet is seldom noted, a Dr. Hooper tells of an entire house trembling during a seance: "I have seen and felt the floor, walls, and contents of a room vibrate with the power of the mighty rushing wind." [11]

The spirits contacted by the shamans are usually anthropomorphic beings of native mythology, usually the "masters" of various animal species. The most important is Mikinak, the Great Turtle, who serves as an intermediary between the medicine man and the other spirits, and who will travel forth to get information about distant situations. Mikinak, who talks in a nasal voice like Donald Duck, is a popular clown who tells jokes and kids his audience.

Now and then, however, spirits of the dead are summoned. On such occasions the messages from the human spirits are almost identical with those in spiritualist seances. The living are assured by the so-called dead that they are happy in a beautiful country where they are never hungry or thirsty and never suffer pain. They are told they must not hurt others and if they always do what is right they will someday join their relatives and friends in this happy hunting ground. There is some suspicion of Christian influence in this belief that eternal happiness or misery after death is dependent upon conduct during one's life here on earth. Despite their belief in their ancient mythology, most of the shamans are at least nominally Christian. On the other hand, there has been a reverse cultural exchange that is startling.

Richard S. Lambert, in his book *Exploring the Supernatural*, traces it back to the first spiritualists, the early Shaker communities where it was believed that they received visits by groups of Indian spirits who had belonged to neighboring tribes. These spirits came to religious meetings and "possessed" the Shakers, causing them to shake, shout and dance in Amerindian style. The Shakers believed that by this means they could proselytize these heathen souls.[12]

Then about the middle of the last century came the seances, using large cabinets not unlike the shaman's tent to contact spirits. Moreover, the mediums, although performers would be the more exact word, were bound hand and foot like the Ojibwa medicine men. The first professional "mediums" were the Davenport brothers, Ira and William, who staged their spurious seances in large halls or theaters. The cabinet, which resembled a large wardrobe closet, contained a table bearing musical instruments, bells and slates. Men from the audience were invited to tie the mediums securely to two chairs placed at the ends of the oblong table. Curtains were drawn and the lights were dimmed.

After a few moments there came the sounds of the musical instruments being played; the bells were rung and thrown out through small windows, and glimmering hands waved at the spectators. When the curtains were opened the brothers were found still tied in their chairs. The performance caused a sensation in America and Europe. The secret was a clever but simple rope tie. As they were being bound, they secretly gained enough slack to withdraw their hands from the ropes. After performing, they replaced their hands in the ropes, and by twisting their wrists the slack was concealed. The Davenports came to grief when, in Liverpool, a knot expert tied their wrists with a special "Tom Fool's knot" which left them helpless. The audience rose up as a mob and the pair had a narrow escape from harm.

The Davenports and their many imitators introduced the cabinet into seances as a limited restricted area for the production of spirit phenomena. These "cabinets" were later modified to simply an alcove or a corner of a room enclosed with a curtain. Thus the trail leads from the medicine man's tent to the seance rooms of modern spiritualist mediums.

And at these seances the medium's voice will undergo a change. The new voice will introduce itself as the medium's guide or control with the name of White Eagle, Red Cloud, Moonstone, North Star, Yellow Feather or some other romantic Amerindian name. It seems that a majority of American mediums and some in Great Britain and on the Continent have Amerind guides.

Just as today's psychic sensitives exhibit ESP, clairvoyance and psychokinetic abilities, so did the shamans of our native tribes. The manner in which he receives his gift argues against conscious deception, at least in the Saulteaux society. One must be chosen to conjure by the higher powers. He will have a particular dream that is repeated four times. If he ignores this command, he will be punished by becoming afflicted with a disease. There is no pooling of trade secrets by a fraternity of shamans. There are no secrets passed from father to son. In fact, a conjuror cannot teach another individual how to conjure. It is a bad thing to conjure for fun, to show off, or to do it too often.

All kinds of tribal problems are solved by the clairvoyance of the medicine man. Joseph B. Casagrande, an administrative consultant with the Social Science Research Council, Washington, D.C., has done field work among the Ojibwa and Comanche tribes and published studies on their ceremonialism. In *Tomorrow*, he writes:

Although the shaking tent ceremony has all but disappeared among the Wisconsin Ojibwa, many of the writer's informants had themselves initiated or attended performances. All attested to the power and authenticity of the conjuror's gifts. In one instance the conjuror determined that two missing boys had drowned and located their bodies near the opposite shores of a nearby lake. Moreover, strong belief in clairvoyance persists even in the absence of the ceremony. Thus, during World War II one tribal elder did a thriving business locating scarce stolen tires and securing information about the health and welfare of Ojibwa boys away in the service.[13]

Among the reports collected by Professor Hallowell the most sensational phenomenon in shaking tent performances is the teleportation of objects, or what the spiritualists call "apports," although he does not use this term. At such seances tobacco is produced which is not the commercial variety used by the Amerinds. This was confirmed by Hallowell, who examined some at a performance. It is credited with properties of magical increase, and its source is a mystery to both the natives and the ethnologist. The tobacco increases in amount, and so is never entirely consumed.

More startling, however, is the recovery of lost objects. Victor Barnouw, in a review of Hallowell's book, writes:

Lost articles are sometimes tossed out of the tent to their owners. One conjuror is said to have produced some keys which a baby dropped overboard on a canoe trip; and the same man is credited with restoring a lost rifle to its owner. In fact, if a canoe overturns in the rapids, the conjuror may hand out all the goods from his conjuring lodge. Similar feats, mentioned by other ethnologists, put to shame the miracles of Madame Blavatsky. A fifty-pound sack of flour, for instance, is magically transported for a hundred miles. One conjuror is said to have had fresh blueberries in his lodge in the dead of winter.[14]

Shaking tent seances today are almost entirely restricted to remote tribes in western and northwestern Canada. Early in the nineteenth century Amerind occult practices began disappearing as Christianity spread and the cultural values of the native Americans degenerated under the impact of European civilization. It began in the east, moving west with the tide of colonists. By the beginning of this century the shaking tent phenomenon had passed almost into the domain of legend.

As early as 1879 Sir Cecil Denny wrote: "I could tell many strange and weird stories about these medicine men and the remarkable things they accomplished. These would not be credited by most people. However, these strange men have nearly all died, and most of the old Indian customs with them." [15]

In 1942 Professor Hallowell listed the most recent performances of the shaking tent as a ceremony at Berens River, Lake Winnipeg in 1930; one at Little Grand Rapids, Manitoba, in 1936; another at

Cass Lake, Minnesota, in 1937; and a report by Regina Flannery of one among the Montagnais of James Bay in 1939.

Perhaps there are still a very few medicine men skilled in the old traditions and customs who can perform the shaking tent ceremony. On the other hand, at this late date, it is possible that the voice of the Great Turtle will be heard no more.

II

Medicine Man Magic

GALLUP, NEW MEXICO, is the scene of the great annual Inter-Tribal Indian Ceremonial, held on the last Wednesday, Thursday and Friday in August. The celebration began in 1921 after the Amerinds' participation in the annual county fair became surprisingly popular. Today it is a world attraction with thousands of visitors from every state in the Union and from a dozen foreign countries.

The white citizens of Gallup play host. Prior to the ceremonial they prepare the exhibition buildings, dig huge barbecue pits, and bring in sheep and goats and quarters of beef. And throughout the west, at every pueblo, tepee and campfire, the red men are counting the days.

As the time approaches, the native Americans begin coming to Gallup. They bring their families "unto the third and fourth generation." They travel in every type of conveyance; some in automobiles and buses, others in covered wagons and a few by train. Many come on foot or by horseback, desert horsemen riding through a world of sand and cactus, some in silence, others singing haunting songs that are echoed back from red-banked arroyos.

From their villages of peace come the Hopis, their faces sun- and wind-burned by years of rugged living. Navajos ride in from the mountains and mesas of their reservation. From Zuñi to Taos come the Pueblos, an agricultural people still tilling the soil that their great-grandfathers tilled before them. Arizona contributes the once-fierce Apaches who fought as few men have to keep their an-

138

cestral lands, but today are peaceful traders in fine horses and beautiful baskets. South Dakota sends the beautifully-beaded and feathered Sioux. Oklahoma sends the Pawnee, Comanche, Kiowa and Kaw. From Utah come the Utes.

Thirty tribes—7,000 Amerindians. A three-mile parade through the streets of Gallup opens the ceremonial. The red men and women march and dance to the sounds of tom-toms, gourds, bells, rattles and an all-Indian band composed of members of eight tribes. Writing in the *New Mexico* magazine, Anna Nolan Clark described this spectacle of colorful splendor as follows:

The Navajo men are in white trousers, gay velvet shirts bedecked with hammered silver and copper, turquoise and shell. Kiowas are like birds of plumage with swirls of feathers on forehead, arms, ankles and back, and beads and little bells and tiny flashing mirrors. The Apaches in the devil dance masks have a fierce brutal beauty. Zuñi girls walk by, large earthen water jars balanced superbly on their heads. The butterfly girls from Hopiland are next, little sprigs of living green held upright in their doll-like hands. Taos women in bright dresses and black shawls waddle along in wide-topped white deerskin boots, their tall, proud men swathed in snowy white sheets beside them.[1]

There is a large hall and rooms devoted to displaying arts and crafts. Here the thousands of visiting Anglos, as white folk are known in these parts, can see or purchase pottery and baskets, silver and copper jewelry, shell and turquoise ornaments, and Navajo rugs. At dawn on each of the ceremonial days a Navajo medicine man begins making a sand painting in the center of the exhibition hall. On a bed of brown sand he forms a beautiful tapestry with lines and figures of colored clays. It is symbolic and of profound religious significance. Throughout the day this master of an ancient art makes his design ever more intricate. At sunset it is dusted with pollen and blessed with prayer. Then it is swept away and destroyed.

Every afternoon there are exhibitions of racing, trick riding, bulldogging, boomerang throwing and games. Scattered throughout the grounds are groups of Amerindians around fires, roasting sheep and sides of beef, visiting, bartering and betting on horses. There are the sounds of singing, laughter and the occasional beat of drums. The spicy odor of cedar smoke fills the air.

The sun sets; with the approach of darkness huge bonfires are lighted at each end of the enclosed dancing arena. Above the arena white spectators crowd into the grandstands. Around the arena the native Americans settle down with their babies, food, and especially coffeepots and blankets, for the evening's events will last many hours and the night is chilly. High in the sky is an autumn moon. The flames leap upward, casting fantastic shadows across the scene. Now the first dancers appear, moving in a line from out of the darkness into the bonfire light, chanting, their moccasined feet keeping time to the beat of drum, rattle and gourd. Joining in the chant are the plaintive songs of the solo singers.

Other dances follow as the night lengthens. The Apaches present their crown dances with its symbols commemorating a lost and great past. The Zia dancers mimic crows to the laughter of the crowd. Syncopated jerking rhythm features the dance of the Kiowas. Taos people offer their hoop dance, their bodies flashing through their hoops like water flowing. The Pueblos perform their hunting dramas, their prayers for increase. Mounting excitement accompanies the war dance of the Utes.

Now comes the turn-to-white dance with twelve participants. They shout and twirl their staves tipped with white eagle down. Their bare bodies gleam with daubed white clay as they leap and prance, thrusting their staves toward the scorching flames. The feathers wither away and the spectators shout, "Turn-to-white." Fresh feathers then replace the withered ones, which is the signal for many feats of magic.

In the light of the roaring ceremonial fires, a kernel of corn is planted in the earth. As the medicine men and their assistants chant, the corn grows out of the ground and up through a blanket. Finally, fully grown, tall and tasseled, it waves in the night wind. Next the Navajo shamans stand a feather in a basket, and as they continue their chant it rises up and sways back and forth in a pendulumlike dance.

Some dancing feather magicians are exceptional. In the 1947 Gallup Ceremonial, Manly Palmer Hall, the philosopher, witnessed the performance of an old priest considered the most famous living exponent of the Navajo feather magic. He tells about it in the magazine *Horizon*, published by the Philosophical Research Society.

The elderly performer walked to the center of the arena with several assistants. One of the assistants carried a wide flat basket in which lay a long decorated eagle's feather. The men seated themselves in two rows, one on each side of an open space where they placed the basket containing the feather. The rows were about ten feet from the basket. The medicine-priest began to chant and his assistants joined in.

Hall continues:

A dancer, carrying long ornamented wands and standing several feet from the basket, began posturing and moving his body with the rhythm of the song. Immediately the feather rose upright and, swaying back and forth, followed exactly the motions of the dancer. As the dance became more rapid, the feather vibrated with great intensity and seemed to jump a short distance into the air. The vibration and motion of the feather continued until the dancer ceased his gyrations, and then the plume fell forward in the basket and remained still.[2]

Hall adds that those who have seen the feather dance at close range in the Black Mountains Reservation where the priest lives have never been able to discover any indication of trickery.

The most spectacular dance at Gallup is the Navajo fire dance. Twelve naked dancers suddenly appear from out of the darkness and begin circling a ceremonial fire. Carrying cedar bark torches, they leap over the fire, bathing their agile bodies in the flames. Their wands flaming, they chase each other beating themselves and one another with their firebrands. Round and round, faster and faster they race, then they return to the darkness. It is said that as long as a dancer shouts his fire song, he will not be burned.

An early account of the Navajo fire dance appears in the pages of the Report of the Smithsonian Institute's Bureau of Ethnology for 1883–84. It was written by Dr. Washington Matthews, a United States Army surgeon, who witnessed the dance in 1884 while on military duty at Fort Wingate, New Mexico. The ceremony was at a place called Niqotlizi, twenty miles northwest of the fort. Dr. Matthews states:

The eleventh dance was the fire dance . . . Ten men, wearing loin cloths, entered [the ceremonial circle]. Every man except the leader bore a long thick bundle of shredded cedar bark in each hand. When the bundles were all lighted at the ceremonial fire, the whole band began a wild race around the fire . . . Then they proceeded to apply the brands to their own nude bodies and the bodies of comrades in front of them, no man ever turning around. At times a dancer struck his victim vigorous blows with his flaming wand; again he seized his flame as if it were a sponge, and keeping close to the one pursued, rubbed the back of the latter for several moments as if he were bathing him . . . When a dancer found no one in front of him, he proceeded to sponge his own back.[3]

Immediately after the dance, Dr. Matthews examined several of the dancers. The puzzled physician reported that he found no trace of burns.

Some tribes have used fire in healing rites. The Iroquois, for example, have the masked false face dancers who formerly held special dances for healing sickness. The patient was laid down beside a wood fire. First the dancers wearing their masks and carrying rattles danced around the patient and the fire chanting an appropriate song. Then they scooped up hot ashes from the fire and rubbed their hands in the embers, showing no signs of pain. Finally they would turn the patient over and rub hot ashes into selected parts of his body.[4]

Among all the Amerindians of the desert Southwest, the most secure economically are the members of the Mission tribe of Cahuilla living in the Coachella Valley of California. Much of their wealth is derived from the leasing of land in sophisticated Palm Springs and environs. Despite this constant association with a large population of Anglo-Americans, their ancient tribal customs and religion remain virtually unknown to the public.

Artist and desert authority John Hilton has given us a glimpse of the ancient magic they still practice. A long and trusted friend of the tribe, he was invited to witness a night ceremony for the purpose of freeing two young men from war psychoses which took the form of continual nightmares of battle. The two men had been through the worst of the actions in the Pacific theatre. Government doctors had failed to help them.

The medicine man said the boys had become "victims of newly released spirits from some enemy they had killed. These spirits had clamped onto their souls and were determined to live with them and torture them the rest of their lives." The ceremony was to remove them and send them on to the spirit world where they could do no more harm.

The healing ritual began in the afternoon with a ceremonial feast, with Hilton and several other invited white friends present. The place was at a secret ceremonial house hidden in the brush. After dark there was dancing and chanting, and the cleansing of the place by brushings and wavings of the owl feathers used by the medicine man. The fire was also cleansed as well as the patients. Chants alternated with songs.

Red coals from the fire were handled freely. One was taken into his mouth by the medicine man and, drawing breath through his nose and blowing from his mouth, he sent out streams of sparks. After holding the brush of owl feathers over the fire and brushing both patients repeatedly, especially about the head and shoulders, the medicine man took them in turn, blowing into the patient's mouth, nostrils and ears. Next he began sucking with his lips at a point between the eyes. With a loud smack, he withdrew his lips and removed from his mouth what appeared to be a wiggling white worm which he threw into the fire.

When this act had been repeated for both patients, they were again brushed with the feathers while they remained kneeling. A short speech was made to them, and the cure was complete. "They slept well that night and have not been bothered since," writes John Hilton. "Call it what you may, psychology, hypnotism, suggestion, black magic or white, whatever it was—it worked! Army and Navy hospitals are full of patients today suffering from the same mental ailments which neither medicine nor psychology have been able to cure."

There is an interesting aftermath. Hilton was told that handling red hot coals was easy if one first thought of his hand as getting hotter and hotter until it was hotter than the fire, after which coals could be handled without burns. He tried this, and to his surprise found that it worked for him. When he tried, however, to put the coals in his mouth, the magic failed and he was burned. His Indian friend explained the failure by saying, "Nobody sang. You can't eat fire without singing" (ritual chant and dance).[5]

Live coal handling is not limited to the Cahuilla. E. P. Gibson, in the *Journal* of the American Society for Psychical Research, tells of a number of fire feats among North American Indians.[6] Early explorers and French missionaries reported that the Amerinds of the St. Lawrence and Great Lakes regions had various fire ordeals. They included successful handling of live coals and hot stones, plunging their arms into boiling water, and walking through fire. Defiance of fire, especially as incorporated in the fire walk, is a world-wide rite.

There are also medicine man Houdinis, masters of escapology. One early acount is by Jonathan Carver, who studied the customs of the Crees in Canada from 1766 to 1768. The shaman, wearing only a loin cloth, stretched out full length on an elk hide, then covered himself with the hide so that only his head was in view. Two men using forty yards of leather thongs then tied the medicine man mummy-fashion and knotted the ends. He was lifted and placed in a small tent. After some shouting and what seemed to be praying, the shaman lapsed into silence. Carver thought the performer was exhausted, but to his astonishment the man merged from the tent free of his bonds.

Having heard that Canadian shamans were escape artists, Duncan Cameron, a nineteenth-century fur trader, made a bet that he could tie one so securely that he would beg to be released. His challenge was accepted. The medicine man was first rolled into a large net, then bound with thongs and placed alone in a small tent. "In sixteen minutes he began to shake his rattle which made me think his hands were free," Cameron said. "Six minutes after that he threw out the net and desired me to examine it and say whether it was cut; finding the net all right I paid the wager." [7]

A more startling performance was an escape during a shaking tent exhibition with the climax an apparent teleportation. Skeptical of escape tales he had heard, Paul Beaulieu, an interpreter for the Ojibwa at White Earth Agency, Minnesota, offered a medicine man a hundred dollars for a successful demonstration. A committee of twelve men, which included an Episcopal priest, went to work rendering the naked shaman helpless. First the performer's hands, wrists and ankles were bound. Next his tied hands were forced down so that his knees extended above them. A sturdy pole was placed over his arms and under his knees; finally his neck was bound to his knees. A black stone amulet was placed on his thighs at his request and he was carried into the tent.

Seconds later strange vocal cries and thumping sounds came from within. As the sounds increased in volume, the tent swayed violently. After a bit the disturbances ceased, and the medicine man shouted that the ropes could now be found in a nearby house. Beaulieu told the committee to keep a sharp watch on the tent while he ran to the house. The ropes were there, still knotted. He hurried back and when the priest saw the ropes he fled, crying that this was the work of the devil. Beaulieu was given permission to enter the tent and he found the shaman seated comfortably, puffing on a pipe. The committee agreed unanimously that the medicine man had earned the hundred dollars. [8]

In September 1960, the New Mexico State Fair hired some Zuñi Amerinds to entertain rodeo visitors with their dance ceremonials. The fair officials didn't pay much attention to the dances because they had a big problem. Attendance was not good because of the late afternoon rains that kept falling. Finally someone asked the Zuñis what ceremonials they were performing. They were the tribe's rain dances.

Name any need or desire of mankind and the Amerindians have a dance for it. But of all their ceremonials, the most publicized has been the rain dance. There is a drought. Some native Americans perform a rain dance. Down comes the rain.

Chief George Watchetaker, a Comanche medicine man from Oklahoma, has acquired quite a reputation as a solo rainmaker in recent years. During the Florida spring drought of 1971 a Pompano Beach radio station employed his services. As 1,500 people stood in a circle around a parking lot, the chief lit a small bonfire, chanted, sipped from a bowl of water, and danced. Four minutes after the ceremony the spectators were running to storefront shelters to get out of the rain. Casey Jones, program director for the sponsoring radio station, said the reaction from the crowd was utter disbelief at first, then wild applause. "We just didn't believe it," he said.[9]

A variation of the dance took place while Calgary Productions, a subsidiary of Walt Disney Studios, was filming the million-dollar movie *Nomads of the North*, near Banff, Alberta, Canada. A trading post had been especially built. Nearby were cabins and a number of trailers to accommodate seventy members of the movie company and almost 100 extras. Shooting of the film was ready to begin, but snow was needed, and although it was midwinter there was only a light film on the ground.

For five days the company waited for snow that did not come. The postponement was costing thousands of dollars daily. One movie maker suggested the use of artificial snow, but since it would have to be shipped over a long distance and cover several acres, the cost would have been exorbitant. Finally, a Canadian mentioned the possibility of a "snow dance" by Chief Johnny Bearspaw and his Stony Indian tribe. Several years before the tribal dancers had successfully brought rain at the Calgary Stampede. The movie makers were desperate and the proposal was worth a try.

Chief Bearspaw was brought to the location and he agreed to perform a snow dance—the first ever put on by his tribe. The fee would be $10 for each dancer. The next morning the chief and thirty-one tribesmen appeared in ceremonial costume and they danced and chanted to the beat of drums. The movie makers and the extras cheered and applauded. The Stonys were paid, and they left with solemn assurances of success. That night seven inches of snow fell.[10]

It is the medicine men with the gift of influencing the weather who announce the time and direct the rain dances. They can apparently prevent as well as bring rain. Such a man was Last Horse who was relied on by the Oglala Sioux for many years to control the weather on important occasions.

In the summer of 1878 the Oglala Sioux were visiting their cousins, the Brule Sioux. Everybody was dressed in his finest clothes. During the morning a feast was held under a sunny sky. Then, in the early afternoon, just as dancing and games were getting started, ominous black clouds appeared, driven by a strong wind. As large drops of rain began to fall and the people ran to shelter, Last Horse came forward.

The shaman was carrying his sacred rattle. He walked to the center of the clearing and looked up at the sky. As the people watched in awe, he shook his rattle and began to sing. Then he moved his hands back and forth and the clouds began slowly to separate, moving farther and farther apart. Soon the sky was clear and the people resumed their festivities under a warm sun.

Once there was a sky battle between rival medicine men. Bull Shield was a member of one of the Sioux tribes, greatly respected not only for his weather-making but for his wisdom and dignity. In his old age there appeared in the tribe another shaman capable of influencing the weather. He was named He Crow, a young man, arrogant and boastful. To the annoyance of the tribe, he insisted he had stronger medicine than Bull Shield. When the time for an important festival approached, he said he would bring in a cloudburst and prove his power was greater than that of Bull Shield. News of the conflict spread, and when the festival day came there were a number of white witnesses on hand, including the noted anthropologist and Commissioner of Indian Affairs, Dr. Clark Wissler, who later wrote a number of books on the Amerindians.

At dawn on the appointed day the sky was cloudy. He Crow boasted that he was responsible for the clouds and that soon he would make it rain. But Bull Shield quietly began singing his song, a prayer to the sun to drive the clouds away. After a time the clouds separated and began drifting apart. He Crow resumed his singing and shouting while beating a drum, calling upon the clouds to return and to pour down rain.

The clouds did return, darker than before, and soon it seemed that it would start raining at any second. But Bull Shield continued singing and praying, and after a time the clouds again separated. From morning to afternoon, for hours, the contest went on, a seesaw battle. To the astonishment of the spectators, the sky alternately turned dark and bright as the shamans dueled. The end came in midafternoon just before the festival when the sun came into full view for the first time. Despite He Crow's shouting and drum beating, the clouds drifted away and the festivities began.[11]

What is the rainmaker's secret? It is a psychic attunement with Nature. It is producing a physical manifestation psychically. And it is a knowledge of certain signs learned by years of practice and handed down to the medicine man from his predecessors.

Although precise observations and rituals vary from tribe to tribe, there are certain basic patterns. First of all, rainmaking is regarded as a sacred occupation. There is a mental and spiritual preparation. George Watchetaker, the Commanche shaman, has stated that it takes him at least ten days of this preparation before the actual ceremonies began.

There are natural signs to be observed. The moon is an important sign. The Navajo say that if the crescent of the new moon has its prongs upward there will be no normal rain for the month; if downward, rain is on the way. Rings around the sun and moon are good signs, as they indicate haze in the atmosphere. The medicine men know too that many clouds have rain-making potential that never benefits the earth. Unless some force is brought to bear, a potential rain remains just that.

According to the signs, the rainmaker names the right day for the ceremony. The Hopi snake dance, however, is an eight-day ceremony, with the public dance limited to a short period late in the afternoon of the final day. Both performers and the snakes undergo purification rituals. At the end the snakes are taken back to the desert and released to carry the message of the need for rain. "Before the night is over," writes J. H. McGibbeny in his book *Children of the Sun*, "the rain will come. It never fails. No sickly drizzle, but a downpour of cloudburst proportions." [12]

Some southwestern tribes use sympathetic magic in their rainmaking ceremonies on the principle that like produces like. Thus, to make rain you use water. Water is poured into a sacred bowl. The water is then taken into the mouth and blown in the four directions, east, south, west and then north.

Sound—chants and the beat of drums—is apparently a require-
ment in the success of the ritual. Nor is the use of sound for this
purpose limited to Amerindians. The white man at one time tried
to cause rain by firing cannons or explosives. That sound has the
power to alter physical conditions or produce manifestations is a
universal age-old belief.

Amerind chants and drum beats are distinctive. The chants are
repetitious; only a few notes are used and there is no melodic pattern. The drum beats can have a hypnotic effect and they are not
comparable to other rhythms we can recognize.

Melba Blanton, writing in *Occult* magazine, describes the probable process as follows:

> It is easy to imagine how certain ceremonies used by some Indian tribes
> might have utilized the sound principle to produce rain. Picture a huge,
> resonant drum, which is situated in the center of a large circle. Place
> around this drum ten to fifteen men, all with sticks to beat out the peculiar
> rhythms of the Indian music. These men, then, begin to chant their spiri-
> tual thoughts. Then around the circle, the light, rhythmic treading of the
> feet of hundreds of dancers begin. It is easy to imagine this formation of
> vibrations and sound could act on the atmosphere, causing water vapor to
> form into droplets. These raindrops would then be drawn toward the big
> drum as if aiming at a bull's-eye.[13]

Another attribute of many Amerindian medicine men is their
ability to experience premonitions. The grandmother of Charles
Eastman, who was educated at Dartmouth and became a physician, was a celebrated medicine woman among the Sioux late in the
last century. Dr. Eastman wrote that on one occasion his family
left Fort Ellis in southern Canada to camp along the Assiniboine
River. This was at a time when there was conflict between some of
the tribes. His grandmother refused to camp at the place chosen by
the men. She had a premonition of danger. Even though it was already dark, the family continued downstream to a new location.

Another family traveling behind them did make a camp at the
spot the grandmother had rejected. The next day it was discovered
that this family had been massacred by a band of enemy tribesmen.

On another occasion the doctor was living with his family at
Lake Manitoba when a messenger came with the tragic news that a
beloved son of the grandmother, Eastman's uncle, had been killed
at a settlement some distance away. As the shocked family began to
mourn, the grandmother told the family not to weep as the news

was false, and her son would soon arrive in the flesh. Sure enough, two days later the son did appear, very much alive.

Another prominent Sioux shaman with the gift of prophecy was Tall Holy, a name he had earned by being well over six feet in height and a man of mystical character. In 1903 he was living at the Oglala Sioux Reservation of Pine Ridge, South Dakota. At that time the buffalo herds had vanished and farming on the reservation was difficult for the natives. There was, however, one exciting source of revenue for the younger Amerinds and that was joining Buffalo Bill Cody's Wild West Show.

Buffalo Bill asked his friend on the reservation, Luther Standing Bear, to take charge of seventy-five young Sioux and bring them to Chicago to join the show. There was no problem getting recruits, and Standing Bear and his men were soon loading their wagons for the trip from Pine Ridge to the railroad station at Rushville, Nebraska.

In the midst of the loading, Tall Holy came up to Standing Bear and warned him not to make the trip. He said he foresaw that something ominous would happen to him if he continued the journey. Standing Bear respected the elderly medicine man, but he was young and this opportunity was too good to lose. He decided he would take his chances.

The train was boarded at Rushville and all went well until it neared Chicago. There it crashed into another train. Three of the Sioux were killed instantly; twenty-seven more were injured seriously. Standing Bear was one of the injured and at first physicians thought he would die, but he finally pulled through.

Premonitions, frequently warning of danger, occur among all peoples, but there are some involving extrasensory perception that are peculiarly Amerindian. Dr. J. Allen Hynek is professor of astronomy at Northwestern University and a former consultant to U. S. Air Force UFO investigators. In his book *The Edge of Reality*, coauthored by another scientist, Dr. Jacques Vallee, he offers two examples of this astonishing phenomenon.

Dr. Hynek states that when he was in Batineau, North Dakota, a somewhat isolated place, he met a historian of Amerind cultures. This man had been adopted by the local tribes, and he participated in their dances and other ceremonies. He related the following incidents.

A young Indian had a very valuable saddle stolen. A ceremony was held and the medicine man said that on a certain specific day the theft victim was to go out along the river until he saw a coyote sitting on a bluff. If he would dig under that bluff below where the coyote had been sitting he would find his saddle, and he did.

The second even more remarkable occurrence also involves animal life. Three young men of the tribe had drowned. Two of the bodies were soon recovered, but the third, that of a youth named Red Horn, could not be found. A wind-shaking dance and ceremony was held. At the climax the Great Spirit comes, and there is a very real wind that sweeps through the village whipping up dust and slamming doors. When the wind came a Catholic priest who had been invited to be present cried out in pain. There was no permanent injury, but he said later that it felt as if every bone in his body had been broken. The Amerinds just laughed and said that's what the Great Spirit does to those who don't believe. After a few minutes there was a wind in the opposite direction, and the medicine man said, "The Great Spirit is gone."

Then the medicine man told the family of Red Horn to watch for three large birds. They were to follow these birds. Soon two of the birds would turn off and one would go straight. They were to follow the one that flew straight and they would find the body of Red Horn. The birds came; two flew in other directions, and one flew straight. Suddenly a shot was fired and the bird fell from the sky into the river. No one knows who fired the shot, but it was not done by any of the family and their friends who were following the bird. Directly below the dead bird floating in the water they found the body of Red Horn.

Hynek's comment is that these "things are pretty hard to believe in a sense; on the other hand, how do we know?" He also refers to Carlos Castaneda's *Journey to Ixtlan* where he "has the power" or he "doesn't have the power," and he is always looking for signs, for a swallow to fly in a certain way, and that sort of thing.[14]

12

Secrets of the Shamans

DURING THE WINTER of 1866 a group of Sioux camped in the Powder River country, near Piney Creek in Wyoming. Food was low, and the tribesmen tramped through the deep snow in a desperate attempt to find game. After a disappointing hunt they returned to the camp, but many of them were snow blind, unable to see from having looked too long at the glare of sunlight on the snow.

The blind men were taken to a medicine man who had learned healing through dreams and visions. The shaman placed snow over the eyes of the afflicted men, then he sang a song he said he had learned in a dream. Next, he placed snow in his mouth and blew some of the flakes upon the heads of the men. Immediately their blindness went away. Snow blindness is usually temporary, but severe cases can last a considerable time, and sight returns gradually.

This was healing by ritual and a song.

Luther Standing Bear, who lived on the Oglala Sioux Reservation at Pine Ridge, South Dakota, was an educated man. One day he was alone in his home with his stepmother when she suddenly collapsed. He carried her to a bed where she tossed and moaned in agony. Standing Bear hurried away and brought back the tribal medicine man, White Crow.

For a few minutes the medicine man watched the woman suffering on the bed. Then from his medicine bundle he withdrew a piece of root which he cut in two. He asked the woman to chew

151

both pieces until they were soft. Finally he had her swallow one of the pieces and rub the other on her chest. Five minutes or so after she did as instructed, all pain left her body and she got up and resumed her work. White Crow refused to tell Standing Bear the name of the plant from which the root came or to sell him another piece of root. That was a medicine man's secret.

This was healing by herbs.

Another remarkable cure was witnessed by Dr. J. M. De Wolf, an army surgeon, and Paul Beckwith, an anthropologist. The patient had been hunting some distance from the camp when he was bitten by a poisonous snake. Hours had passed by the time he managed to stagger home. Dr. De Wolf examined the badly swollen leg and said the poison had been working too long for him to be able to help the victim. Death was not far away.

Then the tribal medicine man was brought to the scene. He gave the stricken man a herb to eat and then performed a ceremony, singing a song as he shook his rattle and beat his drum. In a short time the patient was cured, walking around none the worse for his experience.

This was apparent healing by both herbs and ritual.[1]

To an Amerindian the meaning of the word *medicine* is quite different than its connotation among whites. To most native Americans medicine signifies not just treatments and remedies alone, but an array of concepts and ideas about an entire realm beyond his understanding. In most Amerind cultures the medicine man or shaman combines in his person the attributes of many professions. He functions as a priest, philosopher, historian, politician, family counsellor, and physician.

Nor can anyone dispute the bedside manners of the medicine men who concentrate on relieving anxiety and improving the morale of their patients, according to Dr. Guenter Risse, of the University of Wisconsin:

This is an area in which the modern physician, engrossed in sophisticated medical technology, has fallen short. When a person becomes ill, he loses his self-assurance and becomes depressed and worried . . . the mere presence of the highly respected shaman is an important morale builder. The shaman represents all of the religious and social beliefs of the tribe and can call on the powerful spirit world. His rituals draw attention to the patient and build up the patient's hope. White doctors in Navajo reservations have acknowledged the shaman's power. They say recovery from operations is notably faster if the patient is visited by the medicine man before surgery.[2]

Dr. Robert L. Bergman, a psychiatrist in the Indian Health Service at Window Rock, Arizona, enlisted six Navajo medicine men to teach twelve young tribesmen the elaborate chants that appear to cure Navajo emotional problems. He explained that psychiatrists have come to realize that every culture has brought forth healers of one sort or another who are as effective with their own people as psychiatrists are among Westerners. Cultural expectations appear to play a very important part in the healing process.

There is every indication, Dr. Bergman said, that the twelve trainees will become effective psychotherapists well able to meet the mental health needs of their tribe. Some of the healing chants continue for from five to nine nights in the medicine man's hogan with the patient's entire family present.

"It seems to me," the doctor explained, "that the ceremony is almost always symbolically appropriate to the case. Pathologically prolonged grief reactions, for example, are almost always treated with a ceremony that removes the influence of the dead from the living and turns their attention back to life." [3]

In Navajo land the medicine men are called "singers." They work with as many as thirty-five ceremonials, most of them devoted to healing, and each involves word-perfect memorization of numerous prayers and chants. Very few master any large number of ceremonials in their lifetimes, so there is specialization among the singers. In addition, they must learn how to treat wounds, set bones, and have a knowledge of the medicinal properties of local herbs.

Alexander H. and Dorothea C. Leighton, in their book *The Navajo Door*, tell of the difficult training as follows:

When a man wanted to be a singer, he should start in the summer and get a good crop of corn and harvest it and store it, and then about the time the first snow flies, build him up a good hogan, and then haul plenty of wood there to do a long time, and have a woman there to cook for him, cook that corn and make bread. Then he gets a singer and has him there in the hogan and they work and keep at it.

If they get too tired, then they can take a sweat bath and next day they feel good and can go on with it again. They stay at it until the first thunder, and then quit. Next summer the learner does the same thing again, and the next winter goes on with the learning. Do that for maybe five years. By that time learn two or three ceremonials.[4]

In other tribes becoming a medicine man is no easy matter. A Blackfoot, for example, undergoes a seven-year training course to qualify as a shaman. The Eskimo shaman learns to name all the parts of his body, including every bone, by its special name in the sacred shaman's language. In some tribes the schooling includes learning to recite tribal histories and special proverbs. In addition, the prospective medicine man undergoes examination by a group of men already admitted to practice. They review his life and training, his personal characteristics, and his fitness to be entrusted with the exercise of great power.

Medicine man knowledge is the result of many centuries of observation and practice. Long before Sigmund Freud was born, the shamans practiced dream analysis. To the Iroquois, dreams were the windows of the soul through which an individual expressed his unconscious wishes while his body slept. They realized that there is a conscious and subconscious part of the mind, and that subconscious desires, if frustrated, could cause mental and physical illness. They understood the causes of psychosomatic illnesses and how to relieve them by calling up a patient's hidden thoughts.

This was confirmed by Father Paul LeJeune in the second quarter of the seventeenth century in his study of the shamans of Quebec and Huronia. He and his fellow Jesuits found they had methods of healing the sick which in some cases resembled modern psychoanalysis. In his *Relations* he wrote that the natives believed one of the main sources of disease "is the mind of the patient himself, which desires something, and will vex the body of the sick man until it possesses the thing required. For they think that there are in every man certain inborn desires, often unknown to themselves, upon which the happiness of individuals depends. For the purpose of ascertaining the desires and innate appetites of this character they summon soothsayers, who, as they think, have a divinely imparted power to look into the inmost recesses of the mind."[5]

Thus, as Virgil J. Vogel points out in his book *American Indian Medicine*, whether Indian treatment of disease was less rational than European is debatable. Certainly treatment of external complaints, wherein the origin or nature of the ailment was obvious, was usually rational and often quite effective. However, in cases of persistent internal disorder it was frequently the custom to attribute the disease to a supernatural agency. Especially prevalent among southwestern tribes was the belief in witchcraft as a cause of disease.[6]

The supernatural causes of disease among tribes in general were soul loss, taboo violation, object intrusion, and spirit intrusion. Soul loss occurred when the soul left the body in a dream and began traveling around. Sometimes it was believed the soul had been stolen by enemy shamans or evil spirits. It was the task of the medicine man to bring back the soul through appropriate rituals.

Some diseases were thought to be punishments for taboo violations. These violations included killing an animal without an offering to its spirit, waste of natural resources, and disrespect toward natural elements such as fire by spitting, urinating or throwing offal into the flames. Object intrusion meant that an insect, worm, snake or other small animal had entered the body. Among the Creeks nearly every disease had the name of an animal thought to be its cause. It was the medicine man's duty to remove the object.

As for spirit intrusion, it was a belief shared by the people of medieval Europe and colonial America, and "spirit possession" is still believed in some quarters. It was supported by numerous biblical references to demon possession. Witches and enchanters, poisonous plants and roots, and human and animal ghosts were thought to be possessed by evil spirits that could cause diseases.

There is an element of truth in all these concepts. In our bodies there are microorganisms (and occasionally worms and teratomas). Spirit possession is still a debatable phenomenon in psychical research. In our waste of natural resources we are already paying a price and our punishment will be greater in the future. The poison in plants may be called a spirit, but it is still a poison that can kill. Much of what we accept as fact today will be disproved by the sciences of the twenty-first century and beyond. It is belief that make customs and practices work.

It was, however, in the realm of herbs and drugs that the Amerindians made their greatest contribution to the healing arts. Dr. Arthur S. Freese, in his book *Pain*, states that of the 144 known drugs "the North American Indian medicine men used for a variety of conditions, nearly half are still in our pharmacopoeia." [7] Even in comparatively recent times, Amerind pharmaceutical practices have helped open new frontiers in medical history. Insulin, cocaine and the use of drugs to control the menstrual cycle (which launched the research that led to "the Pill") are examples. Amerind gifts to combat illness include arnica, cascara, ipecac, oil of wintergreen, petroleum jelly, quinine and witch hazel. Some plants were brewed into tea for the patient to drink. Other plants were chewed and eaten or applied as poultices or salves on the affected parts of the body.

Joseph Logan, a resident in Ontario's Ohsweken Indian Reservation, consulted a non-Indian doctor for a routine physical examination some years ago. He was told that X-rays disclosed that he had tubercular spots on his lungs, and he was advised to take a long sanitarium rest. Logan said he would think it over and come back later for another X-ray examination.

Several months later Logan did return to the doctor's office. To the doctor's surprise this time there were no spots on the lungs. Today the elderly Logan bears no signs of tuberculosis. He is one of thirty council members in Canada's Six Nation Indian Confederacy and is a widely respected shaman. In an interview with reporters he said Amerindians believe that "Nature provides all cures for all illnesses. God would not put man on earth without such cures." [8]

An elderly man suffering from cancer of the face was told at the University of Utah Medical School that he would die unless he had radical surgery. He refused and went home to St. George, Utah, to await the end. Several months later he returned to the university, and to the astonishment of the physicians he had made an amazing recovery. According to United Press International, an old Amerind friend, a retired shaman, had advised him to drink cups of "chaparral tea" which is brewed from the leaves of the desert creosote bush.

University researchers found that the tea contained an ingredient called nordihydro-guaiertic acid or NDGA. Later research at the University of Nevada revealed that NDGA is a potent inhibitor of the mitrochrondial functions within animal cells, which is the area where metabolic energy is produced. The acid seems to work only on diseased or cancerous cells. Dr. Dean C. Fletcher, chairman of the department of biochemistry at Nevada, is cautious about its use as a cancer cure and says much more research is needed. "All we can say at this time," he said, "is that the drug appears to be extremely interesting." [9]

Another contemporary medicine man is Louis Prince of the Salteaux tribe living on the shores of Lake Manitoba. He is a healer, but it is his clairvoyance in locating drowned bodies that has brought him fame. For his healing ceremonies he uses a skin rattle filled with shells, a whistle that is said to emit high sighing sounds during incantations, and a pipe.

A detailed account of how he located one body was reported in the *Winnipeg Tribune* (26 July 1954). A five-year-old boy, accompanied by two other boys, went down to the swollen Assiniboine River to bring a bucket of water back to his home. The bank caved in, throwing the boy into the water. All his companions could do was run for help. Royal Canadian Mounted Police dragged the river, and tribesmen searched along the banks and from boats.

Bruce Pashe, a native, decided to enlist the assistance of Louis Prince. On the third day he managed to get a ride to Sandy Bay where Prince has his home. Prince met Pashe and his friend with the automobile at the door dressed up and ready to go. "I knew someone would be coming to get me," he explained. In the car Prince said the search was being made in the wrong location. "The body is down farther, beyond where the white men are building something across the river." This "something" was a net built by the police in hopes of intercepting the boy's body as it passed downstream.

The medicine man first went to the victim's home, then walked alone to the river bank. Returning to the house, he held a seance with five tribesmen and a white farmer friend present. A pipe of tobacco was passed to all the men. Prince spread powder on a plate of hot coals provided by the victim's father, then called on the gods for help. Those in the room said the whistle lying on the floor whistled throughout the ceremony. Sounds like voices were heard coming from the plate of ashes.

"The body will be found six bends down the river caught in tree boughs," Prince finally announced. And that's where the body was found the following morning.

Among some southwestern tribes, especially the Navajo, sandpainting is an ancient art for healing the sick. The medicine man "paints" on the ground or on buckskin or cloth by skillfully permitting sand to flow through his fingers. Instead of sands of various colors, he may use flower pollen, corn meal, powdered roots and bark. The creation of a ceremonial sandpainting is a sacred ritual which the Amerindians believe places the medicine man in contact with spiritual forces to heal and bless the ill.

According to David Villasenor in his book *Tapestries in Sand*, the intricate and beautiful sand paintings and the accompanying chanting and rituals have a miraculous effect upon patients. Villasenor is an artist and sculptor who makes sand paintings at Amerindian ceremonial meetings and explains their meanings. A part Otomi Indian, he was adopted into the Navajo tribe as a youth and learned from the medicine men not only how to make sand paintings, but their spiritual meanings and the beauty and wisdom of native mysticism that they represent.[10]

Next to the Navajo, the Ojibwa are the second most numerous Amerind group in North America. They and other neighboring Algonquin groups to whom the Ojibwa are related through language and culture have gained a reputation as practitioners of the occult arts. The Ojibwa medicine men use a method of healing that is practiced by other cultures, and it appears to be an ancient component of peoples in both the New World and the Old.

Joseph B. Casagrande witnessed this healing seance on the Lac Court Oreilles Reservation in northwestern Wisconsin. He has done field work among the Ojibwa and Comanche tribes and published studies on their languages and ceremonialism. He served as staff secretary at the Twenty-Ninth International Congress of Americanists.[11]

This performance of the sucking doctor or medicine man is the most powerful form of therapy available to the Ojibwa. It is undertaken to cure the victims of sorcery or patients suffering from diseases resistant to other forms of treatment. In the seance Casagrande observed the shaman was John Mink, a nonagenarian and the most respected man on the reservation. The patient was Prosper, a man in his sixties who was a nominal Christian but, like so many Amerinds, owed allegiance to both Christianity and native tradition. The ceremony was held in the medicine man's cabin.

First Mink's assistant and drummer covered the windows to shut out all light and made sure there were no dogs around whose barking would disturb the performance. A candle provided the only light. Prosper was asked to lie on a blanket on the floor. The spectators sat in a semicircle around him, and Mink stood facing them on the other side of the supine patient. The assistant put two finger-length tubes made from the leg bones of a deer into a pie tin half filled with salt water. This tin he placed beside the patient and covered it with a red bandana.

Mink began the ceremony by telling how he had acquired his powers. During a fast he had a dream. Led by a flock of wild geese, he came to a hut inhabited by six spirits. Later there came a beautifully dressed lady whose home was in the sky. These were the ones, Mink said, who taught him how to cure people and taught him the songs to sing in summoning their help.

Accompanied by his assistant on the drum, the medicine man began to sing as he shook his rattle, calling in the spirits that were to help him. After singing several songs, he shook the rattle over Prosper and also around his own body. As the drumming continued, Mink placed one of the bone tubes in his mouth, swallowed it as his body jerked and swayed, dropped to his knees beside his patient, and regurgitated the tube. Bending down, he sucked through the tube several times in the region of Prosper's abdomen, ending each sucking by blowing through the tube into the pan of salt water. Finally he signaled his assistant to stop the drumming and help him to his feet.

After a brief rest the shaman sang another song, followed by a second series of suckings. This time he extracted a small piece of a whitish substance which was passed around in the pie tin for inspection. Mink announced that he had removed only a part of the disease, but believed he could get the rest of it the following night when he would summon stronger spirits.

The group reassembled the next evening and with only minor variations the ceremony of the previous night was repeated. Prosper stated that he had slept well for the first time in months. Mink asked the two women present to assist him, one to shake his rattle and the other to place the bone tube in his mouth. The reason, he explained, was that two female spirits were helping him this time. He had his assistant get him a larger bone tube. On the first attempt he sucked from the patient's abdomen a small maggot and several pieces of the same white stuff. He announced that he had now gotten it all.

Casagrande writes, "Despite his great age, John Mink's performance had force and dramatic quality. Watching the ceremony, I sensed the weight of history that lay behind it—here, I felt, was an expression of the human mind and spirit to which we are all heir."

In many tribes the medicine men are specialists. One may devote his attention to influencing the weather, another to healing, and still another to assuring victory in battle. With the invasion of the Europeans, a new kind of shaman appeared. His duty was to endeavor to bulletproof the warriors.

Two of the most famous of the bulletproofers were Chips, the

Sioux shaman, and Ice, of the Cheyennes. Chips was known as the Stone Dreamer because he sought his magical powers from stones. His visions and dreams, brought about by fasting and meditations, involved the earth-power inherent in rocks and stones. The stone represented strength and solidity. Many a warrior carried a small pebble given to him by Chips as he went into battle.

In 1857 the Cheyennes received word that hostile white soldiers were headed their way. The warriors asked Ice and another medicine man named Dark to make them bulletproof. Leading the way to the shore of a small lake, the two shamans performed their rituals and sang their songs, meanwhile dipping their hands in the water. When it was over, the pair had a warrior shoot at them at close range as they held up their hands. The spent lead fell from their clothing to the ground.

When the soldiers came, the tribesmen simply stood their ground, waiting, believing that when the soldiers fired they had only to raise their hands and the bullets would fall harmlessly to the ground. Instead of firing, however, the cavalry pulled out their sabers and charged the tribesmen. Several warriors were slashed and the rest had to flee. They ran for several miles before the troopers gave up the chase. The soldiers then proceeded to destroy the Cheyenne village.[12]

It was not war parties but individuals who apparently proved the efficacy of bulletproofing medicine. One of these was Roman Nose, a famous Cheyenne warrior. To gain the magical aura of protection from his enemies, he lay on a raft for four days in the middle of a sacred lake, fasting. His mentor, White Bull, an elderly shaman, made him a war bonnet. Projecting from the headband were eagle feathers, and on the headband itself were sewed part of the skins of a hawk, a kingfisher, a swallow and a bat. Each of these creatures gave the warrior some of its qualities—courage, swiftness, strength, maneuverability. In addition, he never married. This was the "no-woman" medicine which was believed very powerful in battle.

In a battle against white soldiers in September 1865, Roman Nose asked the warriors not to charge or fire until he had ridden before the soldiers and caused them to empty their guns. Riding his white pony, he rode within easy range of the soldiers who were standing beside their wagons. Then he wheeled his mount and rode parallel to their ranks.

The tall, brightly bonneted warrior made a splendid target. The bullets enveloped him like rain. He completed three or four passes back and forth before a ball struck and killed his pony. Roman Nose arose, unharmed, as the warriors launched a charge against the bewildered, awe-struck soldiers.

As long as Roman Nose observed the rituals and the taboos he seemed invulnerable. One of the most important taboos was that the bulletproof warrior must not touch any metal with his mouth. Metal in the form of guns, bullets, knives, swords and hatchets had the power to kill. Before a battle he could not eat with metal spoons or knives.

In the autumn of 1867 the Sioux asked Roman Nose and his Cheyennes to join them in an attack on white scouts. The scouts had been sent by General Sheridan to look for Indian encampments for winter attacks. The whites were besieged by the allied warriors at Beecher's Island in the Arikaree River in Colorado. Roman Nose was there, but could not take part in the fighting. He had learned that a woman in preparing his food had used an iron spoon. He would not again be bulletproof until he went through purification ceremonies—to take a sweat bath, burn the sacred sagebrush or cedar branches and stand in their smoke. And there wasn't time for this.

Roman Nose saw his friends and relatives falling in the charges. The chiefs told him courageous deeds and acts of honor would result from his presence on the field. He decided to serve his people without his protection. He led the next charge knowing that he would surely be killed. As he went past the scouts, a shot struck Roman Nose in the back. The end he had foreseen had come to pass.

Sitting Bull was another warrior who understood the bullet-proofing medicine. He was a remarkable man in many other ways. He was a mystic who prayed and meditated. It was said that he was under the protection of the buffalo whose name he bore. It was said that he could commune with animals and the birds and that animals could warn him of danger.

In August 1872, the U.S. Cavalry, serving as escorts for surveyors laying out the route of the Northern Pacific Railroad, came into the Yellowstone River Valley in Montana. Sitting Bull and his Sioux tribesmen were camped in the valley, and they resented this invasion of their hunting grounds. A skirmish resulted.

Leaving his horse and weapons behind, Sitting Bull walked casually toward the cavalrymen. When he reached a point about 300 feet from the firing whites, he sat down on the grass, lit his pipe and started to smoke. Bullets whistled over his head and peppered the ground around him. He was a stationary target. From 50 to 80 percent of the men in the western cavalry units were good marksmen, veterans of the Civil War and the various Indian wars. Yet their shots missed Sitting Bull.

When he had finished smoking, he emptied his pipe of ashes, put it into its case and stood up. He walked back to his companions, his back toward the still shooting soldiers. The story of this courageous act was told and retold around western campfires for many years.

The great Crazy Horse too had a reputation for being bulletproof. General George Crook was an expert marksman both in conflict and as a hunter of deer, elk and bighorn sheep. In the Sioux War of 1876 the General said that he took careful aim at Crazy Horse at least twenty times—and missed.

Crazy Horse, as a boy, went out into the wilderness to fast and pray for spiritual guidance. He had a vision of a warrior riding a horse who fought in many battles but was never harmed. As he fought, a red-backed hawk flew over his head. Yet the man's own people kept trying to seize him from behind to hold him back.

The dream was explained by a holy man. He said the warrior in the vision was Crazy Horse himself. If he dressed and acted like the dream warrior he would be protected and invincible in battle. But in the end his own people would betray him. So when Crazy Horse became a man, he left his hair loose like the dream warrior instead of braided or tied with fur as was the Sioux custom. In battle he wore a red cape and the stuffed skin of a red-backed hawk on his head instead of a war bonnet. As his dream hero did, he led the charges and was first to strike the enemy. He fought in many battles and never experienced defeat.

When in the spring of 1877 Crazy Horse and his tribe surrendered, it was not because of any military defeat. The buffalo were gone and there was no food. He gave up his freedom because his people were starving. At the Red Cloud Agency in Nebraska, he tried to live in peace. However, the Amerindians who had turned to the white man's ways were jealous of the prestige he held among the Sioux. And the officers and soldiers at nearby Fort Robinson believed that at any time he would go back on the warpath. General Crook especially suspected this.

Crazy Horse was arrested and taken to Fort Robinson. He was

told he would not be harmed, but at a hearing the next day he would have an opportunity to deny the rumors that he was planning to continue to fight the white man. They led him to the guardhouse. When he saw the bars, the chains and iron balls on the legs of the prisoners already there, he made a break for freedom. As he started to run, his own people seized his arms and held him. An officer shouted an order to kill the chief and a soldier bayoneted him in the back. He died a few hours later, thus fulfilling the prophecy of his youth.

The North American Indians believed that the Great Spirit had given to all creatures certain outstanding abilities or powers. Some had courage, strength, speed, or cunning. They believed these abilities could be transmitted to those who were mentally or spiritually able to communicate with these animals and birds. Thus the black-tail deer was swift, wary, keen-sensed. He was seldom killed on the game trail since he was protected by living in rough country with abundant vegetation cover.

When one was killed the hunter preserved the entire skin including the head, legs and hoofs. He believed that by wearing this hide in battle he was protected from bullet, arrow and lance. Simply wearing the skin did not provide this protection. The warrior had to pray to the spirit of the dead deer, enlisting its help after performing rituals to contact the spirit.

One of the owners of a protective black-tail deerskin was High Crane, a Minneconjou Sioux. In 1876 in South Dakota an advance unit of General Crook's army made a surprise dawn attack on a small camp of Amerinds. The survivors were driven from the camp into gullies and caves from which the warriors continued to fight. Sitting Bull and Crazy Horse were in another camp at the time, not far distant. A request for help was sent to them.

The two chiefs with about 800 warriors did not hesitate to come to the assistance of the surviving warriors and their families who were now trapped in a cave. This, despite the fact that they had few guns and little ammunition, and would be forced to rely on bows and arrows. The party reached the besieged cave about noon only to discover that General Crook had arrived with the main body of his troops. Now the white soldiers outnumbered the warriors at least two to one. And the soldiers had accurate, far-shooting carbines.

Sitting Bull and Crazy Horse lined up their warriors out of rifle range and held a council. To charge 2,000 armed soldiers with bows and arrows would be suicide. Since they had wiped out Custer and his men three months earlier, the war had gone against the Sioux. Food was scarce and ammunition was short. Then Sitting Bull remembered that one of his warriors, High Crane, had a black-tail deerskin with its magical power against bullets.

The chief asked High Crane to ride alone against 2,000 riflemen. The warrior did not hesitate. He pulled the big hide over his body, head over his head, tied the forelegs to his arms, the hind legs to his own legs, then mounted his pony. He rode out in front of the troops. Bullets whined around High Crane and his pony. Bullets plowed the ground and cut the grass over which he rode. He was in the midst of a storm of lead, yet not one pellet touched the warrior or his mount. Within easy rifle range he rode, back and forth, back and forth.

The soldiers and their officers were awe-stricken, utterly bewildered. In the face of High Crane's tremendous courage and mysterious invincibility, one by one they ceased firing. What weird strategy was this? Were the wily Sitting Bull and Crazy Horse preparing for some other surprise? Orders were given and the line of troops withdrew 500 yards. The next day the troops pulled out completely.

Thus ended the battle of Slim Buttes, in northern South Dakota, in September 1876.[13]

13

Wigwam Wizardry

It was at Fort Fitzgerald in far northwestern Canada that Jean W. Godsell had her first experience with the moccasin telegraph—the Amerindian's extrasensory perception (ESP). It was late autumn, and she and her husband watched the departure of the Caribou Eater Indians for their winter hunting grounds in the Hill Island Lake country to the eastward. They felt a deep compassion for the motherless daughters of the chief, Marie and Therese Cheesie, aged six and seven respectively. They were staggering down the river bank with bundles as heavy as their own slim bodies to load into the boats. In the far wilderness they would help their father with the chores of his life as a hunter and trapper.

"Poor little mites!" she exclaimed.

"It's tough," her husband replied, "but it's part of their life."

As the winter months passed, Jean Godsell occasionally thought of those two little girls far off in the frozen wilderness. "I could picture them," she wrote, "in their caribou-skin dresses setting their rabbit snares; cutting wood to keep the wigwam fire alive, and bending beneath huge loads of faggots as they snowshoed through the silent woods."

One bitterly cold morning John Daniels, their Indian interpreter, burst into the kitchen. "Indians will come today," he said excitedly.

"How do you know, John?" she asked. "We have no contact with the outside world and not a living soul has come into the fort for weeks."

165

"I know, I just know," he answered. "They have had plenty of bad luck, too. They come," he pointed to the meridian, "before the sun reach here."

Shortly after lunch Constable Bob Baker of the Royal Canadian Mounted Police invited Jean Godsell to accompany him outside the fort. "I've spotted a couple of Indians coming this way from the east. Let's see who they are."

Out on the ice a dog team was moving slowly toward the fort. Ahead of the dogs was a diminutive, fur-clad figure wearing snowshoes and breaking a trail for the team. Behind the sled was another small figure. Five emaciated dogs panted and tugged as the sled came up the river bank. By this time Jean Godsell, Constable Baker and John Daniels had been joined by a group of Amerindians.

As the two figures and the sled approached the trading post, the spectators stared in astonishment. It was six-year-old Marie Cheesie who was breaking the trail, and it was seven-year-old Therese who was urging the dogs on with shrill cries and a caribou-hide whip. At last the sled stopped and the weary dogs sat down. The faces of the girls were seared and blackened with frostbite, their hair and clothing white with frost.

John Daniels questioned the girls in Chippewyan and they replied in monosyllables. Suddenly the squaws in the group covered their faces with their shawls and began crying.

"What's the trouble, John?" Jean Godsell inquired. "Where is their father?"

John pointed at the sled. "Their father is there, under the canvas and blankets," he explained. "Chief Cheesie died way out in the bush eight sleeps to the eastward. These kids tied him to the sled and they trek well over a hundred miles through the woods to bring him to the fort so the mission people can bury him proper. I told you Indians who have bad luck come today."

"How did you know?" Constable Baker asked.

"Last night I had a dream," he answered. "Saw everything, just like right now."

Jean Godsell reports another instance of moccasin telegraph, which can include telepathy, clairvoyance and prophetic visions or dreams. It happened at Fort Churchill on Hudson Bay in northern Manitoba. One year the ship bringing supplies was long overdue. The residents were worried since winter was approaching and their very existence depended on this annual cargo. At the log trading store Ashton Alston, the factor, was issuing ammunition to the men so they could hunt caribou along the coast to supplement their slim rations.

"I wonder what could have happened to that ship," said John Tremayne, the inspector, one afternoon. As he spoke an elderly leather-visaged Amerind entered the store.

"Suppose we ask old Shonkelli, the medicine man, here," suggested the factor. He spoke to the medicine man who agreed to locate the ship for a substantial gift of tobacco. After receiving the gift he left the store and went to his wigwam where he went into a trance. He returned at sundown.

"I had a vision," he explained. "I sent my spirit body out over the water. The ship is safe."

Shonkelli said the vessel would arrive late because it had paused to rescue the marooned crew from another ship that had been lost in the ice of Hudson Straits. They had had some bad luck on their own. One man, wearing clothes like a woman, had died and been buried at sea. "Tomorrow, when the sun is there," he concluded as he pointed at the sky, "the white man's ship will come."

The following day, at the time indicated by the medicine man, the ship came into view. After the excitement had died down, Alston and Tremayne learned the cause of the delay from the captain. In the Hudson Straits they had sighted on an ice floe the stranded crew of a foundered vessel. They went to their rescue, and then they were caught in heavy pack ice for days. A final bit of ill luck occurred only a few days out from port. A Roman Catholic priest en route to a Manitoba mission had fallen overboard and drowned. Surely Shonkelli was blessed with Amerind ESP.[1]

Then there was the man who talked with the seagulls. A report of this incident was contributed by a member of the Society for the Investigation of the Unexplained, founded by the late Ivan T. Sanderson, and published in the organization's quarterly, *Pursuit*. The witness was working in a remote area of Alaska in the early 1950s. One morning an older Amerind fellow workman disappeared, and when he returned he was very worried about his wife. He said that she was seriously ill and that he had to go to her. She was 500 miles away. The Amerind explained that he had gone to talk to the seagulls and they had told him about his wife. At the time the only available communication with the outside world was a shortwave radio, and it was not in operating condition.

The radio was repaired, the pilot was contacted, and he stated that upon landing at the island the wife's illness was confirmed. Despite the fact that there had been no advance notice of the Amerind's arrival, the only automobile on the island was waiting to drive them to the village some thirteen miles distant. The pilot had no explanation for the fact that the taxi was there to meet them. Later, when the Amerind returned to his job, he said it was a good thing that he had gone to talk with the seagulls.

In commenting on this report, the journal's editor suggests several possible theories. It is known that psychic sensitives use their crystal balls, tea leaves, etc., not as sources of information per se, but as objects which help them to concentrate as they receive the "message" from some other source.

"It seems unlikely," writes the editor, "that the seagulls as such convey even simple bits of information from one human to another, but it is possible that a tribe or even a family of Amerinds might choose, say, a seagull as a sort of guardian angel and thus an unwitting intermediary in an exchange of news by what is now called mental telepathy. It is unfortunate that the Amerind was not quizzed more thoroughly, but this, of course, may not have been possible for many reasons." [2]

Smoke signals have been used both by some Amerinds and the Australian aborigines. While in some instances the signals themselves convey a message, in others the signals may simply be an attention-getting device, the information actually being sent by telepathy. This seems to be particularly true of the Australians.

In a contemporary instance, telepathy may have been a factor or it may have been simply clairvoyance. Several years ago two explorer scouts, aged fifteen and sixteen, remained behind their troop in the desolate Nakai Canyon in Arizona to search for an ancient ruin. They became lost in the rocky wilderness of the 16-million-acre Navajo Reservation. They suffered from hunger and thirst, blazing hot days and bone-chilling nights. Search parties failed to find the boys.

On the fifth day three members of one search party sought help from Jack Crank, a medicine man. Crank said he would need the assistance of his aunt, Bela Arquot. As Crank recited incantations, the old women went into a semitrance. When she came out of it, she drew a crude map and marked a spot on it. "The boys you seek are there," she said. "They have been found by a Navajo and are unharmed."

The men compared the woman's drawing with an aerial map they had with them. Later they learned that the boys had been found at that exact spot by Neski Yazzi, a Navajo cattleman, only minutes before Bela Arquot went into her trance.

Paul A. Hout, a professional historian, tells the strange and pathetic story of Piks-ah-ki, a Crow Amerind woman. He found it in the diary of Ames Porter, a young New Englander who left his home in the 1870s to live among the Blackfoot Amerinds in Montana.

On an autumn day in 1878 Porter and an Amerindian companion rode their horses out of the Blackfoot camp and into the mountains to hunt. Later, while resting their horses, they observed a woman walking slowly toward them, occasionally stopping to look in all directions. When she finally approached them, they found she was an exceptionally beautiful young woman. Her two braids of glossy black hair signified that she was married.

She greeted them with a smile as she unslung her pack. Her language was that of the Crow tribe far to the south. She gratefully accepted their offer of food, and while it was being prepared she told her story. She was looking for Two Bears, her tall and handsome warrior husband. She had awakened one morning a few weeks earlier to find him gone. Also missing was his gun and his black and white pinto with its distinctive markings. Apparently he had gone hunting. She awaited his return all that day and the following night, then she went to the chief who organized search parties. Finally the search came to an end. "He must be dead," the chief said. "Maybe an enemy or a bear killed him, maybe he drowned." But Piks-ah-ki was certain he was alive. She waited as the days passed.

Then she had her first dream. It told her that her husband was lying wounded and ill in a camp of the prairie people far to the north. She had the same dream on the next two nights. On the fourth night she was told in her dream that her husband was sad and lonely and was crying for her. She must find him! She left the camp and started walking north. Finally she came to a river where she spent the night. There she had another dream. It told her that information she must have would be found in a camp along this river, but first she must go into the mountains. She met Porter and his companion on her fourth day in the mountains.

The two men urged her to come with them to the Blackfoot

camp where she could rest. Since it was on the river that she had dreamed about, she might obtain there the information she sought. Members of many tribes came there to trade and visit. She could ask them about her missing husband. She was welcomed at the camp and given a snug lodge.

Weeks passed. All visitors were asked if they knew anything about her husband Two Bears. The answer was always no. Finally one morning a band of Blood Amerindians rode into camp. One of them was riding a black and white pinto with distinctive markings. With a scream, Piks-ah-ki ran up to the rider. "I know this horse. It belongs to my husband. Where did you get it?"

"It is mine," replied the startled rider.

"It is my man's horse," she insisted. "I'd know it anywhere. You must know about my husband since you have his horse. Where is he?"

The Blood warrior hesitated, then spoke with obvious reluctance. "We went to war. Away to the south. One day I saw this man who had this horse. I struck him with my club. He did not die, and then I was sorry I had struck him. I carried him to my lodge where he lay wounded and sick for many days. Finally one night when the moon was high, he died. I kept his horse."

Sobbing, she turned and ran to her lodge where she covered her head with a shawl. Then she walked up the hill behind the camp to a spot that overlooked the valley. There she remained, grieving for three days, refusing to eat any of the food that was brought to her. Dawn was breaking on the fourth day when she arose, walked down the hill and entered her lodge. After an hour or so the Blackfoot elders decided to find out if she needed any assistance. They found her lying on her bed of furs.

"I am about to die," she said. When the elders remonstrated, she smiled. "You don't understand," she continued. "I die happy because I misinterpreted my dream. I thought I was to seek my man in the flesh. Instead, it was meant for my shadow to seek his shadow. Tonight I start. This time I know I'll find him."

That night, as the moon rose and cast scintillating flickers on the rippling river, Piks-ah-ki died. And as was the custom of the Blackfoot, her body was placed to rest in the strong boughs of a cottonwood tree. This is the story found in the century-old diary of a white man who lived for a time in the camp where she died.[3]

Prophetic dreams and visions are a part of Amerind ESP as they are in the psychic experiences of all races. Two of the famous psychic sensitives who dreamed true were Crazy Horse and Sitting Bull. Both are said to have had premonitions of the Battle of the Little Big Horn. Sitting Bull had his vision of victory during a special Sun Dance held two weeks before the conflict. As for Crazy Horse, his vision revealed how he could attain that victory.

Alvin M. Josephy, Jr., is a historian, an editor of *American Heritage* magazine, and was editor-in-charge of the *American Heritage Book of Indians*. "No question about it," he says, "Crazy Horse had strong medicine. He had very strong supernatural powers—much stronger than those of the average Indian religious leader." [4]

Robert Burnett, chief of the Rosebud Sioux in Rosebud, South Dakota, says he has talked to people who were present when he had his visions. "First he would have a vision," Burnett explains, "then he would tell the tribe what to do, based on the vision, and everything always happened exactly the way he said it would."

As told by the Sioux, Crazy Horse had a prevision of the entire battle days before it took place. It, together with his skill in military tactics, enabled him to defeat General George Custer's superbly trained force. He saw that there was a bluff in the battlefield's center, and through it was a small ravine that was hidden by brush.

In June 1876, General Custer and 264 men of the Seventh Cavalry confronted the native Americans at the Little Big Horn. Crazy Horse (so named because a wild pony was seen dashing through the village just as he was born) charged the soldiers shouting, "Today is a good day to fight, today is a good day to die."

Custer took up a fighting position with the bluff at his back for protection. Crazy Horse, trusting in his dream, sent several hundred men to look for the small ravine. They found it and attacked Custer from the rear. Every man in this surrounded group of cavalrymen was killed in a desperate battle that lasted only half an hour. [5]

Another famous Amerind leader with powers of precognition was Geronimo. Examples of his ESP are given by Geronimo's cousin, Betzinez, in his book *I Fought With Geronimo*. [6]

Shortly before he surrendered, the Apache chief made a final foraging raid into Chihuahua, Mexico. Betzinez was sitting next to him at meal time watching the chief cut a chunk of beef. Suddenly a strange look came into Geronimo's eyes and his body stiffened as he dropped the knife and rose to his feet. "Men," he said, "United States troops have captured our base camp, and our people there are prisoners. We will have to go back."

The Apaches' base encampment was 120 miles away, and Betzinez knew there had been no messenger or smoke signals. They broke camp the same night and started back. Four nights later Geronimo had a vision and made a prediction: "Tomorrow afternoon as we march along the north side of the mountains we will see a man on a hill to our left. He will cry out to us, and tell us that the troops have captured our camp."

The next afternoon, as they came within fifteen miles of the base camp, the messenger appeared just as Geronimo said he would. The messenger came down the hill to inform Geronimo that U.S. cavalrymen, trailing the Apaches into Mexico, had surprised and captured the entire band at the encampment.

Some prophets are specialists, and there is one who in recent years baffled the U.S. Weather Bureau. Chief Billy Bowlegs of the Seminoles forecasts hurricanes. Within a hundred miles of modern Miami, Florida, the Seminoles still live in the Everglades much the same as their ancestors did before the white man arrived. They are known as the only tribe which never surrendered to the U.S. government.

Chief Bowlegs has a little jade statue of Hurakan, the wind god of the ancient Mayans. In some undisclosed manner the storm god through this statue sends the chief warnings of hurricanes days before the U.S. Weather Bureau has any inkling of their existence. This enables him to lead his people deeper into the Everglades to a rock-bound retreat where they are safe from the mighty winds. For three days they travel by boats through the canals and marshes to the retreat where they pitch camp and remain until the chief knows it is safe to return to their homes.

One of the worst hurricanes to strike Florida occurred in 1926, taking 372 lives. After hitting the coast, the storm swept inland straight for Lake Oxahatchee, home of the Seminoles. So strong had been the wild winds that relief workers found the village huts smashed to kindling and even the waters of the lake had been swept away. But the Seminoles were safe in their retreat where Chief Bowlegs had taken them two weeks before the Weather Bureau in Miami had any reason to suspect the hurricane.

It would appear that the jade statue is a focal point for the chief in receiving his ESP information. Asked to comment, an official of the Weather Bureau at Miami said: "The only thing we know about it is that it works. Sometimes our predictions are inaccurate because it is impossible to forecast the capricious turns these storms often take. But those Indians never miss. Somehow they always seem to know whther there is any danger or not."

For example, in 1944 Florida seemed to be the target for two hurricanes. One changed its course and seemed to have missed Florida, only to turn back, strike inland from the Gulf of Mexico and seriously damage the citrus crop across most of the state. The second hurricane was headed for the coast between Miami and Jacksonville. Warnings were out all along the coast. The Navy and Coast Guard moved its planes and personnel inland. But the storm turned, missed Florida and struck far northward.

The Seminoles moved out and went to their retreat before the first hurricane, which seemed to offer no danger. Then, when the second seemed certain to strike, Chief Billy Bowlegs and his people remained quietly in their village.[7]

Another medicine man said to have been able to forecast the outcome of battles and raids was Sky-Walker, also known as *Do-ha-te*, the owl prophet. He practiced his seership during the 1870s when his tribe, the Kiowas, had joined forces with the Comanches and other tribes in their efforts to stop the westward advance of white settlers into the frontier country of Oklahoma and Texas.

The Owl Prophet was an almost legendary character who became master of all medicine men of the allied tribes. According to his fellow tribesmen, his prophesying went far beyond determining the victor in an impending conflict, but included events during the struggle, as well as the number of warriors and the enemy who would be slain. He would bring the chiefs together in council on a hilltop around a campfire the night before an engagement. After he had chanted, from out of the darkness would come the sound of beating wings and the screeching cries of an owl. The prophet would listen to the cries, then interpret their meanings to the chiefs. He said it was his deceased ancestors who spoke to him through his oracle, the owl.

Once, it is said, his oracle informed him that two parties of whites would pass along the old Butterfield Trail in northern Texas a few hours apart. The first would be a small group easily overwhelmed, but it must not be attacked. The second and larger party should be taken. As the war party waited in ambush, a wagon with a small detachment of soldiers passed by. The impatient warriors wanted to attack, but the Owl Prophet restrained them. About three hours later a train of ten wagons came along the trail and was successfully taken. It was learned later that the first party had consisted of General Philip Sheridan and his escort, who had been sent west to investigate Amerind atrocities. If Sheridan had been killed, quite likely full-scale reprisals against the tribes would have been undertaken by the government.

The Owl Prophet, however, is remembered by his people for an apparent display of black magic that marked the end of his life. A powerful Kiowa chief, Kicking Bird, realizing the futility of war, had succeeded in taking a large number of natives, including an estimated three-fourths of the Kiowas, to Fort Sill, Oklahoma, to live in peace with the white man. There is little doubt that by so doing he saved the lives of hundreds of innocent persons. At the same time he made many enemies among the warriors who were still resisting the white advance.

By 1875 the Kiowas and Comanches had been reduced to only small groups of warriors, and in late February of that year even they realized the uselessness of further resistance. They were persuaded to come to Fort Sill and surrender. Among them was the Owl Prophet. The government, however, had decided that the most incorrigible of the warriors and their leaders should be sent to St. Augustine, Florida, for confinement. Kicking Bird was asked to select the ones to go, and he chose seventy-four Kiowas, Comanches and Cheyennes, including the Owl Prophet.

On April 28 the prisoners were loaded into wagons for the long journey. Kicking Bird rode up on his horse and spoke to the Kiowas. He said he was sorry they were being punished, but that he loved them all and would endeavor to get them released as soon as possible. He was interrupted by the Owl Prophet who called him a traitor to his race, and concluded his tirade with the threat, "You will not live long, I'll see to that!"

As the wagons bearing the chained prisoners made their way toward Florida, a medicine man named Eagle Chief asked the Owl Prophet to pray that Kicking Bird soon would die. Despite the fact that the laws of his medicine forbade the killing of a fellow tribesman by magic and he would lose his own life if he were to pray Kicking Bird to death, the Owl Prophet agreed to do it. He told his fellow prisoners that at dawn in just four days, Kicking Bird would die.

On the morning of May 4 the forty-year-old Kicking Bird, a man who had enjoyed excellent health, suddenly collapsed in great pain. The agency doctor was unable to help him, and before noon he was dead. The doctor's report stated that the chief "died suddenly May 4, supposed to have been poisoned, probably through jealousy or anger by some of his tribe." This supposition the Kiowas to this day have refused to accept.

Word of Kicking Bird's death reached the Florida-bound prisoners a few days later. The Owl Prophet knew his own fate was sealed. As the prisoners reached the prison at Fort Marion, he died of "natural causes." [8]

Brad Steiger, in his book *Medicine Power*, tells the story of a century-old curse that doomed the Navajo Long Salt family. About the year 1825 a man in the family began suffering nightmares allegedly caused by the spirit of a slain enemy. The victim's brothers obtained the services of an old, blind shaman who held a three-day ceremony over the afflicted man.

Part of the payment demanded by the shaman was five butchered sheep from the family flock. Several Long Salt men were assigned to slaughter and prepare the sheep, but being lazy and finding that the sheep were grazing at some distance from the village, they decided to substitute five wild antelope in their place. After all, the medicine man was blind. Even the family members who presented the carcasses to the medicine man did not detect the substitution, since the heads and lower legs had been removed.

A few weeks later a man in the family suddenly died. One by one other members of the family became ill and died. Then when the lazy ones confessed that they had substituted the antelope for the sheep, it became apparent that the medicine man had set a *chindi*, an avenging evil spirit among them.

A delegation representing the Long Salts called on the blind medicine man. Yes, the shaman said, he had indeed set a *chindi* against the family with instructions that the entire family should die. He had been very angry about the substitution, which he considered an insult.

The delegation begged the shaman to recall the evil demon. They pointed out that they had been duped as well as he. Already several Long Salts had died. Would he not consider himself sufficiently avenged?

Impressed by their arguments, the medicine man explained that perhaps his anger had been too great over a matter of five sheep, but the act had been a challenge to his dignity and reputation. For a price, he would remove the curse. However, he would have to consider what the price would be, and he asked the delegation to return in ten days.

The delegation left, and when they returned on the tenth day they learned to their horror that the shaman had suddenly died. Moreover, he had not recalled the *chindi* before his death, for when they returned home they found several members of the family ill and dying. At the time there were about a hundred Long Salts. Despite annual additions by births, the number of Long Salts steadily declined as the years passed. By 1900 only ten were living.[9]

Writing in the *Frontier Times* (August–September, 1967), John R. Winslowe tells how he met that last surviving member of the Long Salts in 1925. She was a slender girl named Alice.

"Alice Long Salt was born in 1912," Winslowe states. "There were then only five of the family remaining, and all were young. They were her parents, two uncles and an aunt. Curiously, anyone marrying into the family met the same fate as a blood Long Salt. Alice's mother died when the girl reached seven and while she was attending the Tuba City boarding school at the Indian agency. Alice's father became skin and bones, dying two years later. That left her an orphan. The remaining three Long Salts were ill, crippled and helpless. Friends cared for them, watching them fade into nothing before their eyes."

At the agency school Alice had been the top student in her class. Soon after she became the last of the Long Salts, she became dull and listless. Within a few months she became ill with a disease that puzzled the medical doctors who examined her.

Determined to protect the girl from the curse, a fairly well-to-do man named Hosteen Behegade adopted Alice. He had medicine men from throughout the Navajo country come and conduct their sings. Each hoped he would be the one whose medicine would dispel the *chindi*, but they could not surpass the power of the long-dead blind man.

"By late 1927," Winslowe wrote, "Behegade had expended all his property and was heavily in debt, fighting bravely for the girl's life. That year Behegade evolved a plan. To finish off the stricken girl the *chindi* had to be present. His idea was to keep moving constantly, concealing his trail. By this means he could prevent the *chindi* from locating Alice.

"One dark night an owl hooted close by. At dawn Alice Long

Salt was too weak to leave her blankets. The *chindi* had found its innocent victim again. From then on Behegade always obeyed the owl's hoot, believing that it had come to his aid against the *chindi*."

The man and the girl became wanderers, fleeing back and forth across the Navajo country. During the winter of 1928 they sought refuge from a blizzard in a hogan near the trading post on Red Mesa. With deep snow and howling winds, the blizzard became the worst snowstorm in years. Perhaps the storm was a protection, perhaps it would thwart the demon with its evil mission of vengeance.

As the storm raged outside, the pair slept peacefully. In the morning Behegade arose and walked over to the blanket covered figure of his adopted daughter. Alice Long Salt was dead. The century-long pursuit of a doomed family had reached its end at last.

14

The Curse of Tippecanoe

IN THE WAKE of the white man's advance and the conflict between white and red cultures, there arose prophets who either sought to preserve the old ways or to find a compromise between the beliefs and customs of the races. Only one, the great Handsome Lake of the Iroquois, succeeded in forging a compromise religion that has lasted among a minority of the tribe to the present day.

One of the last of these prophets was a Nevada Paiute named Wovoka. In 1889 he had a vision in which he talked with the Great Spirit. An Amerindian Messiah was coming. He would resurrect the dead, bring back the great buffalo herds, and the Amerindians would once more be masters of their land. His followers performed a trancelike dance, often dancing until they dropped exhausted. It was called the Ghost Dance by the whites because the teaching was that the spirits of the dead Amerindians were present to help the living in this time of their oppression. This is what Wovoka promised:

The Great Spirit told us that all of our dead were to be resurrected; that they were all to come back to earth and that, as the earth was too small for them and us, he would do away with heaven and make the earth itself large enough to contain us all; that we must tell all the people we meet about these things. He spoke to us about fighting, and said that it was bad and that we must keep away from it; that the earth was to be all good hereafter and we must all be friends with one another.

He said that in the fall of the year, the youth of all good people would be renewed, so that nobody would be more than forty years old and that, if they behave themselves well after this, the youth of every one would be renewed in the spring. He said if we were all good he would send people among us who could heal all our wounds and sickness by mere touch and that we would live forever. He told us not to quarrel or fight or strike each other, or shoot one another; that the Whites and Indians were to be all one people. He said if any man disobeyed what he ordered, his tribe would be wiped from the face of the earth; that we must believe everything he said, and we must not doubt him or say he lied; that if we did, he would know it; that he would know our thoughts and actions in no matter what part of the world we might be.

The new faith spread rapidly throughout the west, and then east where it was welcomed by the Sioux. It united the tribes and caused enemies to become friends. It aroused new hopes and intensified the mysticism of the past.

Fearful that this great revival with its mounting excitement might lead to violence and renewed hostilities, the government decided to disarm its followers. Sitting Bull was killed at the height of the tension.

On December 29, 1890, a unit of the Seventh Cavalry rounded up around 300 Hunkpapa Sioux, two-thirds of them women and children, in freezing weather at Wounded Knee Creek, South Dakota. Four Hotchkiss guns were set up and aimed at the camp. As they were disarming the men, a disturbance broke out and a shot was fired. The soldiers immediately began an intensive fire at point-blank range. Many fell in the first volley. The surviving warriors attacked the cavalrymen with their bare hands or what weapons they still had, and succeeded in killing twenty-nine of them. The Hotchkiss guns hurled two-pound explosive shells at the rate of fifty a minute. The hundreds of maddened soldiers fired as long as there was a moving target and long after all resistance had ceased. Some of the women were pursued several miles before they were caught and slain. One surviving squaw named Blue Whirlwind received fourteen wounds. Only a few escaped the massacre.

With the burial at Wounded Knee of the dead in a communal pit went the last hopes of the red men. The white man with superior numbers and arms had triumphed. Their spirits were crushed, their faith destroyed. All they had now were fading memories of a happier time known to their long-dead fathers.

Wovoka died in obscurity in 1932, but some of his teachings were absorbed into the peyote cults that continue to exist. The imagined utopia of yesterday is today a psychedelic dream.[1]

Once there was another prophet—Tens-Ka-Ta-Wah, or Elskatawa, meaning "The Open Door," but called by the Americans simply "the Prophet." He certainly deserved the title, for he made one of the most amazing true prophecies in American history and left a grim legacy that still haunts the United States presidency. His brother was the great Tecumseh (Shooting Star), considered by many historians to embody the highest conception of Amerindian character.

The remarkable crusade of the Shawnee brothers began with a dream. One night while living in a White River village in Indiana, Elskatawa fell asleep. When he awakened he was a man with a vision. He had made a visit to the realm of spirits, he told the villagers, and there he had been given a new religion that would save the red man.

A curious mixture of Amerind and Christian doctrines, the new faith's basic tenets were a return to the simple life of their forefathers and the avoidance of everything connected with the white man's civilization. Abstinence from liquor was advocated, as well as an end to all conflict between tribes. Speaking through the Prophet, the Great Spirit laid down rules governing courtship, marriage, daily bathing and limitations on intercourse and trading with the whites. Inspired or not, it was at least a well-planned program of Amerind reform, and it spread rapidly through the woodland tribes.

Behind this revival was a political menace. A relentless tide of settlers was coming from the east, and by 1808 a series of treaties made by General William Henry Harrison with widely scattered tribes had deprived the Amerind of most of the southern third of the present state of Indiana. The signing of the Treaty of Fort Wayne alone cost the native Americans three million acres between the Wabash and White Rivers.

The Prophet was a man with great oratorical ability and apostolic fervor. His brother Tecumseh was a fearless, upright leader with a deep love for his troubled race. A brilliant statesman, Tecumseh realized the need for political unity among the tribes, and he attempted to make the land the common property of all. By stopping the piecemeal cession of lands, he hoped to stop the westward advance of the whites without bloodshed. His motto was simply "America for the Americans."

Together, the Shawnee brothers labored to create the second great Indian confederacy. The Prophet's faith served to fuse into emotional unity the peoples that his brother was attempting to lead with practical statesmanship. They tried, first, to get an agreement from the tribes not to sell any more land, but the chieftains were reluctant to surrender their traditional rights of making treaties. Nevertheless, some progress was made, and General Harrison, at his Indiana Territory headquarters at Vincennes, decided to act.

He sent a message to all the tribes: "Who is this pretended prophet who dares speak in the name of the Great Creator? If he is really a prophet, ask him to cause the sun to stand still—the moon to alter its course——the rivers to cease to flow—or the dead to arise from their graves."

The Prophet accepted the challenge. He boldly announced that around noon on June 16, 1806, he would cause darkness to come over the sun as evidence of his supernatural powers. To the utter bewilderment of the tribes, his prophecy came true. It is possible, of course, that he had information from a white man who owned an almanac, but during this period he had little contact with whites and was spending much of his time in fasting and long periods of trance.

Meanwhile, Tecumseh was determined to hold the Ohio River as a dividing line between the races. He tirelessly visited tribes from Wisconsin to Florida, seeking support for his confederacy and an end to tribal treaties. "Sell the land!" he pleaded. "Why not sell the air, the clouds, and the great sea . . . Did not the Great Spirit make them all for the use of all his children?"

In June 1808, the brothers and a large band of their followers gathered from many tribes moved to the west bank of the Wabash River, near the mouth of the Tippecanoe, and built Prophet's Town. Intoxicants were prohibited. Crops were planted in the surrounding fields. The town grew rapidly as hundreds of warriors broke away from their stubborn chiefs. Tecumseh too had the help of the British, who hoped to establish an Indian buffer state to the rear of the American colonies. A steady stream of men and arms flowed between Fort Malden in Canada and Prophet's Town.

During the winter of 1809–1810 feeling ran high as the situation grew more tense. For the most part the Miamis and Delawares remained peaceful, but the Kickapoo, Potawatomi, Winnebago and

Wyandot tribes sent war parties to the Wabash where they joined the deserters from the peaceful nations. Turbulent mass meetings inspired by the Prophet's oratory added to the state of angry unrest.

General Harrison became alarmed. He summoned Tecumseh to a grand council at Vincennes in August 1810, and Tecumseh came, still hoping to avert bloodshed. But the conference was futile. The two leaders could not agree on the problem of land sales. Tecumseh then proposed a truce while he visited the Creeks and other tribes in the south, after which he planned to see President James Madison in an effort to solve completely the difficulties existing between the two peoples.

Harrison's opinion of Tecumseh is of interest:

The implicit obedience and respect which the followers of Tecumseh pay to him is really astonishing and more than any other circumstance bespeaks him one of those uncommon geniuses, while spring up occasionally to produce revolutions and overturn the established order of things. If it were not for the vicinity of the United States, he would, perhaps, be the founder of an empire that would rival in glory Mexico or Peru.

One of Tecumseh's complaints at the grand council was that in the Treaty of Fort Wayne signed the year before, other tribes had disposed of lands to which the Shawnees had a claim. Harrison's reply was that he would refer the question of ownership of the land to the President. "Well," said Tecumseh, "as the Great Chief is to determine the matter, I hope the Great Spirit will put sense enough into his head to induce you to give up this land . . . he is so far off that he will not be injured by this war; he may sit in his town and drink his wine, whilst you and I will have to fight it out!"

It was in 1807—a year before the founding of Prophet's Town— that an astonishing prophecy was included in a lengthy message sent to all the tribes by the Prophet. It can only be regarded as one of the most incredible previsions in history. And as R. E. Banta writes in his book *The Ohio:* "There is no question as to the authenticity of either the talk or the prophecy." It was read by Le Maiquois—the Trout—a follower of the Prophet, to a gathering of Chippewas and other Lakes Indians at Michilimackinac on May 4, 1807, and was reported in full in a letter from Captain Dunham, commandant of that post, to General William Hull at Detroit in that same month.[2]

The prophecy was as follows: "Now, therefore, my children, listen to my voice, it is that of the Great Spirit! 'If you hearken to my counsel and follow my instructions for four years, then there will be two days of darkness, during which I shall tread unseen through the land and cause the animals, such as they were formerly when I created them, to come forth out of the earth . . .' " [3] It was the Prophet's plan to have this talk with its forecast of catastrophe circulated among the tribes "during the summer and fall of 1807—four years and a small varying fraction before December 1811."

By the year 1811 the prophecy was being repeated by Tecumseh and had gotten down to actual dates. At the time of the Battle of Tippecanoe Tecumseh was in the south seeking the support of the Cherokees and the Creeks. While visiting the Creek Chief Big Warrior at Tuckhabatchee on the Tallapoosa River, in the late fall of that year, Tecumseh stated that a great earthquake would occur the day he returned to Detroit and the Creek villages would be destroyed.

Thomas L. McKenney, coauthor of the book *History of the Indian Tribes of North America*, obtained the account of this forecast from Big Warrior himself. The chief said that Tecumseh told him: "You have taken my talk and the sticks, and the wampum and the hatchet, but you do not mean to fight. I know the reason. You do not believe the Great Spirit has sent me. You shall know! I leave Tuckhabatchee directly, and I shall go to Detroit. When I arrive there, I will stamp on the ground with my foot, and shake down every house in Tuckhabatchee." [4]

Tecumseh had given strict orders to avoid conflict while he was in the south. There were widespread reports of war preparations at Prophet's Town, however, and General Harrison received an order from President Madison to break up the rendezvous on the Wabash. With an army of about 900 men, Harrison came within sight of the town on the afternoon of November 6, 1811, and camped on a plateau about a mile away.

Following the lead of General Harrison's account, most historians have blamed the Prophet for precipitating the battle. The story is that he assembled the warriors and brought out the magic bowl and the talismans, which he assured the braves would protect them from the soldiers' bullets. Then during the fighting, it is said, he stood on a high rock overlooking the battlefield uttering magical incantations. On the other hand, a settlement of Shakers then living near the town said that the Prophet and some of his followers abstained from the fighting, and that the battle was precipitated in spite of him.

The attack on Harrison's camp came in the misty Hoosier dawn. A good part of the battle consisted of bitter, deadly hand-to-hand struggle. Soon after daylight Harrison managed to organize his forces for a series of charges, and the warriors were driven into a nearby swamp and scattered. His victory was a costly one—nearly a fourth of his men were killed or wounded. In comparison, Amerindian casualties were small. On the following morning Harrison rode to Prophet's Town, now deserted, and burned the village with all its supplies. Then, with his dead and wounded, he returned to Vincennes.

Days later, as Tecumseh was traveling north but still below the Ohio River, messengers told him of the disaster. For him, the work of a decade lay in ruins. Skirting the settlements, he made his way to Detroit. Meanwhile, the Prophet with a group of his faithful followers had reached Fort Malden, at the mouth of the Detroit River on the Ontario side, where they placed themselves under the protection of the British.

A few weeks after the battle a horde of squirrels, stirred by some mysterious impulse, pressed south from Indiana. They poured into the Ohio River, swimming, clinging to drifting bits of wood. Thousands of lifeless bodies drifted downstream, a mute warning of the terror to come.

Then, thirty-seven days after the Battle of Tippecanoe, at two o'clock on the morning of December 16, the earth moved. Amerindians and settlers were awakened by an ominous rumbling that slowly grew in intensity. They hurried from their dwellings into the night. A weird glow lit the sky as the ground swayed under their running feet. Dazed and bewildered, they huddled beneath trees as inanimate objects around them danced and groaned with a sudden life born of chaos.

Through the long night and the light of dawn, shock succeeded shock as the earth buckled and rocked. Centering around New Madrid, Missouri, the quakes were felt over a region of more than 300,000 square miles. A district of 30,000 square miles sank from five to twenty-five feet, while other areas were raised by similar amounts.

Reelfoot Lake in Tennessee, eighteen miles long, was created. At several places the Mississippi and Ohio Rivers flowed backward, and the course of the Mississippi was changed for hundreds of miles. Several hundred lakes and islands were formed on a 300-mile front from the mouth of the Ohio to the St. Francis River. As the convulsions continued, some of these lakes, miles in extent, were formed or drained in less than an hour. Thousands of trees choked the river currents.

Rising and falling in sickening waves, the earth's surface split into fissures, some half a mile long, and sulphurous gases poured out. Trees were bent until their branches interlocked into a leafy ceiling. Landslides swept furiously down bluffs and river banks, the entire cemetery at New Madrid being carried away into the river.

"When the tremors were felt," an eyewitness reported, "houses crumbled, trees waved together and the ground sank. Undulations increased in elevation as they advanced, and when they had attained a certain fearful height the earth would burst, and vast volumes of water and sand and pit-coal were discharged, as high as the tops of the trees, leaving large chasms where the ground had opened." Dust darkened the skies for days throughout the region.

From a scientific standpoint the shock of December 16, 1811, was the worst in American history and one of the greatest on record. Only the fact that the district affected was thinly settled and that most of the structures were cabins and huts well adapted to resist quake damage prevented a tremendous loss of life and property.[5]

The New Madrid Earthquake occurred before word of the Battle of Tippecanoe could reach the Creeks and Cherokees in the south, but they remembered the words of Tecumseh. Writes R. E. Banta:

The earth in the Mississippi and lower Ohio valley *did* shake—such shaking as was unknown to Indian tradition—the sky *was* darkened, and the sun glowed faintly red through those thick clouds of dust. Immediately, by report, the southern Indians seized their weapons and started north—if this was a sample of Tecumseh's stamping, they probably reasoned, 'twere as well to make a propitiating gesture. Before they had gone far they learned that it was too late.[6]

On May 15, 1812, in what is now the pasture of a farm near Peru, Indiana, Tecumseh built the fire for the last great council of the woodland chiefs—his final attempt to organize the tribes of the middle west into a confederation. With tears in his eyes he raised his arms and said: "Our fathers, from their tombs, reproach us as slaves and cowards. I hear their voices now in the wailing of the winds . . ." [7]

But the defeat of Tippecanoe was still fresh in the minds of the assembled warriors. Despite Tecumseh's eloquence, the chiefs arose and stated firmly that they were done with strife. The whites were too numerous, too strong. Their British friends were too far away. And Tecumseh, realizing that his power had waned, slowly and sadly extinguished his last council fire. With its dying embers faded his dream.

Tecumseh returned to Ontario and Fort Malden. Now the remains of the confederacy merged with the greater struggle between Great Britain and the United States—the War of 1812. The surrender of Detroit and the Michigan Territory in August 1812 gave the British control of the Great Lakes region, but a year later the tide of war had changed.

By a curious twist of fate General Harrison was placed in command of the American forces that far outnumbered the troops under General Procter and the Indians under Tecumseh. From Fort Meigs, above Toledo, Harrison pursued the retreating British into Canada. On October 5, 1813, the Battle of the Thames was fought. The outcome was a foregone conclusion. For the final time Tecumseh and Harrison met, enemies to the last. The Amerinds fought desperately until Tecumseh fell, a bullet lodged in his heart. His fellow warriors buried his body in an unmarked grave.

The Prophet lived in Canada on a pension from the British government until 1826, when he returned to the United States. George Catlin, famed ethnologist and artist, painted his portrait in 1832. This painting is now on exhibit at the National Museum of Natural History at Washington, D.C.

As for General Harrison, he entered the White House in 1840 on the campaign slogan of "Tippecanoe and Tyler Too!" And that is when the so-called curse of Tippecanoe began. The curse is said to have been instituted by the Prophet about the time of Harrison's election. Harrison caught a cold on his inauguration day and died a month later from pneumonia.

So began the presidential death cycle. Since that time every president elected at a twenty-year interval has died in office. An estimate of the odds of this against chance must at least be hundreds to one. President Lincoln was elected in 1860 and was assassinated five years later; President Garfield, elected in 1880, was assassinated in 1881; President McKinley, reelected in 1900, was assassinated in 1901; President Harding, elected in 1920, died in 1923; President Roosevelt, reelected in 1940, died in 1945; and President Kennedy, elected in 1960, was assassinated in 1963.

John Kennedy had been warned of this death cycle while a candidate for the presidency. Whenever the matter was brought up, his reply was that if every candidate took such a warning seriously, there would be no one willing to serve as president. The curse is alleged to have been communicated to John Tyler, who succeeded Harrison as president.

Soon after the assassination of President Kennedy, L. Taylor Hansen, the expert on Amerind history and lore, sought out a sachem or wise man, and the story of the visit is told in *Search* magazine.[8] "There are some very good ones left," the writer says, "among the Sioux, the Apache, the Navajo and other tribes to name a few." The visitor wanted to know why an innocent man had been stricken in a curse which took place over a small battle so very long ago?

The wise man explained that the battle took place in 1811, but the curse pronounced by Tens-Ka-Ta-Wah, or the Prophet, was made around 1840. It was not so much concerned with the battle as with the treatment of the Indian people, for it was around 1840 that the various trails of tears took place.

Under a law enacted in 1830 all tribes east of the Mississippi were to cede their lands in exchange for territory in the west. The Choctaw led the exodus during the winters of 1831 to 1834 in pathetic bands of 500 to 1,000. Three years later, the Chickasaw joined them. Then came the Creeks, with their chiefs in chains. Of the 15,000 Creeks driven west, 3,500 died of disease and exposure. The great Cherokee migration began in the spring of 1838. They suffered "indescribable hardships," as the *American Heritage Book of Indians* puts it, from which 4,000 of the 13,000 emigrants perished. In 1838 it was the Potawatomi and the Prophet's own tribe, the Shawnee, that were moved west into Kansas and what is now Oklahoma.

Prodded along by U.S. soldiers, they were allowed to take only what they could carry on their backs. Many left comfortable homes and rich farms with cattle behind. There were outbreaks of malaria and other diseases, and the trails were littered with the dead and dying, but the marches kept on and on to Indian territory. No one was allowed to stop to care for the sick.

"In that horror," said the sachem, "was born the curse for the man who sought the presidency that year with the unforgotten slogan 'Tippecanoe and Tyler Too.' He was the focal point for the agony and fury of a despairing and defeated people."

"But why has the curse continued to this day?" inquired Hansen.

"Because of continued mistreatment down through the years. Massacres like those at Sand Creek and Wounded Knee. Perhaps the curse spectre gains his strength from greed, broken promises."

"What would The Lord of Wind and Water say to curses?" asked Hansen.

"What would Jesus Christ say to broken promises and horrors like the trails of tears? There are good men and bad men among my people, as there are among the whites. Also there are those among my people who have strange power—as you know. Not all of them are good. But I hope, as I know that you do, that in time the curse of Tippecanoe will have nothing to feed on, and the power of the spectre will fade away to nothing."

Of the seven presidents included in the death cycle, four were assassinated. Alan Vaughan, editor of *Psychic* magazine and a psychic sensitive himself, in his fascinating book *Patterns of Prophecy* tells of factors in the death cycle as well as in the more recent assassinations of Martin Luther King and Robert Kennedy. There are meaningful coincidences, or what Carl G. Jung called synchronicities, in the deaths of Abraham Lincoln, J. F. Kennedy, Martin Luther King, and R. F. Kennedy. Their assassinations were all foretold by psychic sensitives, dreams or premonitions indicating that they were playing out preexistent archetypal roles as part of their "blueprints" of life. And apparently sensing their own fates, Lincoln, John Kennedy and Martin Luther King all made statements that were prophetic of it shortly before their deaths.

Whatever the primary cause of the presidential death cycle may be—a prophet's curse or possibly something else—what appears to be operating is an archetypal destiny as given in the philosophy of the late Carl G. Jung.

"What of the president elected in 1980?" Alan Vaughan asks.

Will he be able to cheat the presidential death cycle? Will the curse of the Shawnee Prophet still hold?

Since any answer must be a prophecy, I will make this one: The curse has run its course. Even now the American Indian is demanding his full rights as a fellow American. If allowed once more the dignity of his ancient race, then he will perhaps have vanquished the spectre of the Shawnee's curse. If I seem overly partial to this explanation, it may be because I too have American Indian blood.

Moreover, I have a feeling (psychic perhaps) that by 1980 the election rules for presidents will be changed so that terms will run for five or six years and be nonrenewable, so that the next presidential election after 1976 will be in 1981 or 1982. So perhaps by a technicality we shall see an end to the archetypes of assassination.[9]

15

The Great Purification

In this time of widespread pollution, threatened species of animal life and extravagant consumption of natural resources, we need the lesson of the Amerindian's reverence for Nature. In his animistic religion, the red man was his own priest and the forest, plains and desert his temple. Nature was alive with spirit, with unseen forces. The Great Spirit was in all things, omnipresent. To look at a tree, to listen to a waterfall, to drink in the balmy odor of pine, was to become conscious of God. The Amerindian ceremoniously danced and prayed to the sun and moon, to the earth with its winds, rain, thunder and lightning, to the ancestors of totem birds and beasts. And in our own ways we must all learn to respect Nature again.

Writing in *Psychology Today* Frank Waters, author of the *Book of the Hopi*, tells us:

> To Indians the Earth is not inanimate. It is a living entity, the mother of all life, our Mother Earth. All Her children, everything in Nature, is alive: The living stone, the great breathing mountains, trees and plants, as well as birds and animals and man. All are united in one harmonious whole. Whatever happens to one affects the others, and subtly changes the interlocked relationships of the parts to the whole. This life force or dynamic energy that pervades and unites every entity in Nature is the *orenda* of the Iroquois, the *maxpe* of the Crows and Sioux, the *manitou* of the Algonquins, and the *katchines* of the Pueblos.[1]

Frank Waters says we must realize, as the Amerindians do, that underlying physical ecology is a psychical ecology. All living enti-

190

ties, like man, possess an inner spiritual component as well as an outer physical form. In order to meet material needs, Amerindians may have to kill an animal or fell a tree, but before doing so they invoke its spiritual life as a source of psychic energy also. He tells us we must graduate to this belief and recognize both the inner and outer realities of life if we are to close the widening rupture between our minds and hearts.

"By rupture," he continues, "I mean this: In ruthlessly destroying Nature, man, who is also a part of Nature, ruptures his own inner self. We set ourselves apart not only from the Earth, but from the dark maternal unconscious, its psychic counterpart. For man's unconscious is equated to and rooted in Nature."

Today the Amerindians are experiencing the beginnings of a renaissance, and there is an increasing appreciation of the red man's culture and traditions among whites. In his book *Medicine Power*, Brad Steiger writes:

Although many historians and anthropologists believe that the native people buried their god as well as their hearts at Wounded Knee and that the contest between the white man's religion and the red man's medicine was decided along with the issues of territories and treaties, the last decade has seen a dramatic rebirth of the strength and spirit of Amerindian magic. The old ways and traditions have always been carefully nurtured and quietly cherished, but medicine power has returned in a manner that reveals our Amerindian heritage as laden with spiritual insights fraught with special meaning for our new age of ever-rising awareness.[2]

According to George W. Cornell, religion writer for the Associated Press, the native religion of Amerindians is gaining increased respect today in the churches that once tried to stamp it out. One reason for the change is the need for a deeper reverence for Nature in the face of modern damaging misuse of the environment.[3]

Dr. Benjamin Reist, dean of San Francisco Theological Seminary at San Anselmo, declares that Christian theology is "terribly impoverished when it comes to a doctrine of Nature." He adds that there "must come a day quite soon when American Indian theology must be represented in the highest councils of Christian theology in the world."[4]

Dr. Reist spoke at a 1974 meeting of the National Fellowship of Indian Workers in Estes Park, Colorado. The fellowship is a loosely knit association that includes native Americans from a number of tribes and non-Indians from many Protestant denominations. Its purpose was to find relationships between church teachings and tribal beliefs.

At present a growing number of denominations have set up special Indian departments, headed by Indians, to bolster church sensitivity to their interests. Among these are the Episcopal Church, the United Methodist Church, the American Baptist Convention and the Lutheran Council.

In the past the churches have maintained special missions to Amerindians, and many have been educated in mission schools. The practice, however, has been to replace native religious thought with denominational teachings. Now, with the church perspective changing, it is being realized that Christianity and native American beliefs have some basic tenets in common.

An Indian clergyman, the Rev. Homer Noley of New York, told his listeners at the fellowship meeting that Indian religion may be recognized as "closer to original Christianity than most American whites realize." Vine Deloria Jr., a Sioux and author of the book *Custer Died for Your Sins*, went further. He maintained that native Indian religion excels Christianity both in its tolerance and communal character. It is a "relationship between the Great Spirit and a group of people," he said, adding that in contrast, religion that is "conceived as something personal and only personal" has little impact on the community.[5]

Another Amerindian, the Rev. Cecil Corbett of Tempe, Arizona, who directs the Cook Christian Training School there, said the Indians' deep-rooted "concern for harmony with Nature" offers a special value in today's world.[6]

A "harmony with Nature" is certainly needed, and one wonders if any future efforts to achieve it may not be too late. It's easy to imagine George Washington weeping in polluted Pittsburgh or smog-shrouded Los Angeles. A Sioux prophet eighty years ago said the power of the ghost dance would make the surface of the earth roll up like a vast carpet, taking with it all the white man's works. Underneath, the original Americans would find again the flowering prairie, the clouds of birds, the herds of buffalo. So the Sioux did the ghost dance until they fell from exhaustion. And the dream ended in massacre.

It was not the time for this to happen then, says Lame Deer, a full-blood Sioux and medicine man, who collaborated with Richard Erdoes on a book *Lame Deer, Seeker of Visions*.[7] He believes, however, in the spirit behind the rolling up of the earth. He has had a vision about the return of the rolling up spirit among Indians, whites, blacks and the young. "Let's roll up the earth," he says. "It needs it."

In seeking his visions, Lame Deer refuses to use peyote. "I mistrust visions come by in the easy way—by swallowing something," he declares. "The real vision has to come out of your own juices." [8]

Perhaps the surface of the earth will roll up like a vast carpet after the great purification foreseen in Hopi prophecy. In Hopi mythology we are living in the fourth world, and it is nearing its end. The three previous worlds were advanced civilizations that fell because of the people's extreme materialism and corruption. Each ended in a catastrophic purification instituted by the Great Spirit.

The last purification was by flood, as told in the myths of almost all old cultures. Perhaps it destroyed the fabled Atlantis. At any rate, Hopi legends tell of a materialistic and evil third world, and Frank Waters in his *Book of the Hopi* states that the legends refer to the use of aircraft in warfare. "Some of them made a *patuwvota* and with their creative power made it fly through the air," he relates. "On this many of the people flew to a big city, attacked it, and returned so fast no one knew where they came from. Soon the people of many cities and countries were making *patuwvota* and flying them to attack one another. So corruption and war came to the Third World as it had to the others." [9] Is this mere fantasy or is it a glimpse back into a prehistoric and forgotten time?

A faithful few of the ancestors of the Hopi survived the Great Deluge. The survivors split into four groups and migrated to the north, south, east and west. Only the group that came north, presumably from Mexico or Central America, managed to complete the migration. They were led by a brilliant "star," and some tribesmen, in the light of what will follow in this chapter, believe this "star" was actually a flying saucer guided by the spirit Massau. They were brought to Old Oraibi, Arizona, now held sacred and believed to be the heart of the land of the Great Spirit.

When Massau came to earth, he made a petroglyph near Oraibi on Second Mesa that can be seen today. It shows a maiden with the traditional butterfly hairdo in a dome-shaped object which in turn rests on an arrow. The maiden represents purity, the dome-shaped object is an aerial vehicle, and the arrow stands for travel through space. All this means, say the traditional Hopi, that at the time of the Great Purification the tribe members will be taken to other planets.

The *kachinas*, represented by masked dancers in Hopi ceremonies, resemble human beings, but are spiritlike entities from other planets. The Hopis say the *kachinas* instructed them in agricultural techniques, weaving and other necessary arts. They also taught them the moral and philosophical principles that comprise their culture, and instructed them never to bear arms. Their tribal name means "people of peace." After a time the *kachinas* departed, saying it was time to leave the Hopis, but not yet time to return to their planets. The Hopis believe the *kachinas* reside in Arizona's San Francisco Mountains.

Judging by past performances, Hopi prophecies are not to be taken lightly. Prophecy is an important part of their religion, and their sages seem to be able to tap a psychic source of information. They knew there were races of white, yellow and black-skinned peoples long before they had any contact with other races. The coming of the white man was foreseen along with the period of persecution and hardship that would follow. They knew in advance that a great war would be launched by the peoples of the swastika (Germany) and the sun (Japan). They have a special song that is sung prior to the outbreak of a war that will involve the United States and the young men of Hopiland. In 1914 it was sung during their important Wuwuchim ceremony. It was sung again in 1940 and in 1961 as the United States began its later calamitous involvement with Vietnam.

A delegation of Hopis went to the United Nations in 1959 to warn the assembled world leaders of the impending time of purification. The trip was inspired by an ancient prophecy which described "a House of Glass or Mica [that] would stand at this time, where Great Leaders from many lands would be gathered to help any people who are in trouble." [10] The delegation was received politely, but little attention was paid to their message. Other groups have gone to Washington with their warnings. Copies of the prophecy have been mailed to thousands of world leaders and important individuals.

The Hopis also gave their message at a Council of Mankind held several years ago at the University of Chicago. It was closed to the public and was said to have been largely financed by W. Clement Stone, the insurance millionaire. Spiritual leaders representing the major countries of the world presented their views on mankind's present and future.[11]

What is impending, according to the prophecy, is the return of the True White Brother, also known as the Older Brother, who will protect the Hopi nation during the purification cataclysms. He will bring with him a set of stone tablets to match those broken millenia ago by the spirit Massau when the Hopis first came to Old Oraibi. The matching of the tablets will signal the advent of the Great Purification.

It is said that Older Brother "after many years may change in color of skin which may become white, but his hair will remain black . . . It is known that our True White Brother when he comes will be all powerful and he will wear a red cap or red cloak. . . . With him there will be two great ones, both very intelligent and powerful," the prophecy continues, "one of which will have a symbol or sign of swastika which represents purity and is male. Also he will have this symbol or sign which also represents purity and is female, a producer of Life; the red lines in between the sign represent the lifeblood of a woman." [12]

It should be explained that not all Hopis believe in the prophecy and many simply ignore it. Within the tribe are the modernists who have taken up the ways of the white man, and the traditionalists who preserve the beliefs and customs of the past. The first division occurred in 1906 when the traditionalists were forced to leave Oraibi and settle in nearby Hotevilla. It is, of course, the traditionalists who advocate the prophecy.

Belief in the Great Purification is not limited to the Hopis. The Mesquakie tribe, which has proudly maintained the old traditions, foresees a great catastrophe happening soon which will "rearrange things." Brad Steiger, in *Medicine Power*, quotes Don Wanatee of this tribe as stating:

I think the end might be very near. I am not speaking as a pessimist, but as one who believes in the prophecies of the Mesquakie. A hundred years ago, the Mesquakie prophesied a box that would sit in the corner in which we would see things happening far away and hear people talk who would not be there. They prophesied great trailways in the sky. They said that the animals would be dying. They said that when many species were becoming extinct, man would see unusual things. Floods, earthquakes. It would be as if the Earth were revolting against its inhumane treatment. Other Indian tribes throughout the country are beginning to see these things coming. Many are saying in desperation, "What can we do to revive the old tradition? How can we get back to it?" [13]

The Mesquakie believe the purification catastrophe will leave pockets of men and women who will begin to people the Earth again. These people will return to the traditionalists to learn the tenets of their old religions. There are traditional pockets in the United States and Mexico that they can turn to.

The Chippewa Bear tribe is preparing for the Great Purification. According to Sun Bear, a medicine man, the ancient prophecies say it will come after the white man has built a house in the sky. They believe this refers to Skylab. "The Earth Mother will shake fleas off her back, just as a dog rids itself of its parasites," he insists. "When the cleansing has occurred, good people of spiritual awareness will build a better world." [14]

The cleansing will be accompanied by a terrible famine. The Hopis and other Amerindian traditionalists are storing canned and dehydrated foods, bottled water and water purification tablets, seeds, and drums of kerosene for their lamps in carefully concealed caches.

As in their previous three worlds, the Hopi prophecies state the Great Purification will occur when people turn to material rather than spiritual things; when they pollute and destroy the land; and when "man has invented something which can fall upon the ground, boil everything within a great area, and turn the land to ashes where no grass will grow." [15] Seemingly all of these specifications have been fulfilled.

Another sign that the fourth world is coming to an end is that "your land will be forced to be divided and shall be cut four times, each cut smaller than the other," a prophecy the Hotevilla Hopi say was accomplished by highway construction to Oraibi. [16]

"We know the faithful are to be gathered to escape Purification Day," Chief Dan Katchongva, centenarian leader of the traditionalists, has said. "Therefore when the great fire and explosion takes place, it will be seen all over North and South America and the Earth shall shake. Therefore when the True White Brother comes, listen to him and gather when the power comes from the south." [17] The safest place, say the believers, will be the Southwest United States, especially the area around the Hopi villages in Arizona.

The Hopi prophecy received some publicity in the west as the result of a series of curious incidents involving a strange man named Paul R. Solem.[18] Accompanied by several Amerindians, he first appeared at campfire meetings at the Fort Hall Indian Reservation in Idaho in July 1969. He told his listeners about Hopi prophecies. One prophecy is that there will be mass migration of Indians north from Mexico and Central and South American, led by a 130-year-old chief named Etchata Etchana. They will come to the safe haven of Hopiland. Solem, a non-Indian, said he had the power to "call in" UFOs (Unidentified Flying Objects) and proved it. Barbara Boren, a skeptical reporter for the *Idaho State Journal*, admitted that she observed two "starlike moving lights" high in the air.

Solem claimed he had his first contact with a flying saucer in June 1948, when he, his wife and his brother-in-law watched three glowing objects pass over a field on his Idaho ranch. Four years later he allegedly saw another saucer over his ranch, and he followed it for several miles until it landed in the Lost River Sinks. From it emerged a figure with long hair, dressed in white coveralls.

"At first I thought it was a woman," Solem said. "His hair was blond and shoulder-length and his voice was almost musical in tone . . . There is no reason to fear these people. They are like angels. They come from the planet Venus and they are only here to lend credence to prophecy, not to harm anyone."

The saucer pilot identified himself as "Paul 2," suggesting perhaps that he was Paul Solem's alter ego. Among other things, Solem claims "Paul 2" told him that his assignment was to work with the Amerindians in preparing for the building of the City of Zion, a Utopia where money would no longer be used and all the inhabitants would live communally.

After his 1952 contact, Paul Solem spent the next seventeen years wandering throughout the West. According to a report compiled by the Prescott, Arizona, sheriff's office, two of those years were spent in the Idaho State Mental Hospital. Following his appearances at the Fort Hall Reservation, Solem went to Hotevilla, Arizona, under the guidance, he said, of the Venusians. There he met with Dan Katchongva, chief of the Hopi Traditionalist Sun Clan. When some of the younger members laughed at Solem's claims, the chief defended him.

"This man speaks the truth," he said. "This is all part of our religion."

One Hopi who didn't laugh was Titus Lamson. A few months

earlier, he said, he had seen a rainbow-colored object moving in the sky over Hotevilla. It was saucer-shaped with a dome on top. As he watched, it became transparent, and he could see a man inside with long blond hair, wearing a gray uniform.

The UFOs that began appearing around Hotevilla were more like large stars. Solem claimed they were piloted by a people descended from the Ten Lost Tribes of Israel. He was given a message to relay to the Hopis by Paul 2. "Our leader as spoken of in Hopi prophecy is already here on earth in mortality," the message claimed. "He is known as the Apostle John, the same as in the New Testament." Writer John A. Keel points out that other UFO contactees also claim to have been told about this mysterious "John." Noted seers like Jeanne Dixon have stated that the most important religious leader in history was born somewhere in the Middle East in the early 1960s. Could he be the new Apostle John?

To some of the traditionalist Hopi the belief that Solem's UFOs were actually vehicles or space ships piloted by beings came easily in view of some of their legends. The *kachinas* were supposed to be from other planets. Some believed that at the time of the Great Purification the Hopi who had remained faithful to the old ways and teachings would be transported to other worlds. "We have seen the flying saucers and have heard their message to us," Chief Dan said. "We know they are real, as their pictures were drawn upon stone for all to see . . . Also Hopi Indians know that other planets and worlds have people, and they are watching us."

Chief Dan, however, presided over some stormy council meetings as Solem's claims and messages split the clan. The chief said the division itself was fulfilling the prophecy that there would be three divisions among the Hopi before the coming of the True White Brother. The first was in 1906; this was the second.

Solem left Hotevilla and went to Prescott, Arizona, to bring his message to other Amerindians and whites. He was there in August 1970, when a wave of flying saucer reports hit the area. Since Chief Dan only recently had ordered ten thousand copies of the prophecy distributed to world leaders, Solem claimed that the UFOs had come to confirm the accuracy of the prophecy.

On the evening of August 7 Joe Kraus, managing editor of the *Prescott Courier*, and a group of witnesses had a dramatic demonstration of Solem's ability to "call down" UFOs. As described in the August 9 *Courier*, Solem stood aside, mentally calling for a saucer to appear as he gazed at the sky. About two minutes later,

Kraus reported, "a star appeared that wasn't there before . . . It looked like a star—almost. It rose in the sky, stopped, hovered, wavered to one side, and then continued across the sky, repeating the maneuvers. A flying saucer? Yes, if we could believe our eyes."

As the witnesses watched, Solem repeated an alleged telepathic communication he said he was receiving from a being aboard the ship:

My name is Paul 2, fourth in command of all ships that enter the atmosphere of the planet called Earth. We come to lend credence and as a sign or token that the Hopi prophecy was of a divine nature. Great sorrow and fear will be coming to this planet very soon and few will escape it. . . . The white brother shall be introduced by a huge fire and the earth shall quake at his arrival. We are of the ten lost tribes and we will return several nights unless there is contempt for us.

When Solem finished speaking, the "star" disappeared.

On August 10 Chief Dan, his counselor and interpreter came to Prescott to see the UFOs for themselves. The sky was overcast. Solem said that if the skies cleared, he would call in some space ships. Late on the last night Chief Dan and his companions were in Prescott, the sky cleared and Solem sent out his telepathic call. Shortly later fifteen witnesses saw a bright object come sailing by.

"The craft came in a rolling motion like a moon and was about five hundred to eight hundred feet off the ground," said Nonnie Skidmore, Chief Dan's secretary. "It came from north to south, then turned by the side of the house due west. It climbed and turned off its light like a light bulb."

In the months that followed, Paul Solem visited various reservations seeking to convince the inhabitants that the coming of the True White Brother was imminent. Meanwhile, back at Hotevilla, there was another split among the traditionalists. Chief Dan and his loyal followers believed this was the third split and that the "earth eruption" and Great Purification were at hand.

In November, according to Solem, the Venusians told him the message had not spread as it should have. They would arrange to have four spectacular UFO demonstrations in Prescott, the first to take place on Easter Sunday 1971. The place chosen was over a field owned by a Tim Chapman. Excitement mounted as the day approached.

On Easter morning a crowd of over 1,500 people gathered at the field. Included were two TV camera crews and numerous radio and newspaper reporters. When Solem arrived at the scene, he became angry when he saw bulldozers on the field. Tim Chapman had them moved out of sight. Anxiously the crowd waited and waited and waited. Frustrated and furious, Solem blamed the former presence of the bulldozers for the failure of the saucers to appear and threatened to sue Chapman. He canceled the other proposed appearances. The disappointed crowd drifted away. It was a fiasco.

A few days later a humbled, embarrassed Paul Solem left Prescott. He has not been heard of since. At Hotevilla Dan Katchongva was removed from his position as head of the Sun Clan. The reason given was that his association with Solem had hurt the image of the Hopis and had brought them unfavorable publicity.

In their book *The Unidentified* Jerome Clark and Loren Coleman point out that Solem was "uniquely vulnerable" to his self-deception about the "Venusians." His life had been one of mistakes and failures. He had lost his wife, his ranch, and he had psychiatric problems. He longed for attention; he wanted to be a somebody, a success.

But had he been alert enough, he would have known who the "Venusians" really were, for they themselves as much as told him. Solem thought that the extraterrestrial was "Paul 2"; but perhaps the Venusian was really saying "Paul, too." Either way the meaning is clear. "He" was Solem's alter ego, a subpersonality split off from the contactee's unconscious mind and projected onto the outside world, where "he" seems to have an independent existence and be able to effect paranormal manifestations much in the manner of the "spirit guides" in the seance room. [19]

How was Solem able to "call down" the starlike UFOs so that they appeared as aerial lights to witnesses? Clark and Coleman suggest that the UFOs "were created out of the psychokinetic energy Solem unknowingly generated from himself (contactees, remember, frequently have powerful extrasensory abilities) and from the believers who surrounded him." [20]

As to the Hopis, they continue to await the coming of the True White Brother and the Great Purification. And they dream of a Fifth World in which they will know once more the freedoms and the gifts of Nature that were lost with the white man's conquest.

Back in 1855 Chief Sealth of Washington sent a letter to President Franklin Pierce. It too was a prophecy:

We know that the white man does not understand our ways. One portion of the land is the same to him as the next, for he is a stranger who comes in the night and takes from the land whatever he needs. The earth is not his brother, but his enemy, and when he has conquered it, he moves on. He leaves his father's graves and his children's birthright is forgotten. The sight of your cities pains the eyes of the red man. But perhaps it is because the red man is a savage and does not understand.

There is no quiet place in the white man's cities. No place to hear the leaves of spring or the rustle of insect's wings. But because I am a savage and do not understand, the clatter only seems to insult the ears. The Indian prefers the soft sound of the wind darting over the face of the pond, and the smell of the wind itself cleansed by a mid-day rain or scented with a pinon pine. The air is precious to the red man. For all things share the same breath—the beasts, the trees, the man. The white man does not seem to notice the air he breathes. Like a man dying for many days, he is numb to the stench.

What is man without the beasts? If all the beasts were gone, man would die from great loneliness of spirit, for whatever happens to the beasts also happens to man. All things are connected. Whatever befalls the earth befalls the sons of the earth.

It matters little where we pass the rest of our days; they are not many. A few more hours, a few more winters, and none of the children of the great tribes that once lived on this earth, or that roamed in small bands in the woods, will be left to mourn the graves of a people once as powerful and hopeful as yours.

The whites, too, shall pass—perhaps sooner than other tribes. Continue to contaminate your bed, and you will one night suffocate in your own waste. When the buffalo are all slaughtered, the wild horses all tamed, the secret corners of the forest heavy with the scent of many men, and the view of the ripe hills blotted by talking wires, where is the thicket? Gone. Where is the eagle? Gone. And what is it to say goodbye to the swift and the hunt, the end of living and beginning of survival? We might understand if we knew what it was that the white man dreams, what hopes he describes to his children on the long winter nights, what visions he burns into their minds, so they will wish for tomorrow. But we are savages. The white man's dreams are hidden from us.[21]

Bibliographical Notes

Introduction: Our Indian Heritage

1. N. and M. Rau, "Honest Injun?" *Pageant* (November 1956): 44–51.
2. John Collier, *Indians of the Americas* (New York: Mentor Books, 1948), pp. 117, 121.
3. Paul A. W. Wallace, "People of the Long House," *American Heritage* VI:2 (February 1955): 26.
4. C. Fayne Porter, *Our Indian Heritage* (Radnor, Pa.: Chilton Book Co., 1964), p. 20.
5. Edward Nickerson, AP feature, 1 August 1958.
6. *Ibid.*

1. Whence Came the Amerind?

1. Letha Curtis Mugrave, "Big Dig at Calico," *Westways* (June 1971): 28–32.
2. *San Diego Evening Tribune*, 14, 15 May, 1974; 12, 24 July 1974.
3. AP dispatch, 1 November 1974.
4. *World Almanac 1974* (New York, Cleveland: Newspaper Enterprise Association, Inc.), p. 426. *Also* AP dispatch, 11 September 1970.
5. *World Almanac 1975*, p. 399. *Also* UPI dispatch, 13 November 1973.
6. Ronald Schiller, "When Did Civilization Begin?" *Reader's Digest* (May 1975): 119–123.
7. Frank C. Hibben, *Digging Up America* (New York: Hill and Wang, 1960), p. 41.
8. Paul Radin, *The Story of the American Indian* (New York: Liveright Publishing Corp., 1927), p. 363.
9. R. G. Haliburton, "Primitive Traditions as to the Pleiades," *Nature*

(England: 1 and 15 December 1881); reprinted in *Strange Artifacts*, compiled by W. R. Corliss (Glen Arm, Md.), pp. 95–99.
10. Quoted by L. Taylor Hansen, "Scientific Mysteries," *Amazing Stories* (December 1948): 154.
11. Peter Kolosimo, *Not of this World* (New York: Bantam Books, 1971), p. 114.
12. "Skullduggery, Scientific Style," *Pursuit* 5:4 (October 1972): 89.
13. Hibben, *Digging Up America*, pp. 208–224.
14. *The American Heritage Book of Indians* (New York: American Heritage Publishing Co., 1961), p. 49.
15. William H. Prescott, *Conquest of Peru* (New York: Thomas Crowell Publishing Co.), 1947.
16. Charles Berwitz, *Mysteries from Forgotten Worlds* (New York: Doubleday and Co., 1972), pp. 131–133.
17. Brad Steiger, *Mysteries of Time and Space* (New York: Dell Publishing Co., Inc., 1974), pp. 56–62. *Also* Berwitz, *Mysteries from Forgotten Worlds*, pp. 93–96.
18. Alan Vaughan, *Patterns of Prophecy* (New York: Hawthorn Books, Inc., 1973), p. 173. *Also* Allen Spraggett, *Probing the Unexplained* (New York: New American Library, 1971), pp. 7–11. *Also* Edgar E. Cayce, *Atlantis: Fact or Fiction?* (Virginia Beach, Va.: A. R. E. Press, 1962), p. 24.

2. Artifacts of a World Forgotten

1. W. J. Perry, *The Children of the Sun* (Grosse Pointe, Mich.: Scholarly Press, 1968).
2. Cyrus H. Gordon, *Before Columbus* (New York: Crown Publishers, Inc., 1971).
3. *Ibid.*, Introduction.
4. Berwitz, *Mysteries from Forgotten Worlds*, p. 21.
5. Charles H. Hapgood, *Maps of the Ancient Sea Kings* (Radnor, Pa.: Chilton Book Co., 1966).
6. *Idem.*, *Earth's Shifting Crust* (New York: Pantheon Books, Inc., 1958).
7. *Idem.*, "Piri Re'is Map of 1513," *Fate* (January 1966): 83.
8. *Idem.*, "The Antarctic Map of Oronteus Finaeus," *Fate* (May 1966): 78.
9. *Art and Archeology* (April–May 1966).
10. *Saturday Review* (19 February 1972).
11. Ivan T. Sanderson, *Investigating the Unexplained* (Englewood Cliffs, N.J.: Prentice-Hall, Inc., 1972), p. 184.
12. *Ibid.*, p. 177–178.
13. Giorgio de Santillana, *The Origins of Scientific Thought* (London: Weidenfeld and Nicolson, 1961). *Also* Andrew Tomas, *We Are Not the First* (New York: Bantam Books, 1971), pp. 14–15; 69–72.

14. K. E.· Maltwood, *A Guide to Glastonbury's Temple of the Stars* (London: John Watkins, 1934; revised edition, Victoria, B. C.: Victoria Publishing Co., 1950). *Also* Janet and Colin Bord, *Mysterious Britain* (New York: Doubleday and Co., 1974). *Also* Brinsley Le Poer, *Men Among Mankind* (London: Neville Spearman, Ltd., 1962), pp. 33–42.
15. Peter Tompkins, *Secrets of the Great Pyramid* (New York: Harper and Row, 1971).
16. *Horizon* 8:2 (Autumn 1948). *Also Pursuit* 5:1 (January 1972): 22.

3. Mystery of the Megaliths

1. Quoted by L. Taylor Hansen, "Scientific Mysteries," *Amazing Stories* (June 1947): 131.
2. J. A. Hammerton, *Wonders of the Past* (New York: Wise and Co., 1937), 1:435–444.
3. Berwitz, *Mysteries from Forgotten Worlds*, pp. 71–87.
4. A. Hyatt Verrill, *Old Civilizations of the New World* (Indianapolis: Bobbs-Merrill Co., 1929).
5. M. K. Jessup, *Case for the UFO* (New York: Citadel Press, 1955), p. 153.
6. *The Books of Charles Fort* (New York: Henry Holt and Co., 1941), pp. 568–571.
7. Alexander Thom, *Lunar Observatories* (London: Oxford University Press, 1971). *Idem.*, *Megalithic Sites in Britain* (1967).
8. Janet and Colin Bord, *Mysterious Britain* (New York: Doubleday and Co., 1974), p. 2.
9. Alfred Watkins, *The Old Straight Track* (London: Garnstone Press, 1970).
10. Ivan T. Sanderson, *Things* (New York: Pyramid Books, 1967), p. 73.
11. *American Anthropologist* (1936).
12. Jessup, *Case for the UFO*, p. 148.
13. Berwitz, *Mysteries from Forgotten Worlds*, pp. 79–80.
14. *Guinness Book of World Records*, ninth edition (New York: Bantam Books, Inc., 1970), p. 242.
15. Alan and Sally Landsburg, *In Search of Ancient Mysteries* (New York: Bantam Books, 1974), p. 66. *Also Sunrise* (June 1970): 257–260. *Also* Los Angeles *Herald-Examiner*, 29 July 1973, p. A–7.
16. Ferdinand Anton, *Art of Ancient Peru* (New York: G. P. Putnam's Sons, 1972).
17. *National Geographic* (February 1971).
18. John Brown, "Enigma of Tiahuanaco," *Fate* (December 1952): 32–36.
19. *Transactions of the Linnean Society* I:3 (London: 1939): 32.
20. Immanuel Velikovsky, *Earth in Upheaval* (New York: Doubleday and Co., 1955), pp. 83–89.
21. Curtis Fuller, "I See by the Papers," *Fate* (August 1966): 25.
22. Spraggett, *Probing the Unexplained*, p. 10.

4. Tunnels of the Titans

1. Frank Waters, *Book of the Hopi* (New York: Viking Press, 1963).
2. Harold T. Wilkins, *Secret Cities of Old South America* (London: Rider and Co., 1950), p. 365.
3. Hansen, "Scientific Mysteries," *Amazing Stories* (August 1948): 151–153.
4. Harold T. Wilkins, *Mysteries of Ancient South America* (London: Rider and Co., n.d.), p. 157.
5. *Ibid.*, pp. 162–170.
6. J. Frank Dobie, *Apache Gold and Yaqui Silver* (Boston: Little, Brown and Co., 1939), pp. 74–89; 178–204.
7. Hansen, "Scientific Mysteries," *Amazing Stories* (February 1947): 174.
8. Wilkins, *Mysteries of Ancient South America*, p. 158.
9. Hansen, "Scientific Mysteries," *Amazing Stories* (November 1948): 145.
10. Landsburg, *In Search of Ancient Mysteries*, p. 46.
11. Wilkins, *Mysteries of Ancient South America*, p. 176.
12. Quoted in Berwitz, *Mysteries from Forgotten Worlds*, p. 153.
13. Hansen, "Scientific Mysteries," *Amazing Stories* (April 1947): 154–155; (November 1948): 144–145.
14. *American Heritage Book of Indians*, p. 110.

5. Totem Trails Northward

1. *American Heritage Book of Indians*, p. 382.
2. Harnett T. Kane, *Natchez on the Mississippi* (New York: William Morrow and Co., 1947), pp. 2–4.
3. *Ibid.*, pp. 143–144.
4. *American Heritage Book of Indians*, pp. 147–152. *Also* Radin, *Story of the American Indian*, pp. 183–185; 203–228. *Also* Hansen, "Scientific Mysteries," *Amazing Stories* (June 1945): 185–187.
5. *American Heritage Book of Indians*, pp. 23–24.
6. Hansen, "Scientific Mysteries," *Amazing Stories* (February 1947): 167–174. *Also* Millicent Todd, *Peru: A Land of Contrasts* (Boston: Little, Brown and Co., 1918).

6. Early Old World Contacts

1. James Bailey, *The God-Kings and the Titans* (New York: St. Martin's Press, 1973).
2. Cyrus H. Gordon, *Before Columbus* (New York: Crown Publishers, 1971).
3. *Ibid.*, p. 43.
4. *Ibid.*, p. 149.
5. Quoted by Hansen, "Scientific Mysteries," *Amazing Stories* (June 1946): 197–202.

6. UP dispatch, 21 November 1956.
7. UPI dispatch, 13 April 1975.
8. Garcia, quoted in *Life* (16 October 1970): 12.
9. Alexander von Wuthenau, *The Art of Terra-Cotta Pottery in Pre-Columbian Central and South America* (New York: Crown Publishers, 1970). *Also* Gordon, *Before Columbus*, pp. 21–35. *Also Life* (16 October 1970): 12.
10. *Life* (16 October 1970): 12. *Also Catholic Digest* (October 1974): 24.
11. Neill J. Harris, "New Mexico's Elephant Slabs," *Fate* (October 1971): 76–81.
12. Hibben, *Digging Up America*, p. 57.
13. Thor Heyerdahl, *American Indians in the Pacific* (Chicago: Rand McNally, 1953).
14. Chinese Historical Society of America, San Francisco, quoted in *Los Angeles Times*, 19 December 1974, Pt. I-A, p. 1; San Diego *Evening Tribune*, 26 February 1975.
15. Henriette Mertz, *Pale Ink* (Chicago: The Swallow Press, Inc.), quoted in *Catholic Digest* (December 1973): 67–69.
16. Bill Murphy, *Dolphin Guide to Los Angeles and Southern California* (New York: Doubleday and Co., 1962), p. 349.
17. Robert Marx, "They all Discovered America," *Oceans* (November–December 1973): 22–27.
18. Robert N. Cheetham, "Bear Paws or the Feet of Buddha?" *Fate* (January 1964): 64–65.
19. Cyclone Covey and Bill Buchardt, "What is a Chinese God Doing in Oklahoma?" *Catholic Digest* (December 1973): 67–69.
20. San Diego *Evening Tribune*, 26 February and 16 November, 1975.
21. Pierre Honore, *In Quest of the White Gods* (New York: G. P. Putnam's Sons, 1964).
22. Quoted by Lewis Spence, *The Problem of Lemuria* (New York: David McKay Co., 1933), p. 151.
23. Alexander von Wuthenau, *The Art of Terra-Cotta Pottery in Pre-Columbian Central and South America* (New York: Crown Publishers, Inc., 1970).
24. George F. Carter, *American Antiquity* (January 1953). *Also* Hansen, "Scientific Mysteries," *Amazing Stories* (September 1946): 155–157.

7. Columbus Was Late

1. Gordon, *Before Columbus*, pp. 120–123. *Also* William F. Dankenbring, "Who Discovered America First?" *Plain Truth* (12 July 1975): 8–10. *Also* William D. Conner, "Ancient Rock-Writing in America," *Fate* (June 1972): 40–45.
2. Conner, "Ancient Rock-Writing in America," p. 42. *Also* Gordon, *Before Columbus*, p. 125.

3. Gordon, *Before Columbus*, pp. 182–185. *Also* Dankenbring, "Who Discovered America First?" p. 9.
4. AP feature, 4 November 1970. *Also Grit* (27 June 1971): 13. *Also Pursuit* 4:1 (January 1971): 16.
5. Gordon, *Manuscripts* XXI:3 (Summer 1969), quoted by Dankenbring, "Who Discovered America First?" p. 9.
6. William D. Conner, "Archaeologists Link Georgia Indians to Crete," *Fate* (January 1971): 42.
7. *Ibid.*, p. 42.
8. *Ibid.*, p. 40.
9. *Ibid.*, p. 40.
10. *Ibid.*, p. 39. A copy of Dr. Mahan's thesis is obtainable from University Microfilm Service, University of Michigan, Ann Arbor, Mich.
11. Dankenbring, "Who Discovered America First?" p. 8.
12. Marx, "They all Discovered America," p. 22.
13. Gordon, *Before Columbus*, p. 39.
14. Marx, "They All Discovered America," p. 26.
15. Mack Reynolds, "Did the Phoenicians Reach Mexico?" *Fate* (June 1954): 26–32.
16. Charles M. Boland, *They All Discovered America* (New York: Doubleday and Co., 1961).
17. UPI feature, 17 April 1975.
18. Brad Williams and Choral Pepper, *The Mysterious West* (New York: World Publishing Co., 1967), pp. 22–26.
19. Constance Irwin, *Fair Gods and Stone Faces* (New York: St. Martin's Press, 1963).
20. *Ibid.*
21. *Pursuit* 7:2 (April 1974): 51.

8. The European Wanderers

1. AP feature, 3 September 1975.
2. *Midnight* (2 June 1975).
3. UPI feature, 2 September 1969.
4. Christensen, *Proceedings of the Society for Early Historic Archaeology* (January 1970), quoted in *Pursuit* 2:4 (October 1969): 76. *Also* Copley News Service feature, San Diego *Evening Tribune*, 27 July 1970.
5. *The Literary Digest* (21 February 1925): 24.
6. Earl Chapin, "Mystery of the Mandans," *Fate* (June 1952): 89–90.
7. Quoted by Chapin, "Mystery of the Mandans," p. 91.
8. Wilkins *Secret Cities of Old South America*, p. 421.
9. *Indiana: A Guide to the Hoosier State* (New York: Oxford University Press, 1941), pp. 392–393.
10. *Grit* (25 October 1970): 62.

11. Marx, "They All Discovered America," p. 26.
12. *The Books of Charles Fort*, pp. 147–152.
13. Williams and Pepper, *The Mysterious West*, p. 18.
14. *Ibid.*, p. 19.
15. Gaston Burridge, "Enigmas in Lead," *Pursuit* 4:1 (January 1971): 17–18. Thomas Bent's monograph was published by him in a very limited edition and all copies were distributed years ago.
16. Williams and Pepper, *The Mysterious West*, p. 21.
17. Bill Mack, *Argosy* (March, 1972).
18. *Ibid.*
19. "Ships that Sailed the Desert," *Fate* (January 1973): 63–72.
20. D. and M. R. Coolidge, *Last of the Seris* (New York: E. P. Dutton and Co., 1939).
21. *Pursuit* (January 1971): 18–19.
22. *Ibid.*, p. 16.
23. Marx, "They All Discovered America," p. 27. *Also* AP dispatch, 27 July 1975.
24. Andrew E. Rothovius, "The Scotsman who Discovered America," *Fate* (August 1963): 26–31.
25. *Coal Age* (February 1954); reprinted in *Fate* (July 1954): 8–10.
26. *Ibid.*, p. 8.
27. T. H. Lewis, *American Antiquarian* 11 (1889): 293–296; reprinted in *Strange Artifacts*, compiled by W. R. Corliss (Glen Arm, Md.: 1974), p. 249.
28. Anonymous, *Nature* 45: (England: 12 November 1891); reprinted in Corliss, *Strange Artifacts*, p. 252. *Also* AP feature, 9 April 1956.
29. Arlington Mallery, *Lost America* (Washington, D.C.: privately published, 1951). *Also* William D. Conner, "Ohio's Ancient Iron Age," *Fate* (October 1968): 84–96. *Also* Clyde Keeler, "New Light on Ohio's Ancient Iron Age," *Fate* (August 1972): 88–93.

9. The Lost Colony Enigma

1. John Harden, *The Devil's Tramping Ground* (Chapel Hill, N.C.: University of North Carolina Press, 1949), pp. 79–87.
2. Chicago Daily News Service feature, 28 January 1958.
3. *Ibid.*
4. *Dictionary of American History*, Vol. II.

10. Mystery of the Shaking Tent

1. R. S. Lambert, *Exploring the Supernatural* (Toronto: McClelland and Stewart, Ltd., 1955), pp. 19–20.
2. *Ibid.*, p. 24.
3. *Ibid.*, p. 29.

4. Reprinted in *Tomorrow* 4:3 (Spring 1956): 123–126.
5. *Ibid.*, p. 125.
6. *Ibid.*, p. 123.
7. Publications of the Philadelphia Anthropological Society, Vol. II (Philadelphia: University of Pennsylvania Press, 1942); reviewed in the *Journal of the American Society for Psychical Research* XXXVII:4 (October 1943): 226.
8. *Ibid.*, p. 226.
9. Andrew Ballantine, "Indian Magic of the Shaking Tent," *Fate* (May 1962): 59.
10. Francis Dickie, "Mystery of the Shaking Tents," *Real West* VII:37 (September 1964): 18–19.
11. Edward Lawrence, *Spiritualism Among Civilized and Savage Races* (London: Black Publishing Ltd., 1921), p. 18.
12. *Ibid.*, p. 45.
13. Joseph B. Casagrande, "The Ojibwa's Psychic Universe," *Tomorrow* 4: 3 (Spring 1956): 37.
14. Review, *Journal of the American Society for Psychical Research* XXXVII:4 (October 1943): 224–225.
15. Dickie, "Mystery of the Shaking Tents," p. 18.

11. Medicine Man Magic

1. Anna Nolan Clark, *New Mexico* (July 1937); condensed in "Indians to Gallup," *Reader's Digest* (August 1938): 111.
2. Manley Palmer Hall, *Horizon* 7:4 (Spring 1948): 69–70.
3. Quoted by R. DeWitt Miller, "Forgotten Mysteries," *Coronet* (June 1945): 51.
4. *Man, Myth and Magic* 52 (London: BFC Publishing, Ltd., 1971), p. 1458.
5. John Hilton, "Black Magic of the Cahuilla," *The Desert Magazine* (May 1949).
6. E. P. Gibson, *Journal of the American Society for Psychical Research* XLVI: 149.
7. Milbourne Christopher, *The Illustrated History of Magic* (New York: Thomas Y. Crowell Co., 1973), pp. 71–74.
8. *Ibid.*, p. 74.
9. AP dispatch, 2 May 1971.
10. "The Amazing Snow Dance of the Stonys," *Fate* (October 1961): 33.
11. "Did Sioux Indians Control the Weather?" *Fate* (April 1957): 65–71.
12. Melba Blanton, "The Rainmaker's Secret Weapon," *Occult* 4:3 (October 1973): 32–35.
13. *Ibid.*, p. 35.
14. J. Allen Hynek and Jacques Vallee, *The Edge of Reality* (Chicago: Henry Regnery Co., 1975), pp. 143–144.

12. Secrets of the Shamans

1. "Did Sioux Indians Control the Weather?" *Fate* (April 1957): 65–71.
2. Curtis Fuller, "Government-Trained Medicine Men," *Fate* (March 1973): 26–28.
3. *Ibid.*, p. 28.
4. Quoted by D'Arcy McNickle, "The Healing Vision," *Tomorrow* 4:3 (Spring 1956): 25–31.
5. Lambert, *Exploring the Supernatural*, p. 22.
6. McNickle, "The Healing Vision," pp. 25–31.
7. Quoted by Virgil J. Vogel, *American Indian Medicine* (Norman, Okla.: University of Oklahoma Press, 1970).
8. Curtis Fuller, "Green Medicine," *Fate* (February 1970): 25–26.
9. *Ibid.*, p. 28.
10. David Villasenor, *Tapestries in Sand* (Healdburg, Calif.: Naturegraph Books, 1960).
11. Joseph B. Casagrande, "The Ojibwa's Psychic Universe," *Tomorrow* 4: 3 (Spring 1956): 36–39.
12. *The American Heritage Book of Indians*, pp. 341–342. *Also* Frederick J. Goshe, "Requiem for the Medicine Man," *Fate* (November 1963): 40–47.
13. Frederick J. Goshe, "Bullet-Proof Indians," *Fate* (February 1956): 46–52.

13. Wigwam Wizardry

1. Jean W. Godsell, "Moccasin Telegraph," *Fate* (September 1954): 95–99.
2. *Pursuit* 6:4 (October 1973): 81.
3. Paul A. Hout, "The Crow Woman who Died for Love," *Fate* (August 1970): 46–50.
4. *National Enquirer*, 9 September 1975, p. 34. *Also* Frederick J. Goshe, "How Sitting Bull Prophesied Custer's Last Stand," *Fate* (May 1955): 53–59.
5. *National Enquirer*, 9 September 1975, p. 34.
6. Betzinez, *I Fought With Geronimo* (Harrisburg, Pa.: Stackpole Co., 1959).
7. John D. Murphy, "Billy Bow-Legs and the Hurricanes," *Fate* (Fall 1948): 44–45.
8. Tex Lowell, "Death Curse of the Owl Prophet," *Fate* (September 1961): 76–80.
9. Brad Steiger, *Medicine Power* (New York: Doubleday and Co., 1974), pp. 100–103.

14. The Curse of Tippecanoe

1. Radin, *The Story of the American Indian*, pp. 368–371. *Also* Dee Brown, *Bury My Heart at Wounded Knee* (New York: Holt, Rinehart and Winston, 1970), pp. 417–419. *Also* John G. Neihardt, *Black Elk Speaks* (New York: Pocket Books, Inc., 1970), pp. 217–223.
2. R. E. Banta, *The Ohio*, Rivers of America series (New York: Rinehart and Co., 1949), pp. 210–218.
3. *Ibid.*, p. 214.
4. Quoted by Banta, *The Ohio*, p. 215. *Also Indiana: A Guide to the Hoosier State*, pp. 449–450; 466–467.
5. Ben Kartman and Leonard Brown, *Disaster* (New York: Pellegrini and Cudahy, 1948), pp. 3–6.
6. Banta, *The Ohio*, pp. 215–216.
7. From a reenactment of Tecumseh's speech on the council site by the late Ross Lockridge, professor of history at Indiana University, Bloomington, Indiana.
8. L. Taylor Hansen, *Search* (May 1964): 4–9.
9. Alan Vaughan, *Patterns of Prophecy* (New York: Hawthorn Books, 1973), pp. 52–53.

15. The Great Purification

1. Frank Waters, *Psychology Today* (May 1973).
2. Steiger, *Medicine Power*, Introduction.
3. AP feature, 29 June 1974.
4. *Ibid.*
5. *Ibid.*, *Also* Steiger, *Medicine Power*, pp. 98–99.
6. *Ibid.*
7. William Kittredge "Books," *Harper's Magazine* (November 1972): 120–123.
8. *Ibid.*, p. 121.
9. Quoted by John Keel, "America's Unrecognized UFO Experts," *Saga* (April 1973): 35–37; 68–71.
10. Steiger, *Medicine Power*, pp. 200–202.
11. *Ibid.*, pp. 205–206.
12. Keel, "America's Unrecognized UFO Experts," p. 68.
13. Steiger, *Medicine Power*, p. 204.
14. Brad Steiger, "The Great Purification," *Beyond Reality* 21 (July–August 1976): 33; 54–56.
15. Steiger, *Medicine Power*, p. 203.
16. Keel, "America's Unrecognized UFO Experts," p. 68.
17. Albuquerque *Journal* (New Mexico), 10 October 1970, p. 16.
18. Jerome Clark and Loren Coleman, *The Unidentified* (New York: Warner Paperback Library, 1975), pp. 213–224. *Also* Jerome Clark "Indian Prophecy and the Prescott UFOs," *Fate* (April 1971): 54–61.

Also Keel, "America's Unrecognized UFO Experts," pp. 35–37; 68–71. *Also* Albuquerque *Journal* (New Mexico), 10 October 1970, p. 16. *Also* Steiger, *Medicine Power*, pp. 206–207.
19. Clark and Coleman, *The Unidentified*, p. 221.
20. *Ibid.*, p. 221.
21. Reprinted in *Wassaja* (June 1975).

Index